Changing Landmarks of America

Unique and completely fascinating, this book proves that the development of America's cities and towns is caused by the changing wants and ambitions of the people of the United States.

Presenting a lively panorama of American civilization as it is reflected in the art of our homes, public buildings and civic environment, this provocative volume discusses the changes in city development brought about by the railroad and the automobile, the rise of the industrial mill town, the switch from village greens to large city parks, the growth of the country-club and the suburbs, the origins of shopping centers and other innovations of modern urban living.

In a stimulating, informative manner, the authors urge cities and states to establish art commissions and encourage housing experts, architects, government departments and business groups to consider our cultural heritage in working out large-scale urban improvements and to make their communities "the pride of the region, the pride of the nation and the glory of the America we offer to the world."

CHRISTOPHER TUNNARD has taught city planning and civic art for the past eleven years at Yale. HENRY HOPE REED also taught city planning at Yale and has written many articles on architectural subjects.

American Skyline IS PUBLISHED IN A HARDCOVER EDITION BY HOUGHTON MIFFLIN COMPANY.

Other MENTOR Books You Will Enjoy

COMPANY MANNERS *by Louis Kronenberger*
A penetrating and provocative appraisal by a noted critic of American culture, with special emphasis on art, theater and television as well as individual morals, manners and ideals. (#M156—35c)

THE PUBLIC PHILOSOPHY *by Walter Lippmann*
A challenging analysis of the changing state of Western democracies, by one of America's most influential political commentators. (#M174—35c)

AMERICA IN PERSPECTIVE (abridged)
edited by Henry Steele Commager
Commentary on our national characteristics by twenty-one acute and perceptive foreigners from Tocqueville to Matthew Arnold and Brogan. (#MD169—50c)

THE CREATIVE PROCESS *edited, with introduction, by Brewster Ghiselin*
Thirty-eight of the greatest minds in the world reveal how they actually begin and complete creative work in such fields as art, literature, science, and philosophy. (#MD132—50c)

MACHINES THAT BUILT AMERICA *by Roger Burlingame*
The adventurous and exciting story of the ingenious men and inventions that welded a struggling young country into a great industrial nation. (Signet Key #Ks327—35c)

To Our Readers

We welcome your comments about SIGNET, SIGNET KEY or MENTOR books, as well as your suggestions for new reprints. If your dealer does not have the books you want, you may order them by mail, enclosing the list price plus 5c a copy to cover mailing costs. Send for a copy of our complete catalog. The New American Library of World Literature, Inc., 501 Madison Ave., New York 22, N. Y.

THE GROWTH AND FORM
OF OUR CITIES AND TOWNS

AMERICAN
SKYLINE

CHRISTOPHER TUNNARD
AND HENRY HOPE REED

DRAWINGS BY JOHN COHEN

A MENTOR BOOK

Published by THE NEW AMERICAN LIBRARY

Published as a MENTOR BOOK

FIRST PRINTING, JULY, 1956

A cloth-bound edition of *American Skyline*
is published by Houghton Mifflin Co.

MENTOR BOOKS are published by
The New American Library of World Literature, Inc.
501 Madison Avenue, New York 22, New York

to
Lydia Tunnard
and
Henry Hope Reed, Sr.

KATHERINE LEE BATES

(1859–1929)

O beautiful for patriot dream

That sees beyond the years

Thine alabaster cities gleam

Undimmed by human tears!

America! America!

God shed His grace on thee,

And crown thy good with brotherhood

From sea to shining sea!

"America the Beautiful," Stanza 4

GRATEFUL ACKNOWLEDGMENT IS MADE FOR permission to print the following: Comment on American town planning by Thomas Adams, cited from Thomas Adams, *Outline of Town and City Planning* (Russell Sage Foundation, New York, 1935), p. 21. Quotation from sermon of Jeremy Taylor, see *The Golden Grove: Selected Passages from the Sermons and Writings of Jeremy Taylor*, edited by Logan Pearsall Smith (The Clarendon Press, Oxford, 1930), p. 125. Comment of Albert Gallatin on the American village and town, see George W. Pierson, *Tocqueville and Beaumont in America* (Oxford University Press, New York, 1938), p. 139. The description of New Haven in the first years of the Republic comes from Robert Hunter, Jr., *Quebec to Carolina in 1785–1786*, edited by Louis B. Wright and Marion Tinling (The Huntington Library, San Marino, Calif., 1943), p. 152. Description and illustration of the triumphal arch by Charles Willson Peale is to be found in Charles Coleman Sellers, *Charles Willson Peale* (The American Philosophical Society, Philadelphia, 1947), Vol. I, pp. 226-28. Edith Wharton's observation on the street plan of Manhattan is found in Edith Wharton, *A Backward Glance* (Appleton-Century-Crofts, Inc., Copyright, 1934, The Appleton-Century Co., Inc., New York), p. 23. For advertisement of real estate on Brooklyn Heights, New York, see Ralph Foster Weld, *Brooklyn Village, 1816–1834*, in New York State Historical Series, Dixon Ryan Fox, editor (Columbia University Press, New York, 1938), No. 7, p. 28. Benjamin Latrobe's observation on New Orleans houses is to be found in Benjamin H. B. Latrobe, *Impressions Respecting New Orleans: Diary and Sketches 1818–1820*, edited by Samuel Wilson, Jr. (Columbia University Press, New York, 1951), p. 42. The passage on the collapse of the steamboat business in Pittsburgh is quoted in *Pennsylvania: A Guide to the Keystone State* (Oxford University Press, New York, 1940), pp. 299–300. The description of Butte in the 1930's is taken from *Copper Camp: Stories of the World's Greatest Mining Towns, Butte, Montana*, compiled by workers of the Writers' Program of the Works Projects Administration for the State of Montana (Hastings House Publishers Inc.,

New York, 1943), p. 22. Impressions of New York's ugliness in the 1870's on the part of Edith Wharton come from Wharton, work cited, pp. 54–55. For the landfill map of Boston and data, see James L. Bruce, "Filling in of the Back Bay and the Charles River Development," *Proceedings* of The Bostonian Society, 1940, between pp. 24 and 25. The dialogue between Frank Lloyd Wright and Elbert Hubbard comes from John Lloyd Wright, *My Father Who Is on Earth* (G. P. Putnam's Sons, New York, 1946), pp. 32–33. John D. Rockefeller's comment on economic concentration is found in Allan Nevins, *John D. Rockefeller* (Charles Scribner's Sons, New York, 1941, 1st edition), Vol. I, p. 622. The quotation about real estate speculation in Chicago is from Henry B. Fuller, *On the Stairs* (Houghton Mifflin Company, Boston, 1918), pp. 47–48. The complaint against the railroads on the part of the California legislator is in Glenn Chesney Quiett, *They Built the West: An Epic of Rails and Cities* (Appleton-Century-Crofts, Inc., Copyright, 1934, The Appleton-Century Co., Inc., New York), p. 83. The description of Richard Morris Hunt's palace for William K. Vanderbilt comes from Consuelo Vanderbilt Balsan, *The Glitter and the Gold* (Harper & Brothers, New York, 1952), pp. 10–11. The reference to Andrew Mellon and Henry Frick comes from George Harvey, *Henry Clay Frick: The Man* (Charles Scribner's Sons, New York, 1928), pp. 269–70. Henry Adams evokes the World's Columbian Exposition in *The Education of Henry Adams* (Houghton Mifflin Company, Boston, 1918), pp. 339–40. President Theodore Roosevelt's conception of city planning and civic design for the national capital is in Charles Moore, *The Life and Times of Charles Follen McKim* (Houghton Mifflin Company, Boston, 1929), p. 244. Charles Follen McKim's letter to Lawrence Grant White comes from Moore, work cited, p. 303. Daniel H. Burnham's motto for city planners is in Charles Moore, *Daniel H. Burnham* (Houghton Mifflin Company, Boston, 1921), Vol. II, p. 147. The description of Lower Manhattan by Rupert Brooke is in Rupert Brooke, *Letters from America* (Charles Scribner's Sons, New York, 1916 and Sidgwick & Jackson Ltd., London, 1916), pp. 5–6. The description of the suburb of Zenith is to be found in Sinclair Lewis, *Dodsworth* (Harcourt, Brace and Company, 1929), p. 193. The observation on local government trends by Robert Averill Walker comes from Robert Averill Walker, *The Planning Function in Urban Government* (University of Chicago Press, Chicago, 1950), p. 34. Josiah Royce's pleas for the embellishment of the community are to be found in Josiah Royce, *Race Questions, Provincialism and Other American Problems* (The Macmillan Company, New York, 1908), pp. 62, 64,

107 and 108. The last are quoted with the kind permission of his grandson, Mr. Josiah Royce.

The authors wish to thank the following individuals for information and assistance: Albert S. Bard, Adolf Brez, Horace H. Brown, Jr., Katherine Fenimore Cooper Cary, Margaretta Childs, Professor Thomas C. Cochran, Cleveland E. Dodge, Carl Feiss, W. Hawkins Ferry, James Gallagher, Professor Anthony N. B. Garvan, Professor John Gauss, Professor Talbot F. Hamlin, the Reverend Vincent Hopkins, S. J., the Honorable Charles R. Howell, Professor Serge Hughes, J. B. Jackson, Joe Jones, Professor Victor Jones, Joan Kelly, Arthur Knox, Ellen Kramer, Henry Krotzer, the late Professor Eduard C. Lindeman, the late Reginald Marsh, Clark McLain, Professor Martin Meyerson, William Miller, the Reverend C. Kilmer Myers, Charles McKim Norton, Edward Page, Elbert Peets, Professor Steen Eiler Rasmussen, W. Knight Sturges, Gonul Tankut, Andrew J. Thomas, Charles Thompson, Donald Young, Irene V. Walsh, James H. Ward, Charles K. Warner, Robert C. Weinberg, Samuel Wilson, Jr., and Richardson Wood.

They also wish to thank the following museum and library officials: Adolph Placzek and Professor James Grote Van Derpool, Avery Library, Columbia University; David McKibbin, the Boston Athenaeum; Mrs. T. M. Hofmeester, Jr., Burnham Library of Architecture, The Art Institute of Chicago; Aline Cosgrove and Donna L. Root, Cleveland Public Library; Ruth V. Cook, Library of Architecture, and Katherine McNamara, Library of Landscape Architecture and City Planning, Harvard University; Joseph McCosker, Atwater Kent Museum, Philadelphia; the staff of the Massachusetts Historical Society, Boston; Pierre Verlet, Départment des Objets d'Art, Palais du Louvre; the late Charles Mauricheau-Beaupré, Musée Nationale de Versailles; the staff of the Baltimore Room, Enoch Pratt Free Library, Baltimore; Grace M. Mayer, Museum of the City of New York; Arthur B. Carlson, The New-York Historical Society, New York City; Muriel Baldwin, Ina Cassirer, Jane Waite, Norwood Vail, Naomi S. Street, Takato Saito, Neal Richmond and Margaret Viviano, Art Department, Dr. James J. Heslin and F. Ivor Avellino, American History Room, Elizabeth Roth, Print Department, Gerard Alexander, Edward Gardner and Richard Hitchcock, Map Room, and Rosalie Bailey, Genealogy Room, New York Public Library; Cornelia Strohl, Epiphany Branch of the New York Public Library; Eugene Kingman, Joslyn Art Museum, Omaha; the staff of the Pennsylvania Historical Society, Philadelphia; Mildred Boatman, St. Louis Public Library; Mrs. Julius Steinberg, Sarpy County Historical Society, Bellevue, Nebraska;

Lydia Wentworth, Art Library, and Alexander O. Vietor, Sterling Library, Yale University; Elizabeth Gee, Print Collection, Yale University Art Gallery.

In particular they wish to thank Wayne Andrews, Curator of Manuscripts, The New-York Historical Society, John Barrington Bayley, Alan Burnham, Joseph Hopkins and Professor Carroll L. V. Meeks for introducing them to many facets of American architecture and to descriptions of the American scene; Lamont Moore, Director, Yale University Art Gallery, for valuable suggestions; Emile Durbrule for information on the philosophers, Charles S. Peirce and Josiah Royce; Arabel Porter, Victor Weybright and Craig Wylie for advice on work in progress, and Anne G. Biddle, John Pearce, Ellyn Polshek and Walter Reed for help in preparing the manuscript.

CONTENTS

PLATES

Paul Revere Mall, Boston
Reconstructed house of Paul Revere, Boston
Governor's Palace, Williamsburg
Courthouse and square, King William, Virginia
New Haven Green, Connecticut
Middleton Place Gardens, Charleston, South Carolina
Independence Hall, Philadelphia
Capitol, Richmond, Virginia
University of Virginia campus, Charlottesville
Mount Vernon Place, Baltimore
Entrance to Fort Jay, Governor's Island, New York City
Merchants' Exchange, Philadelphia
"Pirates' Alley," New Orleans
Home of Washington Irving, Tarrytown, New York
Cathedral of Saints Peter and Paul, Philadelphia
Mural in dome of the Capitol, Washington
Central Park, New York City
Pennsylvania Station, New York City
William K. Vanderbilt mansion, New York City
World's Columbian Exposition, 1893, Chicago
The Mall, Washington
Detroit Public Library
City Hall, San Francisco
Buckingham Fountain, Chicago
Manhattan skyline
Miami skyline
San Antonio River Park, San Antonio, Texas
Fireworks over the White House

INTRODUCTION

The Temple and the City

THIS IS A BOOK about the American townscape—the man-made America of industries, homes, skyscrapers, hotels, highways and parking lots. It describes how this scene was shaped, how it became part of the American heritage, how it affects the lives we lead, and how we may in turn shape it toward the future.

Americans and foreigners alike have been prone to describe our townscapes as haphazard, formless or the products of accident. Nothing could be farther from the truth. Although not often beautiful, each street or district of our towns and cities reflects some premeditation or planning on the part of an individual or a group, whether it be a home-owner, a banking institution, an individual corporation or a town government. Granted that these segments of society have not always pulled together and that the results have not always measured up to the highest standards, our business blocks, civic centers, subdivisions and industrial plants are not accidentally placed or designed, and we can find distinguishable relationships between them and the cultures which brought them forth. "It is clear . . . that merits or defects in town planning have not been owing to the presence or absence of planning," one authority on American cities, the late Thomas Adams, has observed, "but to the way in which the planning has been done. The chief defects in modern cities are because of piecemeal planning . . . without adequate consideration for the community as a whole."

How closely the development of our cities and towns reflects our people and history! The snug houses and small, neat town plans of the Colonies were a direct reflection of the Protestant mercantile society before 1720, when a change in taste and new-made wealth brought a greater luxury and extravagance to the scene. The white Greek Revival villas

15

and Romantic gardens of a later period reflect the individualism and laissez-faire politics of their generation, while the post-Civil-War mansard houses and residential avenues were born of an age seeking fashion and closer connections with European culture. The age of spreading cities and giant factories announced in visible form the rise of the corporation, and the Regional City of our own day, in which all differences between town and country are disappearing, is made inevitable by the perfection of mass distribution and new forms of communication like the highway and television, as well as by the rise of labor unions and the dominance of suburban informality in everyday life.

The physical community in America, then, is not the product of accident. Definite forces have molded its many patterns. The barrier that still exists between us and the American city is one of ignorance. We have not been able to relate what we see around us to the economic, social and political forces that have shaped the pattern. This is also a barrier to an understanding of ourselves as a nation distinct from other peoples. One of the purposes of this book is to encourage a knowledge of these forces so that we will be better able to create a city which reflects our national aspirations and desires; for the city, whether we like it or not, dominates the interest of modern society and should be man's supreme creation.

To create the future, to plan for posterity, is an opportunity that has always been present since the American colonies were first planted. Today, unfortunately, the city seems so large and the task so huge that little has been done about the townscape except in the cause of efficiency. But the magnitude of the job should hold no fears for Americans who have been familiar with mammoth undertakings from the beginning. It will be important to remind ourselves in these pages of the bold schemes of the past (some realized and some unrealized) that reflect our own lack of imagination and reveal the hopes and aims many Americans have had for their communities, and of the efforts to bring them to fruition. This shaping process is the art and tradition of city planning which, joining with architecture, painting and sculpture and enlisting the aid of the technical sciences, can create the beautiful American community.

If, as Matthew Arnold pointed out, the people of the United States have established institutions perfectly suited to their national character, the institutions have in turn shaped our cities and towns and raised our temples. Only within the framework of these same institutions, economic and technological, religious and governmental, will be found the explanation for the shape of things about us. It will be necessary, therefore, to begin by examining the major forces that account for the special character and peculiarities of the American scene.

1. *Temples of Commerce*

One great institutional force is that of business. Take the skyline of any city in the United States. Above a low line of houses, factories and commercial buildings, a skyscraper, or a cluster of skyscrapers, announces the urban gathering of

Manhattan skyscrapers seen from the New Jersey flats.

humanity. If there are exceptions, the dome of a capital or the pediment of a city hall, they are so few that they serve to underline the vertical element. There is nothing in the shape of the monoliths to reveal their use, ranging from hotels to the offices of great telephone companies. But they have a message: We are a business society.

The United States is not a great nation because of business alone, but business accounts for its spectacular material progress. If the office tower of Waco, Texas, or The Travelers Building of Hartford, Connecticut, are insufficient evidence, go to the Tribune Tower in Chicago—or, better still, the RCA

Building in New York—and from its eminence stare at the piles of steel, brick and stone. There is no escaping them here, so overwhelming are the number and the variety, the menagerie of shapes and sizes. A thousand monsters, which seem to move and breathe as the noise comes up from the crowded streets below. White plumed monsters in winter, as wisps of steam toss in the clear sharp air; lighted monsters at night, like giant electric eels; headless monsters, when, on occasion, their upper stories disappear in the fog and mist.

Jules Coutan's statue of Mercury above the entrance to Grand Central Terminal, New York. Its design is based on a sketch by the architect Whitney Warren.

What disorder the scene presents from the sidewalk or from the observation tower! There a fifty-story building rises opposite one of ten stories, another looks down on an empty lot, and yet a third stands apart among rows of low houses, stiff as an out-of-season bather in cold water. On the street below the same disorder appears—signs, shop fronts, the now omnipresent parking lot and gas station. Over there a new front is being placed on an old building; farther on an apartment house of twenty stories is being replaced by an office building of thirty, and another is being torn down to save money on taxes. All is change where there is money to be made, for all is business. "Business underlies everything in our national life," Woodrow Wilson once said, and nowhere is it more true than in these cities where American business has created its own work of art, the skyscraper.

There is nothing new in American business society. Its tradition is long and fascinating. The businessman is lost in time, and if we must have evidence of him, it can be found in Ur of the Chaldees, in Tyre and Sidon, along the Silk Route of China, in the great buried cities of the East, for the merchant was to be found wherever there was a city. When they gathered in any number, they reared temples to their gods. The Roman merchants gave the name Mercury (from the Latin *merx, mercis,* or merchandise) to the messenger of the gods and declared him the deity of business. In New York City he takes an easy stand upon the façade of the Grand Central Terminal; with his right hand he welcomes the unheeding crowd below to his wonders, while in his left he holds the caduceus with its entwined serpents of prudence, an essential business virtue.

"We three kings of Orient are . . ." How much more like rich merchants are the crowned and adorned monarchs of the Christmas hymn who spread their precious wares before the Christ Child! The merchant wanders in and out of the mist of time, and yet we know of his presence from the objects he has left behind. How did this piece of Byzantine silk come to be used as a shroud for a prince-bishop of northern Europe? Was it not two merchants of Venice, then an unknown town, who stole the body of Saint Mark out of Mohammedan Alexandria and brought it home where business was to build the Jeweled City of the Sea? The rich burgher comes out of the shadows and finds recognition among the poets who were born to merchants. Boccaccio was the son of a traveling merchant of Florence, Chaucer was born in London to a vintner, and the great humanist

Sior Pantaleone, Carlo Goldoni's prototype of the merchant.

and architect Leon Battista Alberti, was the son of a Florentine merchant. There is the "good Antonio" of Shakespeare, about whose argosy *The Merchant of Venice* is plotted; Molière offers Monsieur Gorgibus, the patient hard-working businessman accepting the importunities of his spoiled daughter; and above all there is gentle Goldoni, who transformed one of the stock characters of the *commedia dell'arte* into "Sior Pantaleone," the honest Venetian draper whose name is best known as the source of the word "pantaloon," an article of apparel still in daily use.

In the eighteenth century of Goldoni the European businessman appeared on a stage cluttered with the actors of another age, feudal and monarchial; *in America he had the stage to himself.* The landed gentry were to disappear from the commercial scene or to be reduced to such minor parts that it was only a question of time before business was to have almost every role. There was, of course, the South and its slave economy, but trade in cotton, after all, came to be controlled by northern businessmen.

The overwhelming presence of business is emphasized in the plans of American cities. The skyscraper is one symbol, the gridiron plan another. There are parallel streets and right-angled streets in every community. With a few exceptions which serve to confirm the rule, the cities of America have been laid out mercilessly "by the compass," as James Fenimore Cooper observed, and no hill, no lake, no river or other natural obstacle bends the straight line.

Consider the fact that land in the United States has always been available for a price and even for the taking. How difficult it is for the American today, seated comfortably in his automobile while driving to his home in the suburbs, to understand the excitement caused in Italy by a few peasants occupying fallow land, the property of an absentee marquis. Can he, the owner of his own home, grasp political events of China, Iran and Egypt which spring from land hunger? *His own land revolution took place three hundred years ago.* If he lacked the money then to buy a lot, he would move onto some land held by a proprietor. "To squat," meaning "to settle on uncultivated or unoccupied land without payment of rent," is a wholly American invention. William Penn, the founder of the Pennsylvania Colony, was continually beseeching his agent James Logan to provide a return on his vast property. "I say once again, let me have a rent roll, or [I] must sink with gold in my view but not in my power," he wrote in 1704. A quarter of a century later his heirs asked Logan to take steps against the squatters who had already occupied 100,000 acres of Penn-owned land, a revolutionary act occurring fifty years before the Declaration of Independence.

As events in our time have so forcibly brought home, land hunger is no more part of the American than it is of all men, but in the United States the hunger has a different pattern. On the one hand, the desire can only be satisfied by living on the land that is plowed—the countryside is set off in freeholds each with its house and barn—and, on the other, the same land will be sold without hesitation if a better living can be made elsewhere. In some countries, such as France and Italy, the aim is to own and hold; in the United States it is to own and to speculate. In their desire to keep their land, early settlers would refuse to leave their tracts, at the warning of an Indian raid, to find refuge in a nearby fort; instead they persisted, and at times foolishly, in staying alone in the wilderness. "Neither the interest nor inclinations of the Virginians," wrote an eighteenth-century observer, "induce them to cohabit towns." But, despite the effort that the settler spent to make a home, he would sell out and move on; "pull up stakes," he would say, the stakes marking the bounds of his land. This was true both of the wealthy and of the poor, and remains equally true today. With the whole country taken as real estate to be bought and sold, the nation itself has been carved into a giant gridiron by a series of land laws beginning

Tucson, Arizona. A typical gridiron plan in a mountain setting.

in 1785 and culminating in the famous Homestead Act of 1862. The desire to live on the land was made a condition of ownership in that the government recognized ownership only when a house was built on the claim. The gridiron pattern, dividing the land into quarter sections of 160 acres each, permitted easy surveying, registration and, inevitably, speculation.

There is, of course, the very size of the country itself. All of nature is big—the rivers, the lakes, the mountain chains, the prairies and the distances. "Chicago," wrote the civic designers Daniel H. Burnham and Edward H. Bennett, "has two dominant features: the expanse of Lake Michigan, which stretches, unbroken by islands or peninsulas, to the horizon; and a corresponding area of land extending north, west, and south without hills or any marked elevation. These two features, each immeasurable by the senses, give the scale. Whatever man undertakes here should be either actually or seemingly without limit." There you have it! Would the skyscrapers have risen in a country with limits? The bigness itself has helped shape the economic pattern as well by creating a market so vast as to rival nature's scale; this market can only be supplied by mass production and mass distribution, two great American phenomena. Interchangeable parts, harvesting machines, the great railroad terminal, the chain store, the inexpensive automobile and its superhighway, all these and other products of what Santayana was the first to call "free co-operation", were not only essential to the economic development of the country, but have conditioned the form of man-made America and have produced its giant farms and spreading cities.

Although co-operative planning and action at the level of big business and industry have been a major factor in the shaping of the American scene, it has been notably lacking in other spheres of our national life; individualism has come first, It is not surprising that a country which has always placed such emphasis on self-reliance, independence and the freehold system should have listened with approval to philosophers absorbed in doctrines centering on the individual as an end in himself. Diverse though their philosophies may be, from John Locke to Emerson, from Herbert Spencer to the modern William James, this has been so, and any voice heard in America extolling the virtues of co-operation has been rare. Santayana pointed out that the neglected American spirit of "eagerness to run and help" could be harnessed in favor of a better life, and Charles S. Peirce, the almost forgotten mentor of William James, saw the crying need for the emphasis to be placed on community as a balance to our laudable but sometimes too fervid individualism. "Does the *genus homo* have any existence beyond the individual?" Does he have "any more dignity, worth and importance than individual happiness, individual aspirations and individual life?" asked Peirce as early as 1871. Do men "really have anything in common so that the *community* is to be considered as an end in itself"? For Peirce the relative value of the individual and the community was the most practical question facing the public of the day, and the existence of the individual apart from the community was meaningless to him. In the American business society of today there is more need than ever to reconcile individual aspirations and community needs, to prove that they are not necessarily antagonistic, and to revitalize the democratic ideal through increased co-operation of all citizens and their institutions.

2. *Temples to God*

It is this business society of ours which constantly invites the comment that "Americans are materialistic" (as if we differed from others in our appreciation of money). It is true that in all the great cities of the world, except in the United States, the temples to God stand higher than the temples to commerce. In Peiping it is the Temple of Heaven, in London the dome of St. Paul's, and even in Paris the Sacré Coeur of Montmartre looks down on the Eiffel Tower; but here in the United States it would seem that the omnipresent office building has taken command. Let no one, looking from the top of

Skyline of Colonial Boston, from the Paul Revere print.

the RCA Building at New York City spread out below, be misled into thinking that business so dominates as to exclude all other human interests. Let those who believe this look once again, for there, in and about and behind the clustered skyscrapers, are the church steeples. Everywhere they are present, not a few but a host, and in New York City so numerous are they that a whole section, Brooklyn, is known as the "Borough of Churches." As early as the 1830's such cities as Cincinnati had twenty-four churches, Philadelphia ninety-six and New York itself a hundred, in every instance a church to each thousand of the population. Today, in smaller communities the steeples still shape the skyline, not just a single tall one, as in a Canadian or European village, but several, each announcing a different sect.

If we leaf through our history we cannot help but see how religion touched events, more especially in its Protestant form. In the fight to free the slaves, the churches, beginning with the Quakers, took the first step. Harriet Beecher Stowe, daughter and sister of Congregationalist ministers, wrote *Uncle Tom's Cabin*, which hastened the coming of the Civil War. Then came the war itself with its hymn singing, its fighting preachers, its appeal to God. There was Lee kneeling in prayer before battle, Stonewall Jackson reading the Bible by campfire, Meade discerning God's hand in his victory at Gettysburg and Sherman's troops marching through a silent Charleston with the streets echoing to "Mine eyes have seen the glory of the coming of the Lord . . . Glory, glory, hallelujah!" We sense the atmosphere of Brooklyn so much better when we know that in its formative years in the last century it was dominated by Congregational merchants and their preachers, or the aura of Pittsburgh when we realize that its great bankers and industrialists are descended from Scotch-Irish Presbyterians, or yet again the faint worldliness of Baltimore when we recognize the role of the Roman Catholic Church in shaping its history.

Our cities would be quite different without the ornament of our churches, and although they are often screened by the towers of commerce, the variety of this ornament is greater than may at first meet the eye. Much is added to the North End of Boston by the Baroque spire of Christ Church, where the lantern once burned for Paul Revere. The plainness of Shenandoah, Pennsylvania, is atoned for by the bulbous domes of the Greek Orthodox church rising on the hill. The interior of Peter Harrison's synagogue of Newport is acknowledged to be one of America's greatest contributions to eighteenth-century architecture. Impressiveness marks the Episcopal cathedral on its elevated site in Washington, and luxury the church of John D. Rockefeller on Riverside Drive, the latter denoting a recent and more sophisticated trend in Baptist church building. The three towers of the Roman Catholic cathedral in New Orleans' Place d'Armes add an interest to the square and the skyline.

Yet these examples of churches which are civic ornaments are few and America's cities and towns, on the whole, have not derived as much physical or esthetic benefit from religion as might be expected from its importance in American life. The reason for this lies in our religious traditions.

If England gave us our free individuality and our free co-operation, as Santayana put it, it also gave us our Protestantism—not the Protestantism of a single state church, but the radical Protestantism in which the individual made his own covenant with his God and turned to the Bible for his own interpretation of God's laws without the help of a hierarchy, ceremony, prayerbook or a magnificently decorated house of worship. It was no gentle Protestantism that first took root here, but the stern religion of the Frenchman John Calvin, first in the seventeenth century with the great migration from eastern England to New England and, later, in the eighteenth, with the migration of the Presbyterians from northern Ireland to the frontier along the Alleghenies. (It was the latter who took the log cabin of the Swedish and German settlers, and made it the symbol of the frontier; while it was the former who evolved the clapboard frame house so prevalent today in the countryside.) When the United States was recognized as a free and independent nation by the Treaty of Paris in 1783, two thirds of the three million population were Calvinistic, being either Congregational or Presbyterian. In New England, where the Congregationalists were the majority by far, their church remained established in three states—Connecticut, New Hampshire and Massachusetts—after the Revolution, and it was not completely disestablished in Massachusetts until 1833.

It is hardly surprising that eventually the mass of the people, needing something more emotional and richer in humanity, turned eagerly to the Baptist preachers and Methodist circuit riders, who, with their message of warm love, of a faith in which all men stood equal before their God and welcome in His sight, not impotent and helpless, offered salvation to all, as against salvation for the few. The new sects came with the Great Revival of 1800, which spread like a flash fire up and down the frontier and east to the great cities. Baptists and Methodists would hold huge camp meetings that were social gatherings as well as spiritual ones, where men preached round the clock, read the Bible and sang hymns, and where people found temporary release from their harsh lives. By 1830 the Methodists had become the largest denomination in the country, with the Baptists a close second. Thus the main currents of the religious stream were fixed: the Presbyterians and the Congregationalists had already made their great contribution in education, which had begun with the founding of Harvard College in 1636 and were appealing largely to the well-to-do and the professional elements; the Baptists and the Methodists, with their sympathetic evangelism, were making their great contribution in the shape of friendliness and good works, which are still so much a part of the American character.

The stream of American religion is broad and deep, and there are other currents—the Lutherans, largely restricted to those of German or Swedish descent, the Unitarians, who represent Boston's revolt against a too severe Calvinism and had won Harvard College to their faith by 1805, and, above all, the Episcopalians and the Roman Catholics, as American as the rest but set apart because they both acknowledge a great past and are marked by continuity of tradition. The Roman Catholic can draw at once on the great heritage of Rome, Christian and pagan, and of all the Latin world, to the general exclusion of things English; the Episcopalian, on the other hand, has in addition to the world of Rome, that English inheritance so superbly symbolized by the Book of Common Prayer, which, with the King James Version of the Bible, is one of England's most precious gifts. The Roman Catholic Church can boast of its great congregation, the largest in the country; although the Protestant Episcopal Church must be content with a restricted flock, it can point to the many sons and daughters who have led America in all fields, from politics to the arts.

Even the Roman Catholic Church has not escaped the distant influence of Calvin. Some maintain that the severity of the American branch stems from Jansenism, the heresy tolerated in France in the latter half of the seventeenth century, only to be condemned in 1713 by Louis XIV and Pope Clement XI. The Jansenist Abbey of Port-Royal in Paris, as Sainte-Beuve reminds us, allowed choir music as its only luxury. Even though Jansenism still has its attraction in French intellectual circles, both Catholic and non-Catholic—it must be remembered that Pascal and Racine were among its defenders—it has not touched these shores. Instead, the Roman Catholic Church in the United States, a nation predominantly evangelical Protestant, has inevitably taken on local coloring as has the Episcopal Church, for example, in producing preachers and exhorters, rather than theologians, among their clergy.

If most of the churches built in America are plain, ignoring the message of Jeremy Taylor, the seventeenth-century divine, that "it is good that we transplant the instruments of fancy into religion: and for this reason musick was brought into Churches, and ornaments, and perfumes, and comely garments, and solemnities, and decent ceremonies, that the busie and lesse discerning fancy being bribed with its proper objects may be instrumental to a more coelestial and spiritual love"— if so, it is no wonder the lesser buildings of the towns and cities are commonly without adornment or sophistication. The religious influence in America has helped foster our genius for education, for individual liberty and for brotherhood, but in modern times it has not yet had its potential effect on our physical surroundings, unlike religion's role in Medieval or Renaissance times, or on this continent in the period of Spanish colonization. The American church today is clean and bare, an echo, no doubt, of John Wesley's dictum that "cleanliness is indeed next to Godliness." Is it not time to couple beauty and godliness, as Jeremy Taylor advised, and increase the influence of the church on the American townscape?

3. *Temples of Government*

If we leave the portals of the church and look once again at the skyline, we may discern other temples rising beside those to commerce and to God: the temples of the State. We usually think of the American government in a more abstract way—in terms of its Constitution, of its elected representatives, its President, its congressmen, the state governors and the mayors of cities, as well as the income tax; and we also think of it in terms of the army and navy, of atomic energy, of the great public works. Yet government in America, more modest than business, less obvious than the churches, has done as much as both of these to shape the scene about us. In the center of Galveston, far removed from the cotton sheds and the factories, a columned building, modeled perhaps after Palladio's Palazzo Chiericati in Vicenza by the nineteenth-century government architect Ammi B. Young, quietly reminds us of the federal power, for it was once the custom house. The Subtreasury Building on Wall Street in New York is another example; better still, New York's City Hall by the architects Mangin and McComb, a building of such exquisite proportion and detail that the surrounding skyscrapers stand back from it as if in awe. Then again there are the domes of the state houses, the golden one of Charles Bulfinch, rising above Beacon Hill in Boston, which still defies competition from business towers, the modest capitol by Town, Davis and Paton in Raleigh, North Carolina, or Cass Gilbert's in Charleston, West Virginia, with its dome raised on a great stone drum, symbol of the State.

Above all the Capitol in Washington reminds us that the State has not been idle in decorating America. The Founding Fathers, having created monuments of democratic government in the Constitution and the Bill of Rights, conscious of their mission attained in the creation of these instruments, were not afraid to symbolize in stone the message of the

Republic, while today we eschew symbolism in building a world capital in New York, the United Nations Headquarters.

The intense pride that Americans once had in government is shown in the history of the Capitol building. At the outbreak of the Civil War the structure was still unfinished. Instead of delaying construction, President Lincoln was insistent that it be carried to completion, as symbol of the Union's strength and determination. On December 2, 1863, Thomas Crawford's statue of Freedom (modeled in a Roman studio) was hoisted to the top of the cast-iron dome as thirty-five guns roared out below, to be answered by the boom of the guns from the twelve forts that then surrounded the city.

Dilatory as it may first appear, the State in America, in all its various divisions, stands out even ahead of business as the most steadfast patron of the arts, and that continuing tradition is underlined by the creation of Washington itself. When Major Pierre Charles L'Enfant first drew up his monumental plan at the behest of George Washington, he saw it as his duty to create a capital worthy of the young Republic. If he suffered the fate of many planners in being forced from his post by ambitious speculators, his work was continued in spirit by Jefferson, who, in his passion for architecture, saw the mission that lay before him. It was he who appointed Benjamin Henry Latrobe, one of the greatest early architects, to be supervisor of public buildings; it was he who retained the services of Giuseppe Franzoni, an Italian sculptor, to work on the Capitol; it was he who persuaded Congress to appropriate moneys for the improvement of the city and spent a third of it in laying out Pennsylvania Avenue in the manner of a Paris boulevard.

The tradition once begun has never been totally neglected, and when the American Roman Style was passed and the country lost in a Romantic mist, an artifact worthy of the ancient world, the giant obelisk called the Washington Monument (it was begun in 1848 and finished in 1884) was placed near the crossing of the axes of the White House and the Capitol. With each revival of interest in the classical tradition, the capital city has continued to grow and expand; with the American Renaissance that followed after the Chicago World's Fair in 1893, all of America came to blossom in the manner of the ancients, and the city of Washington guided and set the measure. Again when the classic had all but been forgotten, Washington continued in our time to sponsor tradition in the shape of the National Gallery of Art by the architect John Russell Pope with Otto Eggers and D. P. Higgins, consultants. This building stands for much that is the United States—a wealthy businessman, Andrew Mellon of Pittsburgh, contributing to the nation under the sponsorship of the State, a believer in private enterprise joining in support of government patronage of the arts.

Government buildings in American cities have taken the form of public palaces, Federal Hall in New York being an early and splendid example. Here in 1789 Washington was inaugurated in a chamber rich with American marble, designed by L'Enfant, his first effort to serve the new nation.

The old United States Capitol, looking up Pennsylvania Avenue from the White House, as it was at the time of President Andrew Jackson.

It is largely through these public palaces that Americans have expressed their desire for splendor, and the visitor to our cities must go to the state houses, post offices and courthouses to find the mural painting, sculpture and ornament that are missing elsewhere. If it were not for government patronage of the arts, admittedly spasmodic and casual, our communities would be much farther from satisfying the need for symbols of civic and national pride, which the people of a republic demand—and ours have demanded—no less than kings and popes.

Instead of dismissing our physical creations for sameness,

ugliness and want of order, it is good to look again, as did Matthew Arnold, who thereafter found himself treating our "institutions" with increased respect. The American tradition in giving the physical patterns of the country both shape and variety is far richer than we realize. As we have seen, our business society has planned communities, our churches have helped to decorate the cities, and the State, although the federal government does not as yet count a Secretary of the Arts in the President's cabinet, has some tradition of patronage. American cities and towns have been touched in one way or another by each succeeding generation. All communities, even the youngest, have some mark of time, and their temples, notably those of the Church and the State, have become the treasure houses of the best we have created. By studying them we will learn to know the American urban tradition.

Beyond the physical problems that have come as a result of increasing urbanization, there is the responsibility thrust on the United States by its position in the world today. It is not mere chauvinism to suggest that world leadership demands a splendid physical setting. And there is a choice of direction for the design of our new buildings, new works and facilities. Will they emphasize expediency, provincialism and a negative approach to city planning, or can they be molded into a more noble form? Can our institutions—business, religion and government—be made aware of their responsibility as patrons of civic arts? This is possible, when they understand their great traditions, now obscured by the obsession with technology.

Like a child fascinated by his new toy, the American is seduced by the idea of technological advance. Material progress and scientific development are, of course, to be fostered so that we may enjoy their priceless benefits in hygiene, comfort and convenience. This book will show how important technology has been in shaping our communities, but it is all too easy for Americans, like children, to point to the great bridges and highways, mass-produced automobiles and television sets, imagining that they are emblems of a new, bright and shiny culture, and forgetting that the machine is only a tool for achieving greater things. Permanent monuments are measured in terms of art and humanity, and as we wander, often quite obliviously, among the temples that have been built in America, it would be well to pause and examine what has been created here. The scene about us, of which mechanical objects are only a part, has after all something greater and more lasting to offer, because here

he artist has contributed his invaluable gift and has, in his
vay, brought solace and pleasure to the citizens and some-
imes glory and honor to the Republic. Let us turn once again
o our temples, be they of Commerce, God or Government,
nd see what the past has given us and where the present
ails. "We are one of the most luxurious nations in the
vorld; one of the most developed in all that relates to con-
enience and the practical requirements of life, one of the
nost accomplished in all the so-called useful and mechanical
rts," wrote the American sculptor William Wetmore Story
eventy-five years ago, "but in the ideal spheres of art we
ave accomplished little, because we have desired little; our
eeds and necessities have been amply supplied, but the
eart and soul have been fed upon husks. Use has its build-
ngs and habitations, but beauty has not yet its temple."

Beauty cannot find its shrine in the modern city, and since
Story's time the city itself has been rejected as a way of life.
f we desire little today, we do so at our peril, for above
everything the times call for the highest human aims, which
nclude the creation of beauty. The objective should be
Peirce's American community of "dignity, worth and impor-
ance," in which personal happiness and individual aspiration
vill exist in surroundings shaped by the artist's hand. America
he Beautiful!

PART I

The Colonial Pattern

1607-1776

In an era of conveniences and comforts we cannot remind ourselves too often of the struggles of our ancestors in laying the foundations of the nation. The homes of the early settlers had to be hacked out of the wilderness, and the first communities often suffered frightful disasters before they could be called permanent. Happily, the Atlantic seaboard of the United States is broken by bays, inlets and river mouths that provided the newcomers with a certain amount of shelter. For the colonists the ocean was a fearsome bond, but a bond, nonetheless, with Europe and between settlements that grew rapidly up and down the coast.

Nearly everyone farmed or fished during this period and took their produce to town by water. At first industry, when it existed, was carried on in the simplest mills of stone or wood, but it was chiefly confined to handicrafts in the home. The air of the country was everywhere; even in the city streets pigs and stray cattle roamed freely. Cow pastures and cultivated fields greeted the traveler once he had left behind him the small cities of the pre-Revolutionary days. Beyond the seacoast in the North he came on rare villages and towns; in the South he moved from plantation to plantation or stopped at an occasional courthouse town. As he pressed on beyond tidewater, the world of the new frontier greeted him. The simple cabin, alone in its clearing, reflected the combination of courage and hardship of pioneer life. Because of the absence of towns and cities in this region the settlers led a very primitive life; sometimes the pioneers adopted the habits and the costumes of the enemy Indians.

To a frontiersman, accustomed only to the bare necessities of life, the tidewater cities and towns must have appeared magnificent and, no doubt, corrupt. But to our eyes they are tiny and inoffensive, since even by 1776 no city contained over 40,000 souls. Ropewalks, shipyards, sail lofts, the smell of tar, foreign accents and numbers of ships were constant reminders that water gave life to the community. Some aspects of present-day Salem in the North and Charleston in the South still recall the day when American cities had not yet turned their backs on the ocean or river. And, of course, there was ubiquitous wild nature. On a summer evening in 1750, a boat for Albany had scarcely left its wharf in New York when a mist of fire descended over the Hudson and, behold, the ship was bright with fireflies on the rigging. Ever present nature, Calvinism, mercantile capitalism, the philosophy of Locke and Montesquieu, the early church lantern and the late Baroque steeple, all formed part of the brave venture that was the colonial settlement, clinging, like lichen on rock, to the Atlantic shore.

1. *The First Communities*

Boston was the first important city in American history— "the Metropolis of the whole English America," Cotton Mather called it in the seventeenth century. It was a reflection of the Gothic, a maze of narrow winding streets confined to what is now called the North End. Built of half-timbering, i.e., of a heavy beam frame and timber interstices filled with rubble, brick and stucco, its structures belonged to the Middle Ages. Clapboard came in only toward the end of the century, as did white paint and ornament. Small, crowded, with the second story hanging out over the first, and thin walls pierced by leaded casement windows, the homes of the early Bostonians were humble enough. The restored house of Paul Revere, dating back from about 1676; is a useful reminder of the style, although it was built when clapboard sheathing was coming into use and shingle had replaced thatch. Public buildings were equally plain in a community where art and all that tasted of giving pleasure were banned. Meetinghouses (the building still standing in Hingham is an excellent example) were severe barnlike structures; among public edifices, only the Town House of Boston, three-storied, wooden, gabled and topped with lanterns, might have passed as at all showy or remarkable in the early days.

The struggle to build in the wilderness began up and down the coast when the first immigrants stepped ashore. The relief expedition sent to Jamestown to help Captain John Smith in 1608 found the settlers living in mean cabins and holes in the ground. Dugouts were the only shelter for most of the colonists in their first years, and these were followed by flimsy cabins of vertical stakes and wattles or rectangular wigwams with curved roofs, covered with skins or bark. A visit to the Pioneer Village, a careful reconstruction of Salem, Massachusetts, as it was in the early years, well reveals the rudeness and frailty of the first dwellings.

No such structure as the log cabin existed for the Puritans or the First Families of Virginia; this building type was imported by the Swedes and the Germans along the Delaware at the end of the seventeenth century. Not until fifty years later did the Scotch-Irish spread it along the Allegheny frontier. As soon as practicable the New England settlers replaced their initial wretched quarters by well-built houses of half-timbering in the English fashion; in New Amsterdam the Dutch favored brick houses with gabled roofs and corbiesteps. Rarely did the settlements of our first century achieve anything but a very provincial echo of the Medieval. The most elaborate Medieval building still with us is the delightful St. Luke's Church (1682) at Newport Parish, Virginia, a remote colonial expression of the parish churches across the water.

The prevalent form of American community before the coming of the modern American city was the agricultural market town, today fast disappearing. Many prominent observers fall into the error of calling our towns "villages," notably in the instance of the "New England village," although the latter is the home of the "town meeting." Albert Gallatin, Secretary of the Treasury in Jefferson's administration, was well aware of the distinction. "We have no villages, that is to say centers peopled by farmers," he reminded the Frenchman Alexis de Tocqueville in 1831. "The landowner lives on his land and the houses are all scattered through the countryside. What you call villages [here] deserves rather the name of town, since the population is composed of merchants, artisans and lawyers." Only in the early days of the colonies did the village exist, and it changed very quickly into an agricultural market town with the country's increase in population and trades. The true American village was the product of a very different society.

The Indians lived in villages, for the most part temporary. The Iroquois, for example, moved theirs every ten or twelve years. Only in the Southwest do we still find Indians living in village communities, called *pueblos*. Large multistoried communal edifices of stone and adobe still rise four or five stories on the mesa or the desert. The Pueblo Indians built them without doors for defense reasons and entered them by ladders. The first floor served for storage and the upper floors for living. Their strange form, their hand-smoothed walls of warm yellow-brown adobe often covered with white gypsum, and their austere monumentality offer a sharp contrast to the cluttered modern town nearby.

Another form of village which has fortunately long passed from the American scene is the slave village. Few, except on the largest plantations, were elaborate; in most instances a double row of overcrowded plain log or brick cabins ranged

An early American village, Taos Pueblo in New Mexico.
Originally there were no doors on the ground level.

along a dirt path near the main house. No attempt was made to house the slaves in permanent quarters, forming part of the main buildings—in the way that servants and retainers were housed in a French château, an English country house, or a Palladian villa on the Brenta—with the result that most of the slave cabins, including those built in the nineteenth century, have disappeared.

As Gallatin correctly observed, the village—essentially a product of feudal and slave economies—could not exist for long in a nation of free landlords. Two strong social forces transformed it: the communal drive on the one hand, and the individual drive on the other. The first created the market town, cited by Gallatin; and the second the American land-

scape dotted with farms. In Massachusetts the original settlers joined in groups and obtained land from the General
Court of the colony to form a settlement, which was given the
name of "township." As a township grew in population, it
cast off members who in turn formed a new township with a
grant of new land. In this fashion Cambridge planted the
town of Billerica, and in Connecticut, Hartford mothered the
town of Farmington. The houses were strung along one main
street, with the plots stretching behind for as much as a mile,
while common land was set aside for grazing, as well as a few
lots for a meetinghouse, school and burial ground. The houses
might also be placed about the fenced-in common, which
would take a variety of shapes. Instead of joining with each
other as in the typical European village, the houses stood apart
on their large plots; in the case of Enfield, Connecticut, the
strips measured 192 feet on the street end and stretched some
1920 feet behind. The remainder of the land in the township,
amounting to several square miles, was held in common, the
property of the first settlers. Unlike the European village clustered outside a château—as at Balleroy in Normandy or the
area below the great Farnese villa at Caprarola, Italy, where
the villagers have several miles to walk before they come to
their acres—the houses of Enfield were set back from the
street and separated from one another, and the townsman had
only to step into his long "backyard" to farm. The open lot,
so much a part of the American suburban scene today, stems
as much from dividing the land in this fashion as from the
clearing. Once the population grew, once the sons and daughters of the original settlers came of age or other settlers appeared in the village, the common lands of the township beyond the settled limits were divided, given, or sold and farmed
by scattered individuals. Although this took place on a more
modest scale than in Virginia, the American farm punctuating
the landscape became a typical pattern in the North. Land
hunger increased individualism and began to make a mockery
of the tight theocratic communities the church authorities
wished to perpetuate. By the 1680's the practice of living alone
apart from the community had become so general that Increase Mather was protesting: "People are already [sic] to run
wild into the woods again as heathenish as ever, if you do not
prevent it." In Pennsylvania, under a milder faith, the same
thing was happening.

By 1685 the harassed William Penn was writing to England,
". . . many that had right to more land were at first covetous to
have their whole quantity without regard to this way of settlement, tho' by such wilderness vacancies they had ruin'd the

country, and that to our interest of course. I had in view," said he, explaining why he wanted closely-settled towns, "society, assistance, busy commerce, instruction of youth, government, of people's manners, conveniency of religious assembling, encouragement of mechanicks, distinct and beaten roads . . ." The early Virginians also preferred the open country. In fact, when the General Assembly of the colony ordered in 1680 that nineteen towns be established, one to each county, seeing "the great necessity, usefulnesse, and advantage of cohabitation," Charles II was forced to veto the act on the objections of the planters who refused to ship tobacco by way of the towns, preferring their own plantation landings. Not until 1691, under William and Mary, when towns were made ports of entry, did they appear in numbers; and communities like Urbana, on the Rappahannock River, took shape in the South.

Evolution of the clearing: first stage.

If the land revolution placed the farmhouse in the distant landscape, the manner of clearing the land ultimately produced the "open lot." Houses stood in the open—all were welcome to see and be seen, perhaps the result of claustrophobia brought about by the dark forest. Timothy Dwight, president of Yale College, described the process of clearing the land for a farm, but it was no less true of a new town. "To clear a farm covered with a thick growth of large trees, such as generally abound in this country, is a work of no small magnitude," he warned in what he claimed to be the first descrip-

Evolution of the clearing: second stage.

tion of the process. "Especially is this true when, as is usually the fact, it is to be done by a single man, and still more especially when that man is poor and obliged to struggle with many other discouragements." How clearly our inheritance is revealed by these lines! The forester or pioneer built himself a temporary shelter and, living by his gun, set about in the autumn or very early spring girdling or felling trees, the latter becoming the more general process. "After they have lain a sufficient length of time, he sets fire to them, lying as they fall. If he is successful, the greater part of them are consumed in the conflagration. The remainder he cuts with his axe into pieces of a convenient length, rolls them into piles, and sets fire to them again." He left the ashes to enrich the soil or

Evolution of the clearing: third stage.

gathered and sold them to a manufacturer of "potashes" and obtained enough to pay for the cost of clearing. "After the field is burned over, his next business is to break it up. The instrument, employed for this purpose, is a large and strong harrow, here called a *drag* with very stout iron teeth, resembling in its form the capital letter A. It is drawn over the surface a sufficient number of times to make it mellow, and afterwards to cover the seed. A plough would here be of no use as it would soon be broken to pieces by the roots of the trees."

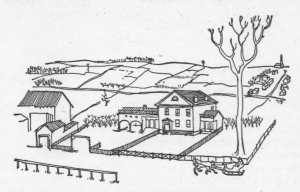

Evolution of the clearing: fourth stage, showing
the Greek Revival Style of the 1830's.

Faced with such back-breaking work, it is little wonder that the pioneer did not look on the tree with any great affection; Dwight noted that many had "cut down their forests with an improvident hand." If trees were left, they stood well apart from the house, as if warned to approach at their peril, nor were hedges or walls permitted to obstruct the approach to the house, except for the occasional picket fence.

Yet, having destroyed the forests, the descendants of the first settlers acknowledged the loss and in homage placed trees along the streets in their towns. The practice began in the latter part of the seventeenth century with great elms or maples relieving the openness once so eagerly sought. "Almost every one has an elegant row of trees and many of the houses have gardens adjoining with fields of Indian corn," reads a description of New Haven in the early years of the Republic, "which gives the town the appearance of so many houses situated in the middle of fine gardens." The leafy, open American community, now to be found everywhere, but more particularly in the suburbs of our great cities, was well established by the time of the nation's birth.

2. Courthouse Square and "Village" Green

The most distinctive feature of the New England town was the common, or green. This open space took many shapes. It might be a wide strip of green down one side of a large main street as in Easthampton, Long Island, a triangle of land formed at an intersection of roads as at Lexington, Massachusetts, with its modern statue of the Minute Man by Henry Hudson Kitson, or a charming oval like that of Woodstock, which is Vermont's best known town green. The first example of city planning in the colonies was the laying out in 1638 of the New Haven Colony in the form of nine large squares, the central one being reserved as the common green, a market place and pasture. Although the construction of tall buildings on three sides has since destroyed the earlier scale, the New Haven green remains much the same. It was this square green that came to be the chief exportable commodity of New England in city planning, as her sons and daughters moved across the Hudson into New York State and the Middle West in the years after the Revolutionary War, founding settlement after settlement in the Western Reserve, and farther west in Illinois and Wisconsin, where almost every town has a square, often elm-shaded in the New England fashion. Usually this feature is the town's proudest possession.

Although the New England green is a conspicuous contribution to the American townscape, it is by no means the only one, nor is it the most important. Certainly, in contrast to many communities where it is absent, the green offers solace, but it lacks a very important quality to give it body, that of formal architectural grouping, open space alone being insufficient to satisfy the eye. The strong medieval strain of the early settlements, to be seen in the half-timbering, the use of thatch and the overhanging second story, rarely produced the enclosed arcaded market square found in Europe. Part and parcel of the walled town, the architectural enclosure could not be expected in open towns where the individual rather than the community counted. "There are no city gates here," wrote Peter Kalm, the Swedish naturalist, of Albany, New York, in 1750, "but for the most part just open holes through which people pass in and out of town." He noted "two market places in town" that consisted simply of very wide streets.

The architectural square in the United States, like the *plaza mayor* of Spain, stems not from commerce but from government, and it originated in the Virginia Colony. In New England, where the township was the paramount unit of government, it does not exist; only where the county comes strongly into the picture can it be found. County government demanded a setting of importance. In 1634 the Virginia government created nine shires (the name was changed to county soon after) and fixed them as the local government units. The county seats did not rise at once; court sessions were held in houses or taverns about the county. With the coming of towns around 1700, several courthouses were built which are still standing: Prince George, seat of the county of the same name, dating from 1702; Hanover, dating from about 1733, set in a wide brick-walled green; and Gloucester (1766), one of the handsomest, surrounded by a walled enclosure. The old courthouse of Yorktown is no longer standing, nor is the one designed by Jefferson for Buckingham County, which was burned in 1869. The courthouse town was, in the days of early Virginia, and remains today throughout the country a social nucleus as well as a political and trading center, a place of congregation for the surrounding county. Such is the contribution of Virginia—the tiny square with a handsome courthouse, perhaps a library, several churches, a lawyer's office, and groups of pink or orange brick houses and shops ranged closely around the green center, small in scale and rich in detail. As an article for export it proved its worth in the Ohio country and throughout the West when the Virginians settled fertile lands beyond the Alleghenies. (Farther south, in Mississippi, the courthouse town forms the setting for the novels of William Faulkner and Eudora Welty.)

Interesting architecturally were the few French communities along the Mississippi River, some of which still survive. Driving down a street lined with one- or two-story houses, with porches and low-pitched roofs, today's motorist may find himself in Ste. Genevieve, Missouri. A trading town founded in the 1750's, its houses originally were of *poteaux-en-terre* construction—upright posts set in the ground with the wall spaces packed with clay and rubble—a method of building found nowhere in this country except in the French towns; but it is the porch, or *galerie*, in many instances carried all around the house, which makes this building type indigenous. Much farther down the river, at Natchez, Mississippi, and Hahnville, Louisiana, others remain to recall the day when the whole valley was once part of the Kingdom of France.

More frequent are the many communities founded by the

Germans. In 1683 Francis Daniel Pastorius led a band of Rhinelanders, forerunner of the great stream of German migrants, to the outskirts of Philadelphia. Here he built Germantown, the first linear community in eastern Pennsylvania, consisting of a double row of gray-stoned houses on either side of the main street. They were joined together and faced directly on the street, presenting an architectural unity seldom found in America. This style of building was repeated by other Rhenish immigrants (the Pennsylvania "Dutch"), copying

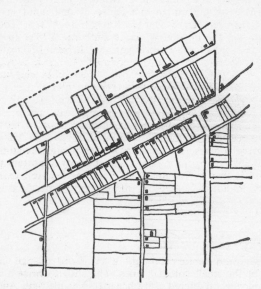

Kutztown, Pennsylvania, founded in 1771, a close-knit Pennsylvania "Dutch" community laid out in linear fashion.

the villages of their homeland; although traces of it remain in Germantown and elsewhere, the pattern has virtually disappeared before the commercial front and the open lot.

Among the few examples of American colonial architectural squares and groupings, the missions and presidios of the Southwest and California are outstanding. A church with an elaborate convent attached and often built about a patio identifies the work of the Franciscan friars. The tower and façade of the church and the quality of the decoration inside and out reveal that the Anglo-Saxon, when it came to the arts, had much to learn. In these communities the Franciscans tried to bring the Christian way of life to uninterested Indians, much as did the Jesuits of Paraguay in their famous "Reductions"—with somewhat more success, for the missions are still with us while the Reductions have almost entirely disappeared. ("Reductions" were the communities founded in the early part of the eighteenth century by the Jesuit fathers to help the Indians protect themselves against the Portuguese and Spanish colonists. These unique settlements figure at one point in Voltaire's *Candide*.) San Xavier de Bac (1784–97) at Tucson, Arizona, and the mission at Santa Barbara (1786) in California are among the best, bringing the Hispano-Mexican Baroque within the limits of the country. The rich façade of San Xavier, with its volutes, scrolls, arabesques and statue-filled niches, as well as the splendor of the interior ornaments, leaves us with the regret that the Franciscans did not build more settlements and give shape to larger towns. The presidios and civilian towns in California founded by Spanish and later Mexican authorities consisted of one-story adobe buildings built around a plaza. Of these very modestly constructed buildings few survive except in name, and the only important plaza inherited is that of La Reina de Los Angeles, still existing, although radically altered, in the center of that sprawling metropolis of the West Coast.

3. *The American Baroque*

The eighteenth century brought a profound change in the aspect of the small colonial cities. The shift to brick—inevitable, since wood offered a fire hazard—was the first. Another was the use of lead paint, a sign of growing prosperity. Right-angled streets, paved and lined with trees, was a third improvement. Most important, a skyline came into being where none had existed before. Although there had been cupolas, it was not until 1740 that the first steeple in the Baroque manner of Sir Christopher Wren was raised on Christ Church (Old North) in Boston. The Calvinist churches met the Anglican challenge by slowly following suit. The white steeple, which is today the symbol of New England, had come into being; the meetinghouse had been transformed into a church.

We know the measure of Wren's influence in this country by the presence everywhere of his steeple. From him and his followers came the English work inspired by Italian and

French churches, palaces and villas; but whereas in Europe most of the work was done in stone, we adapted the style to our wooden architecture. The famous doorways of Westover, Virginia (ca. 1730–34), have pediments of richly carved volutes which betray the shadow of Rome. So too the doorway of the Wentworth-Gardner House (1760) in Portsmouth, New Hampshire. Elaborate chimney pieces, such as the one in a parlor of Philipse Manor, Yonkers, New York (ca. 1720), were another expression of this most exuberant of styles, which became the rage up and down the coast.

In confining himself to wood and brick the colonist did not let the lack of materials curb his penchant for the elegant. If he could not find marble for his interiors, he would imitate the stone in paint and wood. In our current fashion for the plain and the bare, we accept too willingly the notion that monochromy, especially white or off white, was standard in the colonies. This is underestimating our forefathers' taste for art. The rich carving was matched by rich marbling, i.e., imitating marble on wood or stucco, or by graining, an imitation of the grain of expensive wood on ordinary wood. In the Metropolitan Museum of New York we have an example from Marmion, King George County, Virginia, in which marbling and gilding are rivals for honor. The lately restored Hunter House, now open to the public, in Newport, Rhode Island, offers fine examples of graining on pine in imitation of cedar.

The most effective form of imitation was often on the exterior of houses. Wooden walls imitated blocks of stone, as at George Washington's home, "Mount Vernon," in Virginia, and the Redwood Library in Newport. In more modest buildings pretense was concentrated on the front alone, so that it might be properly called "false." The "false front," once so prevalent in the East and now found mostly in the West, stems from the American Baroque. "Houses built of both wood and brick have only the wall towards the street made of the latter, all the other sides being of boards," noted Kalm as he rode through New Brunswick, New Jersey, in 1750. "This peculiar kind of ostentation would easily lead a traveller who passes through the town in haste to believe that most of the houses are built of brick." An example of this "ostentation" exists in several ancient houses on Grove Street in New York's Greenwich Village and in other communities. George Santayana has explained this pleasant vanity as practiced by the Italians, whom the colonists were aping on a provincial scale. "What we admire is not so much a façade as a triumphal gateway," wrote he of the Roman palace, "set up in front of the house to be its ambassador to the world, wearing decidedly richer apparel than its master can afford at home." This was the spirit of the American Baroque; it established a tradition which, even in this day of the efficient and the functional, is echoed in the elaborate shop fronts or richly ornamented lobbies of our great office buildings and hotels.

Intricate gardens were another form of art beloved by the colonists. The style was the formal French garden, which Baroque England had made its own. The *jardin à la française* of Le Nôtre, rather than the *jardin à l'anglaise* of William Kent, was the fashion in the colonies throughout the eighteenth century. In the South, especially, the country mansion was given a splendid setting of formal box, and an elaborate springhouse, stables and even an orangery where exotic plants were stored in winter were built on the grounds. One such orangery has come down to us, an elegant little building at Wye House on the Eastern Shore of Maryland. Whoever has been fortunate enough to visit Middleton Place outside Charleston will know the meaning of elegance in terms of the American Baroque garden. No more beautiful *pleasaunce* exists in this country, and it is the only Baroque garden that has remained intact, although the main house is regrettably no longer there. With its great canal, the banked camellias and azaleas and the superb terraces sloping down to the Ashley River, the pools in the shape of butterfly wings and the moss-covered live oaks, here is American splendor to match the European.

An era that gave so much prominence to entrance ways and gardens did not neglect the appearance of its cities. City planning and civic design had come into their own in Rome with the work of Michelangelo in the sixteenth century and in Paris under Louis XIV in the seventeenth. In the colonies city plans were drawn for Charleston (1680), Philadelphia (1682) and Annapolis (1694), following Wren's London plan of 1666, but these were eclipsed by Williamsburg in 1699. In the new capital of the Virginia Colony civic design took its proper place beside city planning: the town was laid out by Theodorick Bland to display the buildings. The Duke of Gloucester Street, ninety-nine feet wide, forms the major axis running from the capitol to the College of William and Mary where it breaks into a goosefoot street pattern, so often used by Baroque civic designs. The broad Palace Green is a minor cross axis, leading to and displaying the Governor's Palace. As for the main buildings, if their exteriors are so plain and lacking in ornament to have warranted Jefferson's comment that the palace was "not handsome without" and the college and hospital "rude, misshapen piles which, but that they have roofs, would be taken for brick-kilns," the formal gardens, the painted and gilded wrought-iron gates and the sumptuous interiors offer sufficient compensation. The palace itself, today reconstructed, was considered the finest residence of the colonies. The woodwork, the furniture, the hangings, the silverware and even the *chinoiserie* wall decorations disclosed that richness and beauty were at home in the America of the 1750's.

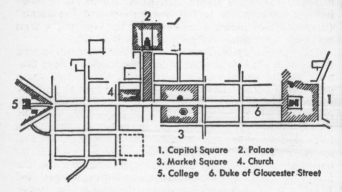

1. Capitol Square   2. Palace
3. Market Square   4. Church
5. College   6. Duke of Gloucester Street

Williamsburg, Virginia, an example of
the American Baroque city plan.

Public buildings of an elegance unknown in the previous century, such as those found at Williamsburg or at Boston in the Old State House and Faneuil Hall, bespoke a new sophistication. Newport could even boast of the country's first professional architect in the person of Peter Harrison, whose Redwood Library (1748–50) is a monument to the fashion of Palladio. The Touro Synagogue (1759–63) and the Brick Market (1761–72) in the same city are other celebrated buildings of his design. New York, where the Dutch and the Flemings had brought their native brick architecture, was an early brick city. Few structures of the eighteenth century remain on Manhattan Island today, the best by far being St. Paul's Chapel (1764) by James McBean, modeled after St. Martin's-in-the-Fields, the famous London church by James Gibbs.

If Boston was to offer the most substantial public buildings in the colonies, New York the handsomest church, Charleston such refinements as a museum and a theatre, and Savannah a sufficiency of squares, they were all to be surpassed at the close of the period by Philadelphia. By 1776 Penn's city had a population estimated at 40,000, the second largest after London in the British Empire. Unlike the others, which went through a long period of development from sod huts, to thatched half-timbering, to brick, Philadelphia sprang almost at once into stone and brick after the pioneer Philadelphians gave up their temporary shelters in caves on the banks of the Delaware. Penn had founded the town in 1682 and three years later he was writing to London of the admirable cheap brick to be manufactured in the future metropolis. Population crowded into the newborn city so fast that three-storied "tenements" (the word then meant a multiple dwelling and not a slum building), were rising alongside one-family houses.

The city plan, rather than the plain brick dwellings, showed Penn's dream to be a product of Baroque London, just as Boston's winding streets recalled medieval London. Here was a gridiron plan, the typical merchant's plan of the age, with the streets laid at right angles, dividing the city into a series of rectangular lots; but because it had five squares it was a novelty for the colonies. The main square, today covered by the city hall, consisted of ten acres set aside for commercial, religious and civic purposes, a future civic center which proved too far out of town to be of any use in the eighteenth century. The four other squares, Rittenhouse, Washington, Logan and Franklin, were pleasure grounds for the people. One street, one hundred feet wide, at first called High Street in the English fashion, ran down to the Delaware. It served as a market place, the name being changed to Market Street only in 1859, when the abandoned market sheds, or shambles, as they were called, were removed. Along the fifty-foot wide residential streets trees were planted after 1700. Twenty years later they were paved and the first sidewalks of brick and flagstones followed soon after, with stone posts to protect the pedestrians from horses and carts. The first civic center in the country was Independence Hall and its surrounding buildings in Philadelphia. In 1730 the Provincial Assembly of Pennsylvania ordered a state house to be built with two flanking wings; this was the initial step in creating one of the most delightful urban complexes in America, although today Independence Hall is somewhat dwarfed in scale by its neighboring skyscrapers.

A novelty in that day, but one which would seem to our eye perfectly normal, was the straight tree-lined street. Again and again travelers commented on the city's neat symmetry, the first important example in America of the order so desired by the merchant and the trader. This and the prosperity that made it the commercial center of colonial America and the main port of entry for immigrants gave it a substantial appearance by the 1750's—Benjamin Franklin had not been mistaken in forsaking his native Boston in 1723 for the greater promise on the Delaware.

Delightful as the city must have been in 1776, with its paved streets, its trees and the five hundred public water pumps, which were its proudest boast, we must not let the distance of the past offer too rosy a picture or too great a contrast with the city of the present. "By the eve of the Revolution," the historian Carl Bridenbaugh reminds us, "Philadelphia had assumed the appearance, and something of the ugliness, of any prosperous and rapidly growing city."

PART II

The Young Republic

1776-1825

ALL COLONIAL COUNTRIES find new energy on becoming independent nations. The fluidity that we see in modern India, Pakistan, Burma and Indonesia was no less apparent in the American republic after the Revolutionary War. At once the frontier shifted west as war veterans and immigrants sought land beyond the Alleghenies in the Western Reserve and Tennessee. Upper New York State, relatively untouched, was invaded by bands of New England settlers, much to the annoyance of the native "Yorkers." Transportation had improved very little since colonial days, despite the coming of the turnpike and the first steamboats, yet the new America was on the move and experimenting. Alexander Hamilton issued his famous *Report on Manufactures* in 1791 and even attempted a planned industrial town for textile manufacture at Paterson, New Jersey, which was premature. Manufacturing on a large scale was not properly established until after the War of 1812, at the close of the era.

A triumphant spirit created the Constitution and gave it a shrine in the federal capital. The times called for bold plans and there were men on hand to make them. Architecture, too, under the inspiration of Jefferson, strove to meet new standards with a stricter interpretation of the classical tradition, but the fact that only one in ten persons lived in towns of a thousand or more set limits to any extended planning in the grand manner. Energies turned elsewhere in the town, building for immediate needs, and the city plans almost exclusively followed one pattern: the gridiron. Attempts at long-term leaseholds were swept aside and landownership in fee simple became the rule. In much the same spirit, town houses of identical design were set in rows because the process was simple. A suburb

49

occasionally appeared on the outskirts of the larger cities wherever easy transportation became available.

In the city center, more steeples rose above the roofs and the ship masts, as Wren's contribution was universally adopted, and congregations welcomed new faiths with the coming of the Methodists, the Baptists and the Unitarians. Merchants were prominent among the elite—the role of John Jacob Astor of New York and Stephen Girard of Philadelphia in financing the War of 1812 showed that we were producing businessmen of power and substance. The American businessman, now independent of his British cousin, built himself large commercial exchanges, whose pediments and domes appeared on the horizon, changing the skyline of the merchant city. During the summer our businessman betook himself to a country villa, while the artisan and his family sought the "pleasure garden."

Inland from the coastal cities new towns were being built on rivers and lakes. The hardships remained much the same, but the American was by now accustomed to the wilderness and knew how to fight it. The New England green and the Virginia courthouse found a new home, often together in the Ohio country and farther west. In the East and South new community types developed in the state capital and the college town, both of them innovations of the era.

1. *The American Roman Style*

On the evening of May 10, 1784, all Philadelphia streamed to Market Street to hear the sheriff proclaim the peace signed at Versailles, officially ending the Revolutionary War. This was one reason, but there was another: to see the triumphal arch of the painter Charles Willson Peale, erected in honor of the occasion. Processions, music and the customary speeches marked the celebration. Crowning the scene was the edifice of wood and canvas set up near Independence Hall. Fifty-five and a half feet wide and forty feet high, it announced the virtues of the new Republic, the glory of its heroes, our friendship with France and the coming of peace. The figure of Peace held her bright torch aloft, while about her stood the cardinal virtues amid heavenly clouds. Painted reliefs and Latin inscriptions recalled the past and foretold a glorious future. In one panel blazed the sun of France and the thirteen stars of the United States. *Coelo sociati,* or "Joined in the Heavens," was the message beneath. In another Washington was shown returning, like Cincinnatus, to his plow as *Victrix virtus,* or

"Victorious Virtue." Supremely confident, the spandrels of the center arch carried the capital letters S P Q P, SENATUS POPULUSQUE PENNSYLVANIANUS. Such was the introduction of the American Roman Style.

Peale's arch was the joint product of private financing and the artist's vision, but the architecture of the next generation, also known as Federal, was to be essentially a government architecture. The man who fixed the style was a public leader,

Ceremonial arch by the painter Charles Willson Peale, erected near Independence Hall in 1784. (Drawing made from reconstruction of Lester Hoadley Sellers.)

Thomas Jefferson. Independence had created a demand for numerous public buildings, even the necessity of building a new city for a capital. For Jefferson the challenge was to show the world that we could build as well as we could legislate. "You see I am an enthusiast on the subject of the arts," wrote he to James Madison in 1785. "But it is an enthusiasm of which I am not ashamed, as its object is to improve the taste of my countrymen, to increase their reputation, to reconcile to them the respect of the world, and procure them its praise." His enthusiasm was matched by a knowledge of architecture unusual even for the times. As our minister to France in the

1780's, he spent every free moment viewing buildings, statues, paintings, and studying at close hand the greatest monuments that Paris had to offer. His architectural library was unrivaled in America, including as it did Perrault's *Vitruvius,* Palladio in several editions, Scamozzi, Serlio, Alberti, Inigo Jones, and many other great authorities. Not unnaturally he led the taste of the young nation in the arts.

Jefferson was impatient with the American Baroque, as his comments on Williamsburg, cited earlier, reveal. The older style lacked the breadth, the scale and the monumentality he believed essential to convey the majesty and pomp of a great republic. What he wanted was nothing less than the Grand Design of buildings, grounds, and town planning—linked to the classical tradition. Compare any large building of the American Roman with the American Baroque (the columned capitol in Richmond, Virginia, with the more modest capitol at Williamsburg, for example), and at once the beholder will sense Jefferson's aim. Just any style would not do for him; it must have passed the test of time. "Whenever it is proposed to prepare plans for the Capitol," he wrote in 1791 to Major L'Enfant, who was designing the federal city, "I should prefer the adoption of some one of the models of antiquity, which have had the approbation of thousands of years . . ." Unlike the matter-of-fact John Adams, who is reputed to have said, "I would not give sixpence for a statue of Phidias or a painting by Raphael," Jefferson was passionately interested in all the visual arts.

He had been in France when the question arose of a new capitol building for Virginia. Taking the initiative, he retained the services of the French architect Charles Louis Clérisseau, and together in 1785 they designed the building that is substantially the one we see today in Richmond (the wings and flight of steps were added in 1904–5), the first permanent structure in the new taste. The model for the building was the famous Roman temple at Nîmes.

Influential as he was, Jefferson's dream would have faded had it not struck a sympathetic chord in George Washington. We know of the first President's interest in architecture and gardening from the love and attention he gave to Mount Vernon. He was in full accord when L'Enfant enthusiastically outlined what could be done with the federal city. Hardly had the Constitutional Convention decided on the site in 1789 than the artist-engineer dispatched a note to his former general, asking to be allowed "to lay the foundation of a Federal City which is to become the Capital of this vast Empire." His appointment followed, and although he was to be discharged two years later, George Washington always remained grateful to him for his vision, and for the plan.

The question of the capitol building was next on the agenda. Here Washington showed his taste for the monumental by picking the design of Dr. William Thornton with its two great wings, its high portico and its central dome. Jefferson, of course, advised in the matter; his sketch for the Capitol has the dome set on a drum, much as we see it today. Although others, notably Stephen Hallet and George Hadfield, had a hand in the final design, the honors go to Thornton. Next to Thornton comes the name of Benjamin Henry Latrobe, in

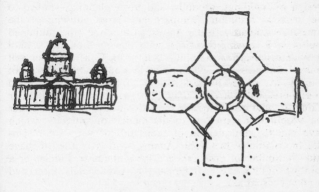

Jefferson's sketch for the Capitol in Washington. Elevation and plan.
(The original is in the possession of the
Massachusetts Historical Society.)

charge of its construction from 1803 to 1817, when the interior of the central portion was done. Here Latrobe placed his corncob and tobacco leaf capitals, the old chamber of the House of Representatives (Statuary Hall), the former Senate Chamber, and above all, the great Rotunda. Latrobe was not to see his designs completed, but he was fortunate in having as successor Charles Bulfinch, Boston's great architect of the period, who saw the old Capitol finished by the end of his service in 1829, the dome and wings being added later by Thomas U. Walter.

To Jefferson also goes the initiative for retaining the succession of Italian sculptors from Giuseppe Franzoni to Giuseppe Valaperti, who were responsible at this time for most of the sculptural ornament and the statues. Even in retirement in

Monticello he helped Colonel John Trumbull obtain the commission for the historical paintings that are now in the Rotunda, "The Declaration of Independence," "The Surrender of Cornwallis" and "The Resignation of Washington," first of the many famous canvases adorning the building. Before he died in 1826, Jefferson could point to the Capitol not only as a great temple of government but as a temple of the arts.

2. *City Planning of the New Nation*

Just as we are struck today by the extreme primitiveness of the reconstructed Pioneer Village in Salem or the tiny log cabins of Valley Forge, we are surprised and often delighted by the modest scale and miniature detail of colonial buildings. Not until after the Revolution and the coming of national mercantile capitalism did a new scale appear. Courthouses, city halls, state houses and custom houses, all to rise between 1786 and 1825, were monuments consecrating the triumphs of the past and promising greater triumphs for the future. They demanded a nobler setting, and in consequence various attempts were made to break away from the mercantile grid.

L'Enfant, in his design for Washington, chose a combination of radial and gridiron to set off the proposed monumental architecture. Seth Pease surveyed Cleveland in 1797 and laid out three radiating avenues from the Public Square, one of them being the famous Euclid Avenue. Joseph Ellicott planned Buffalo two years later in the same fashion, and Judge Augustus Woodward, who devised the "honeycomb" plan of downtown Detroit in 1805, followed the style of L'Enfant. Grand planning was in the air, enough for Verlé, in his 1802 map of Philadelphia, to propose a plan for the western part of the city, where the University of Pennsylvania now stands, in a series of large squares and radiating avenues.

The circuses (circular places), avenues and squares of the early 1800's occurred sporadically and were by no means universally adopted. The residential square, so important a feature of London in this period, was rarely to be found in the growing American city. A suitable form of planning for a country of fixed social classes like England, it probably seemed too sophisticated for the merchants and wealthy families of a community rapidly filling up with people from many countries, all eager to make money quickly. Also, investment in urban land was still risky; not until the next era were the first great urban land fortunes accumulated. In the 1790's speculation in urban real estate had proved disastrous to the bold Robert Morris, who tried to win a fortune in Washington lots only to end in a debtors' jail. The Boston merchant Harrison Gray Otis complained of his Beacon Hill speculation in the 1800's as a costly venture and "the sales slow and far between."

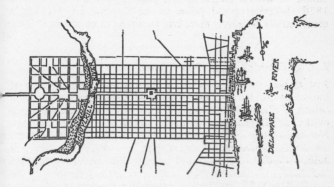

At left, a proposed western extension in the Grand Manner to William Penn's plan of Philadelphia, drawn by the mapmaker Verlé in 1802.

The ground-rent system, common in England, which might have encouraged residential-square building was rarely used. (Under the ground-rent system, the landlord rents his property by a long-term lease, giving the leaseholder for all practical purposes the rights of ownership over the leased land.) An exception was to be found in Baltimore, because of its peculiar kind of land ownership, but there the system only served to perpetuate the row house. The long-term lease in America is particular to Baltimore. Beginning in the 1750's Thomas Harrison, for whom Harrison Street is named, and the Fell family, who gave their name to Fell's Point, leased their land, after the London fashion, with a ground rent of ninety-nine years. John Eager Howard, Revolutionary patriot who gave the land for the Roman Catholic cathedral and Mount Vernon Place, conveyed much of his estate in this manner. Even now the municipality pays fifty-six dollars a year rent for part of the land on which the city hall stands. With the coming of urban redevelopment the city has bought in many of the ground rents, but they continue to be created on the outskirts, although the Maryland legislature allows tenants, under certain conditions, to buy the land after renting it for five years.

Trinity Church in New York City, one of the wealthiest Episcopal parishes in the country, had acquired in the course of the eighteenth century a number of farms which it converted into ninety-nine-year leaseholds. In 1803 it created St. John's Park, or Hudson Square, which once existed just south of the approaches to the Holland Tunnel, one of the rare examples of residential planning in the London manner. Here the parish attempted to build a fashionable quarter by keeping control of the land through the ninety-nine-year lease. By the 1820's their prosperous tenants were complaining and demanding to own their own land in the American fashion. Trinity was forced to convert the leases into freeholds and sell them.

There is cause for regret that the American Roman period was not able to match its buildings with its city plans. Only the perceptive saw the opportunity and the challenge. The illustrious Timothy Dwight of Yale was the most outspoken of these. In a visit to Boston in 1796 he observed: "Had ten open squares been formed at the proper intersections of the principal streets, the largest containing ten, and the smallest five acres, all beautified with selected ornaments, or had some other plan, substantially resembling this, and directed by the nature of the ground, been completed, Boston would even now have been the most beautiful town that the world has ever seen." Americans, by neglecting to break up the grid with squares and open spaces (Savannah, laid out by General Oglethorpe in 1733, is an exception), and by ignoring the advantages of magnificent natural sites, have let too many opportunities slip through their fingers. Although squares in numbers came to the South End of Boston in the 1850's, they were outside the central district, and Timothy Dwight's appeal was too late to remedy the situation.

The attempts at grandeur, few and far between, were shortly swept aside by the progress of the gridiron. There was a variety of patterns to draw from: the linear plan of Germantown, the winding streets of Boston and the Baroque plans of Williamsburg and Savannah; but the grid predominated. In the early days of the Republic municipal commissioners applied the gridiron pattern to all cities, much as the undeveloped land west of the Alleghenies was being carved into a series of giant sections. Baltimore, which had expanded rapidly after 1776, was raised to the status of a city in 1796 and its street commissioners automatically laid the streets out in right angles. Philadelphia (disregarding Verlé's dream), Richmond in Virginia, Reading in Pennsylvania and many others mapped their rectangles to receive houses and people; but when New

ork fixed its famous plan the practice became thoroughly
spectable.

After the disastrous Revolutionary War years, during which
had remained in enemy hands, New York expanded even
ore rapidly than Baltimore and passed Philadelphia and
oston in the race for the title of the country's largest city.
1807 the state legislature, which has played and still plays
important role in the city's life, appointed a commission of
ree to draw up a plan to cover the whole island of Man-
attan. Four years later the three commissioners, Gouverneur
Morris, Simeon de Witt and John Rutherford, offered the all-
o-famous solution that we see today. With the plan came
apologia. Using the third person, it reads: "One of the
rst objects which claimed their attention, was the form and
anner in which the business should be conducted; that is to
ay, whether they should confine themselves to rectilinear and
ectangular streets, or whether they should adopt some of
ose supposed improvements, by circles, ovals and stars,
hich certainly embellish a plan, whatever may be their effects
s to convenience and utility." The complacent document
ontinues: "In considering that subject, they could not but
ear in mind that a city is to be composed of the habitations
f men, and that strait [sic] sided and right angled houses are
he most cheap to build, and the most convenient to live in.
he effect of these plain and simple reflections was decisive."
he document explains uneasily: "If it should be asked, why
as the present plan adopted in preference to any other? The
nswer is, because, after taking all circumstances into con-
ideration, it appeared to be the best; or, in other and more
roper terms, attended with the least inconvenience." Edith
Wharton, a New Yorker of a later generation who has given
s some of the most perceptive analyses of the city in her
ovels, called the plan and report "naif," the product of "a
ociety of prosperous businessmen who have no desire to row
gainst the current." American city planning was tied to the
rid from that time on, until the City Beautiful Movement of
he 1890's.

Equally important was the division of the rectangles (200 ×
00 feet or 200 × 425 feet) into lots 25 × 100 feet. This automatically limited the size of the house. Sometimes the house
was made even smaller than the width of the lot; the enter-
rising builder would put four houses 18.7 feet wide on three
ots, or five 20-foot houses on four. The rectangle and the lot
ize varied from city to city, but the pattern was standard.
Thus preparation was made for the spread of the row house.

3. The Merchant's City

Although there was a move toward uniformity in city houses prior to 1776, it was during the days of the young Republic that the different cities accepted the small London house as a model, with each city having its peculiar variant. "A development of republican days new in America," Fiske Kimball reminds us, "was the block of several houses of unified design," or the row house. Architects were retained to do plans for whole streets. The first so commissioned was Charles Bulfinch, who in 1793 designed Franklin Crescent in Boston, unfortunately destroyed. Several buildings remain from later developments by this important architect, notably the altered Ticknor House on the upper end of Park Street. Philadelphia has several early rows remaining, the Sansom Street Row (1800–1801) by one Thomas Carstairs and the Franklin Row (1809) by Robert Mills. Baltimore, the home of the row house, still has one or two examples dating from the turn of the century—nine houses on Aliceanna Street (1800) and the better known ones at Waterloo Row on North Calvert Street (1815) by Mills. These and their descendants, "expressed in repeated vistas of little brick-faced and protrusively door-stepped houses," suggested to Henry James "rows of quiet old ladies seated, with their toes tucked-up on uniform footstools, under shaded candlesticks of old-fashioned tea-parties." Early versions of the row house can still be seen in the neighborhood of Independence Hall or in the shadow of the skyscrapers of downtown New York on Greenwich Street and in the famous "Village," or yet again on Beacon Hill and in the North End of Boston. Today many of them have disappeared before street-widening and highway schemes and careless "improvements" on the part of property owners.

Baltimore and Philadelphia had their marble "toes" or steps, but New York insisted on its stoop, as if to proclaim its Dutch heritage (the word comes from the Dutch *stoep*). This consisted of six or more steps, with a landing well above the sidewalk; beneath it was the area and stairs leading to the basement. In Boston the steps were pulled inside the house; not until the 1850's did the stoop invade the Boston street. All cities adopted the peculiar custom, begun by Bulfinch, of painting the brick (often porous in those days) in a brighter imitation of the brick itself. The charm of the early rows depended partly on such attempts at color and ornament, as well as on their interiors with their furniture by Duncan Phyfe and others in this great era of American cabinet-making. The

Typical row houses in Baltimore
with white marble steps.

white trim, the green shutters, and the handmade wrought
iron work, especially in New York, together with the silver-
plated knocker and name plate made for a cheerful welcome.

Little was done to create special buildings for different uses.
The row house was taken over for a store, a warehouse or a
multiple dwelling. The modern shop window stems from the
Paris of the Directoire, in the late 1790's, but Americans of
the early nineteenth century followed the English practice of
the day, by placing a large flat many-paned window or a glass
bay in the row house. The first floor was given over to commerce, the second and third reserved for the family and clerks,
and a fourth perhaps for storage. People lived and worked in
the same house or at least in the same neighborhood.

In some cities the steeple was overtopped by a large shot-
tower where the molten lead was raised and then let fall in
drops which, as they fell, became round and hardened into
shot. One still stands in Baltimore. A new challenge to the

supremacy of the steeple made its first appearance in the business architecture of this age. There had been merchants' exchanges in colonial times. Charleston had one that still stands, by Peter and John A. Horlbeck (1767–71), but for the most part the tavern and the coffeehouse served as trading centers for the merchants. In 1815 Benjamin Latrobe and Maximilian Godefroy designed the Exchange, which was to be a fixture of Baltimore's skyline for seventy-five years. A handsome exchange was built on Wall Street in New York; destroyed by fire several times and rebuilt, the last of the succession was designed by Isaiah Rogers after the fire of 1835 and is now encased in the main building of the National City Bank. Perhaps the best architectural example that is still with us is by William Strickland in Philadelphia, built in 1832.

American society continued to revolve about the church, which dominated its leisure moments. Even the grogshop, the refuge of the working man and the mechanic, found itself in competition with the Methodist and Baptist churches. Church design, under the influence of the American Roman, disregarded the steeple, as can be seen in Latrobe's Baltimore cathedral. The new sects, Baptist, Methodist and Unitarian, frowned on such display. Typical of the small church of the period is the delightful domed First Unitarian of Baltimore (1817–18) by Godefroy. In New England and the Middle West the steeple was not deserted for the dome; steeples crown the Center Church (1812–14) by Ithiel Town and the United Church (1813–15) by David Hoadley, both on the New Haven green, showing a lingering fondness for the American Baroque.

Distractions such as the theatre began to exercise their fascination. The pleasure garden was a new form of diversion, apparently brought to America by Frenchmen. Here, for the delight of the whole family were offered vaudeville, *tableaux-vivants*, plays, music and fireworks. New York had an early pleasure garden in 1796, although Philadelphia enjoyed the most fantastic in the Chinese Pagoda built in 1828 by John Haviland.

The first years of the Republic also saw the founding of many cultural institutions. Some had existed prior to 1776, but a rash of new ones now appeared. The Pennsylvania Academy of Fine Arts and the Academy of Natural Sciences in Philadelphia, the American Academy of Fine Arts in New York and the Peale Museum and the Maryland Academy of Science in Baltimore date from this time. Numerous athenaeums, lyceums and subscription libraries invited all to learning as Americans did honor to the arts and sciences. Most, at first, found humble shelter in a row house or, perhaps, in a public building grown too small for its original use. Charles Willson Peale had his private museum for years in Independence Hall.

The colonial city had been transformed when the building of the Erie Canal announced another era. To be sure, the skyline had changed little. It was somewhat higher, and here and there the roof of a merchants' exchange or a public

One of the first textile mills, Samuel Slater's
in Pawtucket, Rhode Island, built in 1793.

building revealed a new shape among the steeples. The street showed the greatest change, with its solid fronts of row houses on every side, bearing witness to more money and more comfort. In the older cities the white clapboard frame house could still be found here and there, but it was disappearing as an urban type. The distinguishing contribution of the age was its monuments and public buildings, constructed in the American Roman Style. Baltimore perhaps could claim most honors here. This busy mercantile city, where Francis Scott Key composed the national anthem in the War of 1812, could point to its cathedral, to the Battle Monument (by Godefroy) and to the Washington Monument (by Mills) on Mount Vernon Place. With justice it had assumed the name of the "Monumental City."

4. *State Capital and College Town*

The first improvements in transportation made possible a few early examples of the suburb, an institution far more familiar today. The first commuters were probably the residents of Charlestown crossing the Charles River to Boston, or those of Society Hill, formerly outside Philadelphia and today covered with row houses. Most of the dwellings on the fringes of the modest urban centers of the eighteenth century, if they were not farmhouses, were country villas where the prosperous could escape the summer heat.

The first suburb in the modern sense of the term was hard by the village of Brooklyn across the water from downtown Manhattan. "Families who may desire to associate in forming *a select neighborhood and circle of society, for a summer's residence, or a whole year's,* cannot anywhere obtain more desirable situations," ran an advertisement for lots on Brooklyn Heights in 1819. The site, the health of the location and, especially, its proximity to the business center were extolled. When Robert Fulton, the inventor of the steamboat, obtained the concession for a Brooklyn steam ferry in 1814, his friend Hezekiah Beers Pierrepont, New York merchant and real estate dealer, had invested in some sixty acres on the Heights. Here he hoped to establish a genteel suburb of large houses, and around the brow of the hill it was his intention to have an ample public promenade. He was disappointed in both aims. He made the fatal mistake of adopting the grid of the Commissioners' Plan of 1811 for Manhattan and even its lot pattern of 25 × 100 feet, and he left no land for his promenade. The grid and the dimensions of the lot opened the door to speculation, and although a few large houses were built, the rapid growth of Brooklyn, thanks to Fulton's Ferry, made the splitting up of the awkward-shaped lots profitable. As for the promenade, he expected the co-operation of the new owners in setting aside land for public use, only to be stopped by a neighbor who saw no reason why he should sacrifice a portion of his land for the public. Not until 1950 did the Heights obtain a walk from which to command New York's most magnificent view, and then it was executed with so little finesse as to exhibit a comfort station as its main architectural feature.

Although too early for the spread of the select suburb the age was notable for its country houses outside the merchant cities. Between 1792 (the date of the Lancaster Road) and the end of the 1820's, turnpikes were extensively built, and country houses in the new Roman style began to appear along the main routes, a reflection of the new money in tobacco, shipping or trade. "Woodlawn," built in 1805 by Dr. William Thornton not far from Mount Vernon, and the handsome bow-fronted brick mansion of Gore Place at Waltham, near

Boston—recently rescued overnight from the wrecker and restored by public-spirited friends—are good examples. Perhaps the most celebrated architectural gem of the age, Monticello, was given its present form by Jefferson between 1796 and 1809. But it should not be imagined that climate and countryside had been conquered so early in the struggle with nature. James Fenimore Cooper describes the mansion of his father, an attempt at wilderness splendor, as it was in 1803, with its porch fallen apart and suffering terribly from the weather, while the appearance of the settlement, Cooperstown, also laid out by the novelist's father, gives us a hint of the rough provincialism of many new towns of the age:

> Immediately on the banks of the lake stood the village . . . [runs the description in *The Pioneers*]. It consisted of about fifty buildings, including those of every description, chiefly built of wood, and which, in their architecture, bore not only strong marks of the absence of taste, but also, by the slovenly and unfinished appearance of most dwellings, indicated the hasty manner of their construction. To the eye, they presented a variety of colors. A few were white in both front and back, but more bore that expensive colour on their fronts only, while their economical but ambitious owners had covered the remaining sides of their edifices with a dingy red.

In spite of the cruder attempts at town building, certain more permanent contributions were made, far from existing cities in the centers of the newly created states. Partly because transportation difficulties suggested the sites and partly because of the perennial fear of the "corrupt" metropolis, new towns were carved out of the forests to serve as centers of state government. Montpelier, the capital of Vermont, is such a town, and we have a description of clearing the forest and laying the roads before the first state house was occupied in 1809. The forest covered most of the site of Columbia, South Carolina, when the state legislature chose it for the new capital in 1786 and laid out a town in the same year. Columbus, Ohio, was platted as a grid in 1812, although the state capitol building, surmounted by a great drum, was not completed until 1861. Indeed, it is not for their street design that these early state capitals are interesting, but for their often handsome domed government buildings, which, like the courthouses, bear testimony to the fact that all levels of American government have given a place to art in cities which would otherwise be so lacking in decoration, painting and sculpture.

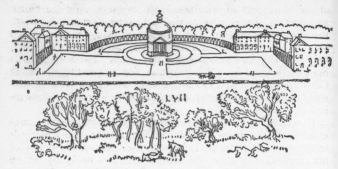

Joseph Jacques Ramée's design for Union College, Schenectady,
New York, antedating Jefferson's University of Virginia.

Again it was the myth of the virtuous small town which determined the location of institutions of higher learning. Like
the government town, the country education town seems to
be another American phenomenon, echoing perhaps the spe-
cialization of certain towns in the Middle Ages, when Cambridge, Padua and Bologna were centers of education and no
university was to be found in London, Milan or Venice. Like
their European equivalents, the campuses of American universities very frequently form centers of order and beauty in
otherwise undistinguished small communities. The best known
of this period is Jefferson's "academical village" built in 1819,
the University of Virginia at Charlottesville. Its chief building was modeled after the Pantheon in Rome, but it is an
ensemble characteristically American, with its red brick and
white porticos that shelter professors and students hurrying
between classes. Less well known and somewhat earlier is
Union College, in Schenectady, New York, founded in 1795,
planned as "a court of honor" by the French architect, Joseph
Jacques Ramée, in 1813. A product of the Age of Enlighten-
ment, Union College had been created by petition and established to avoid sectarian domination. Ramée turned the campus inside out and established an open treatment completely
different from the monastic seclusion of the medieval quadran-
gle. As if to express young President Eliphalet Nott's policy
that education was no longer for the chosen few, he opened
the campus to all who cared to enter, as a gesture, and provided a rectangular court with a central pantheon at the rear.
This was flanked by a colonnade, a mark of the dignity of
education which anticipated Jefferson's use of these elements

at the University of Virginia. Unfortunately, only the North and South Colleges were carried out under Ramée's direction, the circular pantheon and colonnade being erected much later, in the Ruskinian Gothic manner. Bowdoin (1794), Williams (1793), Dartmouth (chartered earlier but with its first building erected in 1784–91), and the University of North Carolina (opened in 1795 and one of the oldest state universities in the United States) are other examples of the "academical village" of the era.

It was fitting that the age which began with a great ceremony in Philadelphia in honor of Washington and America's triumph should close in 1824 with a celebration in honor of his companion-in-arms, the visiting Marquis de Lafayette. In honor of the Frenchman, who symbolized the friendship between the two nations, more arches and triumphal routes were created than at any time since the passage of Louis XIV and his Spanish bride across France in 1660. In Philadelphia no less than thirteen arches, symbolizing the thirteen original states, were raised by the architect William Strickland, aided by the sculptor William Rush and the painter Thomas Sully. ("Wisdom" and "Justice," Rush's statues from the largest arch, are today in the Philadelphia Museum of Art.) These arches were a fit ending to a brief but magnificent period in architecture and civic design, not to be matched again until the end of the century. The age that opened with one triumphal arch had closed with another.

PART III

The Romantic Era

1825-1850

THE AMERICAN CITY of the romantic era produced certain important changes, although they were not dramatic. The steeples continued to rule the skyline, but they now shared it with the Greek Revival banks and the new hotels, as well as with the merchants' exchanges and the shot-tower. On the street the shop fronts were larger, but the shops themselves were not big enough to prevent the overflow of goods onto the sidewalk. New buildings put on a Romantic dress. An important change took place in transportation with the coming of the steamboat into general use, the canal, the first railroads and the horse-drawn omnibus. These made possible new cities and towns away from the coastal areas and enabled the older centers to spread out. It was the heyday of the great river and canal cities: Cincinnati on the Ohio, St. Louis and New Orleans on the Mississippi and Albany, Syracuse, Rome and Buffalo on the Erie Canal. Industrial towns appeared for the first time in any number.

The populations of all American cities expanded as rapidly as they had in the previous generation. New York City rose from a population of 123,000 in 1820 to 515,000 in 1850. The rapidly expanding nation increased its production of goods, especially textiles. Lowell and Lawrence (both in Massachusetts), Nashua and Manchester on the Merrimack (in New Hampshire), Manayunk on the Schuylkill, then outside of Philadelphia, and Troy on the Hudson River arose as rivals to the cities of the English Midlands to turn out cottons, linens and woolens needed. Cincinnati, long before Chicago, became the great meat-packing center of the world. In older centers shipbuilding, iron foundries and machine works developed and expanded. With the growing population and better transportation, urban real estate speculation was rife; with the 1830's came the first nation-wide town booms. Speculation was by no means confined to cities; the countryside, especially in the Middle West, was infected with the fever, and town platting took on fantastic proportions. All this was accelerated by the banking policy of President Andrew Jackson, his advocacy of cheap public lands, and his hostility to internal improvements at federal expense. The laissez-faire economy of his administration and the optimism and individualism of the Emersonian philosophy dominate the age.

Another form of town flourished at the same time, the utopian community. Together with the blueprinted mill-towns, these were planned centers, outside the pattern of land speculation. The age also saw the beginning of the first summer colonies about large columned hotels. Modest suburbs continued to appear, and villa architects, working in the Romantic Revival styles, chose the new fashion of landscape gardening to decorate the open lot. A bucolic atmosphere pervaded everywhere, despite the presence of the growing city and the new railroad nibbling at the city's edge. Trees were leaving the downtown areas and reappearing on the streets of the outskirts. But around 1850, the close of the age, the sky above the city grew darker, and a smell of coal smoke could be detected in the air.

1. *The Speculative Pattern*

The abandonment by New York's Trinity Church of its ninety-nine-year lease was a sign of the new age, in which all emphasis was placed on individuality in the development of land and the building of the city. Trinity's difficulty with its tenants, who preferred the freehold system, foreshadowed the pattern of land ownership in New York and all other American cities—with the exception of certain parts of Baltimore. The long-term lease persisted in isolated holdings like those of the Sailors' Snug Harbor on Washington Square, but it was very rare.

It is significant that John Jacob Astor, who amassed the first great urban land fortune, was also the first to discover the potential value of New York's rocky acres. He did so in the 1820's, in a country that had speculated in "wild land" since its beginning but until now had had no opportunity to develop urban land as an investment.

Astor was an enterprising German who came to America as a young man and made money in commerce, first in the fur trade and then in the China trade. He had toyed with city land in the early 1800's, but only by the 1820's did his income from real estate equal his commercial profits. About the year 1825 he disposed of the last of his ships and devoted himself entirely to his land investments. At first he bought parcels to sell at a quick profit, or, following Trinity's example, he granted long-term leases. By the 1830's, however, he was selling with the help of five-year mortgages at 7 per cent, or he leased on a yearly basis. When he died in 1848 he left a fortune worth from $20,000,000 to $40,000,000, the bulk of it in Manhattan real estate. "Could I begin life again, knowing what I now know, and had money to invest," was his deathbed message, "I could buy every foot of land on the Island of Manhattan."

If Astor represented the sober element of real estate investment, a wild side existed elsewhere, especially in the new cities of the West. Chicago, still prairie, boomed in 1833. In anticipation of a canal that did not come until fifteen years later, real estate was bought and sold and lots staked out for a population of a million. A parcel of land would change hands ten times in a single day. The jumps in price were made possible by a sales system that called for a 10 per cent down payment only, the remainder being in the form of a lien or a mortgage. As the prices climbed, the 10 per cent came to absorb all the purchaser's equity and his only hope lay in a quick resale. When the bottom dropped out of the market, the land returned to the original owner. This was the pattern of "land booming" which has continued, unvaried, to our own time. The Florida Boom of the 1920's operated fundamentally in the same manner, with newer huckstering methods to give it a contemporary flavor.

From the shores of Maine to the banks of the Missouri the speculator haunted the land in packs.

> *Behind the squaw's light birch canoe,*
> *The steamer rocks and raves;*
> *And city lots are staked for sale*
> *Above old Indian graves*

wrote Whittier. The town-jobbing mania was helped by an unspectacular invention that made building quicker and easier. Abandoning the log cabin, westerners had taken over the New England frame house with its heavy posts and beams. Although the construction was simplified, it proved cumbersome: studs and planks had to be cut and sawed, then mortised and tenoned before being set in place. Nails were too costly an item to be widely used. Mass production of nails was impossible until after 1817, with the coming of improved nailmaking machinery, and then their use was held back by tradition—it was feared that they would not serve to hold the studs and beams in place. Thus construction took a great leap ahead with the invention of the balloon frame. Given the name in mockery, it made possible new farmhouses, new city homes and whole cities. It is generally conceded that the first building in the new construction was St. Mary's, the earliest Roman Catholic church in Chicago, built in 1833 by the carpenter-architect Augustine Deodat Taylor. The difference between Taylor's method and the traditional one lay in the substitution of thin plates and studs (2 × 4 inches, as a rule) held together by nails, instead of large beams and posts held together by tenon and mortise. A hammer and a handful of nails replaced the carpenter's toolbox. The old method required a skilled carpenter and an army of assistants to lift the heavy timber into place, but with the new, "any farmer who is handy with the saw, iron square and hammer, with one of his boys . . . to assist him, can go to work and put up a frame for an outbuilding and finish it off with his own labor," remarked Solon Robinson, "King of the Squatters," pioneer agriculturist from Indiana. "If it had not been for the knowledge of balloon-frames," he told a group of New Yorkers in 1855, "Chicago and San Francisco could never have arisen, as they did, from little villages to great cities in a single year. It is not only city buildings, which are supported by one another, that may be thus erected, but those upon the open prairie where the wind has a sweep from Mackinaw [sic] to the Mississippi, for there they are built, and stand as firm as any of the old frames of New England, with posts and beams sixteen inches square."

Aided by this new construction method, the speculating town builders tried to choose a site so perfect that a metropolis would rise at once. Convinced of the wisdom of their selection, they would buttress the town's future prospects by contriving to have it chosen as a county seat or a capital or possibly the home of a college. The site, in most instances, had no influence on the plan, which was the customary gridiron set about a square or on both sides of a main street.

Exceptions cropped up in towns built on what are now called breaking points of transportation, where freight and passengers were transferred from ship to shore or canal to rail, and here a more distinctive tradition could be found. The mark of the river town is a wide street going down to a dock or wharf at the river's edge. Even more than the plan, it is the settled architectural quality of many of these towns which gives us pleasure today. They have preserved the appearance attained in the short burst of prosperity they once enjoyed before slipping into somnolence. Market Street, now called Broadway, which bisects Hannibal, Missouri, runs down the bluff to the river, It was at the foot of Broadway, known as one of the widest streets in Missouri, that "once a day a cheap gaudy packet arrived upward from St. Louis and another downward from Keokuk." "S-t-e-a-m-boat a-comin'," someone would yell, and the town would wake from a summer sleep for ten minutes or so, a scene to which Mark Twain consecrated one of his best passages in *Life on the Mississippi*.

With such unusual sites, many of the river towns could not fail to take advantage of the scenery. Paradise Hill in Hudson, New York, provides a terrace with a sweeping view of the river. In New Richmond, Ohio, a promenade skirts the Ohio, and when the river is high those who feel so inclined may dangle their feet in the water. Keokuk, Iowa, overlooks the artificial Lake Cooper, formed by damming the Mississippi, a view in which small white boats fleck the blue water on a summer day. At Bellevue on the Missouri, the first settlement in Nebraska, we pause because time has stopped; there is an attraction in the scale of the architecture, in the use of trees, in the untouched square; or at New Richmond we are held because the riverbank was made an amenity, and we wonder why we lack such common sense today and why we cannot match such pleasant scenes.

In the main, the picture of new towns is a dark one. The first industrial age in America, as in Europe, paid little heed to the call of amenity. The cry was for gold, and the gold was black. In the 1820's canals joined the newly worked anthracite coal mines of eastern Pennsylvania to Philadelphia, inviting wild speculation. Pottsville, in eastern Pennsylvania, is sometimes considered the first boom town in our history. People dug everywhere for anthracite and, often as not, dug their graves instead. Speculators welcomed the hopeful with prettily printed maps and were at pains to show the exact spot where the future metropolis would soon appear. The influx of population created a tremendous market for houses. Lumber was framed at Philadelphia and transported to the coal town by canal, ready for the joiner. To replace the primeval forest with a thriving town, a city was brought along the canal by boat in sawed-off lengths of wood —an early example of prefabrication methods applied to building.

Speculation was just as active around towns chosen to be state capitals or county seats. Springfield, Illinois, founded in 1821, was chosen as the county seat because the legislature, then meeting in Vandalia, had been tricked into choosing it instead of its now forgotten rival. With the opening of the Erie Canal in 1825 the state's population grew to such a point that it was decided Vandalia was too far to the south to be the capital and that a more central location would be better. Led by Abraham Lincoln, a group of state legislators, known as the "Long Nine" because of their height, engineered the selection of Springfield in 1837. In the case of Missouri, the legislature first chose a village called Côte sans Dessein, an appropriate name as it turned out; hardly had word gotten abroad of the choice than speculators swarmed into the community expecting to profit from the land boom; and the legislature, annoyed, turned instead to Jefferson City, which has remained the Missouri capital ever since.

The least remembered towns within the speculative pattern of this period are the "road ranches" and canal towns—forgotten because the means of transportation that created them have disappeared. The toll road, the turnpike and the post road had knitted much of the hinterland together by 1825. In Ohio and Indiana, where the National Road continued the older Cumberland Road west from the Virginia line, the numerous tollgates and inns gave rise to towns. "As many as twenty four-horse coaches have been counted in line at one time on the road," recorded one historian, "and large, broad-wheeled wagons covered with white canvas stretched over bows, laden with merchandise and drawn by six Conestoga horses, were visible all the day long at every point, many times until late in the evening, besides innumerable caravans of horses, mules, cattle, hogs and sheep. It looked more like the leading avenue of a great city than a road through rural districts." New Concord, Ohio, grew out of an inn serving the road; so, too, Lafayette, whose Red Brick Tavern was one of the many stops. In Indiana, Centerville consisted of two walls of houses on either side of the road, a true linear plan typical of the "road ranch," as it came to be known. West of the Missouri, where the prairie remained long untouched by rails, roads led across the continent from the railheads or river landings and perforce road ranches were built along the main highways. These soon expanded into small towns to serve the eager travelers, but they faded from the scene with the coming of the railroad.

In the canal era of the 1820's and the 1830's, New Jersey, New York, Pennsylvania, Ohio and Indiana were crisscrossed

A canal town. View of Dayton, Ohio, about 1830.

with man-made waterways whose ports drew settlers. Middletown, Ohio, now famous as the home of the American Rolling Mill Company, which developed the high speed strip-steel mill, was formed around a port on the Miami and Erie Canal, midway between Cincinnati and Dayton; hence Middletown's name. Towns such as Little Falls and Frankford, New York, still retain the flavor of the canal—the placid Erie, which brought prosperity to the Mohawk Valley. Abandoned locks, stretches of dry or still-watered canal and grassgrown towpaths are to be found throughout the East and the Middle West. Only recently Justice William O. Douglas of the United States Supreme Court took a three-day walking trip with a following of reporters along the old Chesapeake and Ohio Canal, which ends at the nation's capital. His intention, and it turned out to be successful, was to preserve the ancient waterway as a national park and prevent its desecration by a highway. The forgotten canals add a picturesque note to the countryside, a ruined monument to the coming of the railroad in the Age of Steam and Iron.

2. *Labyrinth and Milldam*

Two forms of community outside the speculative pattern —they are the consciously *planned* towns of the period— make strange companions in the story of American urbanism. These were settlements laid out by religious and socialist idealists and the blueprinted milltowns of the Boston Associates, a group of individualistic businessmen who, in an age when the state existed only to protect property, threw private dams across the rivers and drew workable plans for industrial towns.

The most curious pattern in the history of American towns is that of the many sectarian and utopian communities, riding precariously on the speculative sea in an attempt to bring heaven to this earth. The Shakers, the Rappites, the Fourierists and others are easy enough to mock and easy enough to dismiss, for they built few towns permanently and well. Nevertheless, there is a fascination about their experiments, the fascination of observing Man in his attempt to reach the Promised Land, like the ant seeking salvation on the straw. In the United States the spectacle had color to it, for here it went beyond the books and here it occurred in greatest variety. More than one hundred communities with a total population of over one hundred thousand attempted utopian living, and several lasted for an astonishingly long period. The tradition goes back to the seventeenth century with the founding of the strongly theocratic New England colonies, but the stamping out of heretical sects in eighteenth-century Europe sent others to the new country. Ephrata and The Woman in the Wilderness, Pennsylvania, Winston-Salem, North Carolina, and Bethlehem, Pennsylvania—the last two Moravian communities—were modest, scrubbed and plain stone villages, in which the one diversion was music. Today in Bethlehem, on the hills above the plant of the Bethlehem Steel Corporation, a trombone choir greets Easter Sunday, continuing an old Moravian tradition begun in 1754.

Of the many religious groups the Shakers were the most inventive, creating their own brand of folk art, particularly in furniture. This once unpopular sect, established by Mother Ann Lee in Watervliet, New York, had colonies as far west as Indiana and Kentucky. Severe in their dress, art, way of living and religion, and advocating celibacy, they gave themselves to work in farming and the handicrafts. Where amusement was barred, release took the form of ecstatic religious services, often ending in the strange shaking dance that gave rise to their name. "In the Church of Christ and Mother, Carnal feelings have no place," they chanted. "Here the simple love each other, Free from ev'ry thing that's base." Their furniture exercises a special attraction today, since it resembles, in its plainness, that which we call "Functional." It is interesting to know in this connection that contemporary Danish furniture makers first drew their inspiration from a pattern book of Shaker furniture which fell into their hands.

Another sectarian community was the colony established at Economy, Pennsylvania, by George and Frederick Rapp in 1825. Leading a group of German dissenters from Harmony, Indiana, to the banks of the Ohio River, they built an elaborate settlement, which had a museum (one of the paintings was "Christ Healing the Sick" by Benjamin West), a grotto and that too rare adornment in America, a labyrinth! The Rappites were extremely prosperous, and the community lasted until the turn of the century, when it was finally abandoned. Happily, Economy, now part of Ambridge, Pennsylvania, has been preserved, through the restoration effected by the Works Progress Administration in the 1930's. It is now a historical monument belonging to the state of Pennsylvania.

All religious sects were eclipsed by the Mormons and their Holy Experiment, which converted a desert into a garden and built one of the great cities of the West. Founded by Joseph Smith in the 1830's, the Church of the Latter-Day Saints made many converts, and its popularity was jealously watched. In 1844 resentment against Prophet Smith and his followers turned into mob action; Smith was murdered and the Mormon city of Nauvoo in Illinois threatened. Under his successor, Brigham Young, they moved in a body to Utah, far removed from the violence of their former neighbors, and settled at Salt Lake City. When the religious communities had leaders with a strong business sense they often made their mark on the world outside, but when the leadership was Napoleonic, as in the person of Young, the community became an empire of scores of towns and irrigated farms.

These were evangelical fundamentalist communities. The sophisticated and non-religious communist communities lasted on an average of only two years and they left behind little of permanence in the way of building. In comparison with the sectarian communities they offer a brilliant gallery of figures: Robert Owen at New Harmony, Indiana (the Harmony of the Rappites, purchased by Owen), Frances Wright at Nashoba, Tennessee, Bronson Alcott at Brook Farm, Massachusetts (preserved for us in Hawthorne's *The Blithedale Romance*), John Humphrey Noyes at Oneida, New York, and even Horace Greeley with his Fourierist Phalanxes. Greeley, the publisher of the New York *Tribune,* became interested, turned Fourierist and, With Albert Brisbane, helped found the North American Phalanx near Red Bank, New Jersey. At New Harmony on the Wabash, Owen gathered about him in the 1820's Thomas Say, leading geologist, Charles Lesueur, French naturalist, and others. He brought with him his sons David Dale Owen, another accomplished scientist, who was to become United States Geologist, and Robert Dale Owen, who was the leader in establishing the public school system in the Middle West. When visiting the lonely town on the Wabash, one may well wonder at the excitement caused by Owen, but the appearance of the "Boatload of Knowledge" on the river in 1826 was no small event in the frontier days. Owen and his sons were far ahead of their time. A Gothic villa is the only architectural gem of the community. Fortunately, the direct descendant of the founder, the present Robert Dale Owen, and his wife are gradually restoring New Harmony, so we shall soon see it again as the world once did, when it waited in curiosity for the results of the experiment and the bulletins of its scientists.

The strangest of all experimental communities—a combination of sectarian and utopian features—was that of John Humphrey Noyes, who founded in 1847 the Oneida Community at Oneida, New York. (The name is familiar through advertisements of Community Plate, the silverware still made in the old Noyes Mansion.) "Opposed to random procreation which is unavoidable in the marriage system," he favored "intelligent, well-ordered procreation." To control reproduction he devised the theory of complex marriage. Any man or woman could live together in the community, although prolonged attachments were discouraged by mutual criticism on the part of members. As for the propagation of children, it was supervised by the older people of the community, who designated the couples, Noyes having condemned formal marriage. Although it may be imagined that Noyes had created a Hell instead of a Heaven on earth, the experiment was popular. Handicraft kept the community financially stable, although complete security did not come until one member invented a steel animal trap, the manufacture of which proved extremely profitable. With development and expansion of the community, a large mansion was built to house all. In one of the wings was the Children's House, where the children were completely removed from their mothers, even at night. Parents could visit their offspring whenever they wished to do so. The coming of a second generation, the growing criticism from outside and the resignation of Noyes eventually brought the experiment to an end in 1879.

If Oneida was successful for so long, the stability was due in part to its economic base; likewise a sound economic base ensured the triumph of the most important of the new community types of the period, the New England milltown. In November 1821 the prominent Boston merchants who inspected the Pawtucket Falls on the Merrimack decided to harness the river and build the town of Lowell, Massachusetts. Two years later canals, a mill race, mills and boardinghouses for operators had been constructed; the first wheels began to turn. The pattern of the New England milltown had been created and fixed.

Driving along the Merrimack, the Connecticut or other New England rivers, one can easily pick out the planned towns of dark red brick. Along the riverbank stretch the great mills rising four or five stories, nearby stands the separate

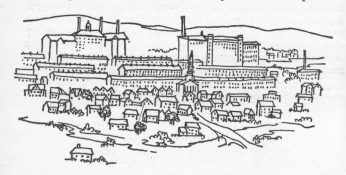

Lawrence, Massachusetts. A typical mill town of the 1830's.

building that houses the offices and the quarters of the supervisors, and beyond, on the streets running at right angles to the mills, come the dormitories for the single workers and the group houses for the family men. It was all according to a blue print—the grass strip along the canal, the perspective of the factory at the end between walls of compact row houses and, on a hill above the water and meadows, the group of Greek Revival temples which marked the houses of the overseers and the merchants. These New England milltowns had a solid well-built atmosphere and were altogether different from Pottsville or the wooden towns of the prairie.

Into these cities of spindles and looms streamed the daughters of the New England farmland, country girls from Maine, New Hampshire and Vermont with strange first names like Samantha, Triphena and Plumy. Welcomed by the overseers, the "mothers" of the boardinghouses and the church pastors, they were assured of proper care away from home. As always in the American scene, the religious note was pervasive without being conspicuous. In one Lowell boardinghouse eight sects, no less, were represented, and just as on the frontier, religion proved to be the chief leisure occupation.

To Francis Cabot Lowell, for whom the prototype city was named, goes the distinction of perfecting the method of converting cotton to cloth under one roof and of improving the living conditions of the millhands. He had seen the milltowns of England and Scotland, and while Robert Owen, yet unknown, was still experimenting in New Lanark, Scotland, he had instituted the boardinghouse scheme for single employees at Waltham, Massachusetts. He did not live to see the system reach perfection in the City of Spindles, but visitors from Charles Dickens to President Jackson made their pilgrimage to the city he created, where the young female millhands, despite their long working day, had their literary clubs and even their magazine, *The Lowell Offering*. Early American career women, their thought was always of betterment. Wrote Lucy Larcom, the Spindle City poetess:

> *Not always to be here among the looms,—*
> *Scarcely a girl she knew expected that;*
> *Means to one end their labor was,—to put*
> *Gold nest-eggs in the bank, or to redeem*
> *A mortgage homestead, or to pay the way*
> *Through classic years at some academy;*
> *More commonly to lay a dowry by*
> *For future housekeeping.*

By the 1850's farm girls no longer came to Lowell, Lawrence, Nashua, Manchester, Chicopee, Haverhill, or wherever the dark mills clustered by a New England river. Instead the once excluded Irish and French Canadians were moving along the valleys and replacing the Yankee maidens. The Irish had had a part in building the milltowns. They did the backbreaking work of digging the canals and raising the stone dams, only to find themselves segregated in miserable shack villages called "Paddytown" or "New Dublin," away from the native Protestants. As the nation grew the Irish were eventually invited to come into the mills, but for them there was no industrial utopia, and the New England factory towns, the orderliness of their plans and their cleanliness apart, came eventually to resemble all the others.

3. *The Coming of Amenities*

The Industrial Revolution did not by-pass the growing city for the meadow by the waterfall. Factories (other than textile, which were dependent on cheap water power) cropped up in all the existing large towns. Shipyards, foundries, machine works and other forms of industry brought a busy hum to the urban scene. The appearance of the city was changed by the introduction of the large warehouse, and the creation of a warehouse district, still to be found apart from the heart of downtown Boston, Providence, Baltimore, Richmond, Cincinnati and other mercantile centers. Ithiel Town, one of the architects of New York's Subtreasury Building, is supposed to have designed the first large warehouse with stone piers in lower Manhattan, around 1830. Some warehouses still survive in that area, on Water Street, and in Baltimore the brick Old Sugar House (1849) is standing. Although these buildings were massive, especially in Boston where they were often built of granite blocks, they did not change the street scene as much as another new architectural form, the templed bank. A French traveler, Michel Chevalier, noted in the 1830's that the bank was rivaling the church for honors as the finest building in town. Whereas the church had Wren's Baroque steeple as its chief symbol, the American bank chose the Greek-columned porch. When Samuel Blodgett designed the still existing First Bank of the United States in Philadelphia in 1796, little did he realize that he had created the first temple of business which could be literally so named, the ancestor of all the columned banks in the country. The fancy spread slowly until after 1825, when every community boasted one. Examples are found as far apart as Gideon Shryock's Bank of Louisville (1837) in Louisville, Kentucky, the Greek bank in Shawneetown, Illinois (1836), and the bank by William Kelly in Erie, Pennsylvania (1839), today sheltering the Erie County Historical Society.

Although not as prevalent as the bank, the most striking newcomer was the hotel. Before the construction of the famous Tremont House (1828–29) in Boston, designed by Isaiah Rogers, the traveler here and abroad looked to the comforts of the inn, which were modest under the best conditions. There were many reasons why the hotel should have been so successful in America. As a people we had been, as we still are, constantly on the move. No such convenience as an apartment house then existed, nor did lodgings in the English fashion. The hotel offered the transient and the permanent guest most of the comforts of home with none of the cost or the burden of housekeeping. Perhaps most important of all was the need for a place in which to meet and entertain in the city. Although our government and business buildings have always been open to the public, they were hardly equipped to provide relaxation and entertainment. Being a democratic people, with no royal palaces or court, Americans perforce created "People's Palaces," as the hotels were called when new, open to all for a fee; they became, and to some degree they remain, the social centers of our cities.

The Tremont House, Boston's pride, had many rooms and suites off straight corridors, a large staircase, a central rotunda, a row of luxurious public rooms and a splendid columned dining room. Locks on every door, free soap in every room, water closets and bathrooms excited the admiration of all, and bellboys reached for the traveler's luggage. With some justice Rogers, who went on to design the Astor House in New York (1836) and the famous Burnet House in Cincinnati (1850), has been called the father of the modern hotel.

There were additional conveniences in the city of the Romantic Era. Improvement of the water supply permitted water on every floor and the raising of the building height. By the 1840's indoor toilets had become more commonplace, largely because of an increased distribution of water. Philadelphia had replaced its well water with water from the Schuylkill River as early as 1801, at the instigation of the architect Latrobe. The city expanded the system between 1811 and 1819, giving Robert Mills the opportunity to create a most delightful architectural setting in the well-known Philadelphia Water Works (now the Aquarium). More spectacular was New York's Croton System, completed in 1841, after a portion of the city had been razed by fire and the need for large quantities of water had been dramatized. Boston followed suit in 1848. Baltimore, which had established the kernel of a system in 1804, enlarged it with the building of the Lake Roland Reservoir in 1858. The handsome engravings made at the time indicate that people fully recognized the blessings of a good water supply, which made possible better health, better plumbing, more rapid urban expansion and, an aspect not neglected by some, increased real estate speculation.

A very important innovation of the age, which saw the triumph of the steamboat, was the coming of the horse-drawn omnibus, first seen in the streets of New York in 1830. By the 1840's the lumbering vehicles were carrying as many as thirty passengers. Their virtue was not lost on the developer, who knew the value of land adjacent to routes of transportation. Building tended to concentrate along the entrances to the city, where ready transportation was present, and the built-up portion of the urban fringe came to look like fingers stretching from a hand. To cheer the traveler on the omnibus, gas-

A New Orleans cemetery showing the influence of
the Greek Revival Style.

light, introduced in New York in 1827 and in Philadelphia
and Boston ten years later, illuminated the way.

Changes also occurred in the American urban house. In
the West the city was built of frame houses on open lots; in
the East the row house continued its triumph, as more financial capital became available and more customers appeared.
More capital meant a bigger investment in improving the
land, which in turn meant that the lot became more crowded.
Buildings rose in height. Gone were the hipped roofs and
dormer windows of the early Republic; a third, and even a
fourth story with flat roof was added. In the late 1820's the
extensive rows began to reflect a new style, not in the main
body of the building, which remained unaltered, but in the
ornament. White Doric or Ionic columns and classical detail
transformed the house into a Greek Revival temple, as they
had transformed the bank. Examples of the columned porch
or entrance can be found in Baltimore on Cathedral Street or
Mount Vernon Place; Philadelphia can boast of many, like
those on Franklin Square. In New Orleans the new style pene-
trated even the French Quarter, and determined the architecture of the raised cemeteries, where little temples to the dead
have created cities in miniature.

In spite of the change in architectural taste, the practice of
the previous age of building town houses in rows continued,
even down to the 1880's. Behind the identical façades were

identical plans. Slight variations occurred city by city, each
having its particular row house with its particular façade and
plan. "The building is of bricks, painted and lined . . . and
modestly ornamented, in very good taste, with caps, sills, cor-
nices, etc., etc., in the dark red freestone [brownstone] of the
country," noted Cooper in the 1830's, of what he termed "a
species of second-rate genteel houses." He was describing a
four-story New York house. First came the half-sunken basement, next the main floor of the house, reached by a stoop.
The entrance was to one side of the front, Cooper tells us,
and it led to a vestibule, which in turn opened on a long hall.
At the end of this hall came the stairway to the second floor.
Off the hall on the first floor were two large identical rooms,
the one in front being the parlor and the second the dining
room. Sliding doors separated them, an early example of
"open" planning, which has since become a distinctive feature
of the American house. The master bedrooms were on the
second floor, and the children's and servants' rooms on the
third and top floor. In the basement were to be found the
kitchen at the back and the children's playroom or a pantry
at the front. "The whole building is finished with great neat-
ness, and with a solidity and accuracy of workmanship that is
rare to meet in Europe, out of England," Cooper observed.
"The doors of the better rooms are of massive mahogany, and
wherever wood is employed, it is used with great taste and
skill." The Old Merchant's House, now a museum at 29 East
4th Street in New York City, follows Cooper's description
almost exactly. In the red brick houses—now divided into
apartments—which every tourist to New York sees on the
north side of Washington Square, the dining room took the
place of the pantry in the basement. The room allotted to
dining in the Old Merchant's House formed in the Washington Square houses an additional parlor. Such was the type of
house described in Edith Wharton's *The Custom of the Country* and Henry James's *Washington Square*. The narrow rectangular lot, twenty to twenty-five feet wide, dictated similar
patterns in most cities of the eastern seaboard. Only the New
Orleans town house differed radically. The architect Latrobe
had noted in his diary:

> Altho' the sort of house built here by the French is not
> the specimen of French arrangement, yet it is infinitely,
> in my opinion, superior to that arrangement which we
> have inherited from the English. But so inveterate is
> habit that the merchants from the old United States who
> are daily gaining ground on the manners, the habits, the

opinions, and the domestic arrangements of the French, have already begun to introduce the detestable, lop-side, London house, in which a common passage and stairs acts as a common sewer to all the necessities of the dwelling . . .

His denunciation of the Eastern house-type concludes with a vain plea for the stuccoed French buildings of New Orleans. But we must remember that the open courtyard and rear wing of the New Orleans house were suited to the climate and the plethora of servants, which made possible a more generous spatial arrangement.

The builder knew no other type than the single family house that was patterned so closely on the London standard. Paradoxically, many houses became multi-family dwellings as soon as they were completed; families desperate to have a home of their own took in boarders in order to pay for it. Timothy Dwight had observed boardinghouses in New York and Philadelphia in the 1800's. "The peculiarity of living in boardinghouses, instead of keeping house or occupying private lodgings, is one of the most distinguishing features of society in New York," wrote James Silk Buckingham thirty years later, and this was equally true of other American cities. The English traveler offered three explanations: too many houses built of too large a size, the already present servant problem and the fact that Americans changed jobs and homes too frequently. He then gave a description of boardinghouse life:

The early hour at which all are rung out of bed by the sound of a great bell, as if at school—the rapidity with which persons rush to the table exactly at eight o'clock— the certainty that if you are five minutes after this, the breakfast will be half-consumed, and what remains will be cold and unpalatable—the haste with which everything is despatched, and the air of indifference with which parties rise up and go away to business when they have done—the earliness of the dinner-hour, three o'clock, with a repetition of the same hurry and bustle over again . . . and the preference of showy appearance to cleanliness—are but a part of the many evils of a boardinghouse life . . .

After reading this description it is no surprise to discover that he and his family did not become accustomed to the boardinghouse even after several years' stay in America.

The boardinghouse persisted well into the 1880's, even for the moderately well-to-do. "Do explain the Millers to the doctor, Edward," remarks the hostess in *The Elevator*, a farce by William Dean Howells. "They board," was the blunt reply. "That accounts for their willingness to flutter round your evening lamp . . ." The boardinghouse joke was once standard in America and lingered on with vaudeville through the 1920's. It was not so long ago that all children knew a song which threatened to become a nursery rhyme. Perhaps it is still sung in Baltimore, Philadelphia, Washington or wherever there is a Boardinghouse Row.

> *There is a boarding-house not far away,*
> *Where they have pork and beans most every day.*
> *Oh! How the boarders yell*
> *When they hear the dinner bell,*
> *Calling them to beans.*

Today the hot-plate and the corner drugstore or cafeteria, unforeseen in the Romantic Era, have made possible that widespread institution, the rooming house, so that the occupant at least does not have to partake of his landlady's fare.

4. Romantic Taste

The Romantic movement came late to America, although the way had been prepared by the novels of Charles Brockden Brown, especially *Wieland* and *Arthur Mervyn: Or Memoirs of the Year 1793*. Brown's Romantic inclinations extended to architecture, in which he had the interest of a passionate amateur. A close friend recalled that "he would for hours be absorbed in architectural studies, measuring proportions with compasses, and drawing plans of Grecian temples or Gothic cathedrals, monasteries or castles . . ." Literature and the new fashion went hand in hand. When in 1832 Alexander Jackson Davis, the most talented architect of the Neo-Gothic, built on the outskirts of Baltimore an early Romantic Revival mansion, his client chose for it the name of "Glen Ellen" as a tribute to his wife and to Sir Walter Scott.

The successive Romantic revivals in architecture began with the already mentioned Greek temple style. This was confirmed by a speech of Congressman Gulian Verplanck before the Academy of Fine Arts of New York in May, 1824. "We must return to those pure forms and scientific proportions of Grecian art which have been admired for ages," advised the author of *Evidences of Revealed Religion*. He castigated "that conception of the Roman, or rather Palladian architecture which delights in great profusion of unmeaning ornament in piling order upon order, in multitudes of small useless columns and mean and unnecessary pilasters, in numerous and richly decorated windows," and pointed out as an example of "this false taste . . . our most splendid and costly public building, the Capitol of the United States." The mixed Greco-Roman manner that had appeared at the beginning of the century soon gave way to the "pure forms" advocated by the Democratic congressman, and the Greek Revival enjoyed an extraordinary vogue. Lacking the intricacy of the American Baroque and the splendor of the American Roman, its features were readily adapted to all kinds of buildings.

> *I love thy rocks and rills,*
> *Thy woods and templed hills,*

sang America in 1832 with Samuel Francis Smith, the Baptist minister who wrote the words of "My Country, 'tis of Thee." Greek temples crowded the city of Syracuse and other new towns. James Fenimore Cooper, who disliked the style, found on his return from Europe the Hudson hills "fairly dotted with them." Greek columns shaded the porches of summer hotels like the Catskill Mountain House, and the style was to be seen in the spas of Virginia and western Pennsylvania, where the wealthy retreated from the city in this period to sip the spring water and marry off their daughters. Perhaps the most outstanding architectural example is Girard College, built in Philadelphia in 1833 by Thomas U. Walter, eminent architect of the Greek Revival who completed the Washington Capitol. Domestic architecture also put on a Greek tunic from Maine to Louisiana, in the South influencing especially the plantation house, with its huge columned porches and plain Greek pediments. Although chaste and often cold, the style can fairly be termed Romantic. It was an idealistic architecture, "casting on the screen of an imaginary past the projection of its unfulfilled desires." Ancient Greek architecture was never as severe as the white-painted wooden temples which are still found even beyond the Mississippi. In America it was associated with ideas of freedom generated by the Greek War of Independence then inflaming the world, and its severity suited it to the plain Protestant religious feeling of the time.

The Gothic villa and castle followed hard on the Greek Revival and soon there were so many Romantic styles that the brewer or banker who wished to build a house on a few acres close to the growing city could indulge in almost any architectural fancy he chose. With the coming of the new manner Wren's church found a most powerful rival. Gothic spires replaced the Baroque steeple, beginning with Trinity Church (1839–46) in New York by Richard Upjohn. Upjohn, an Englishman trained in the Neo-Gothic Style of Augustus W. N. Pugin, brought the new church architecture to this country, just at the time that the Oxford Group and the High Church innovations were making themselves felt in the Episcopal church. The growing interest in ritual on the part of Episcopalians called for a richer church architecture, and their congregations looked to the new style.

Alexander Jackson Davis, chief architect of the age of revivals, listed some of them: "American Log Cabin, Frame House, English Cottage, Collegiate, Gothic Manor House, French Suburban, Switz [sic] Cottage, Lombard Italian, Tuscan from Pliny's villa at Ostia, Ancient Etruscan, Suburban Greek, Oriental, Moorish and Castellated." Davis created his masterpiece in the turreted Paulding mansion on the Hudson River (now owned by the Duchess of Talleyrand); indeed the Hudson River valley is symbolic of the period, as its spiritual center. The romantic valley was the home of the painter Thomas Cole and the Hudson River School of painting, and of Washington Irving, whose Gothic home, "Sunnyside," has lately been restored by John D. Rockefeller, Jr. For foreign visitors a trip from New York to Albany by steamboat was compulsory; a comparison with the Rhine inevitably followed.

The landscape soon felt the new fashion. Jefferson had laid out a part of Monticello in a semi-formal way, showing the influence of the English "natural" gardening style. One of the earliest forms of the Romantic landscape was the American cemetery. Mount Auburn Cemetery in Cambridge, Massachusetts, famed today as the resting place of Mary Baker Eddy, founder of Christian Science, was laid out by amateur gardeners in 1831. The fact that the grounds were formerly those of an arboretum gave the first "rural cemetery" in the world its aboreal variety, a planting tradition that has been preserved. "The Garden of Graves" stands out in strong contrast to the Père Lachaise in Paris and the St. Louis Cemeteries in New Orleans, where temples and sarcophagi inspire an architectural tone, rather than the leafy atmosphere of Mount Auburn. Greenwood Cemetery in Brooklyn and Laurel Hill Cemetery in Philadelphia, the latter designed by the architect John Notman, were laid out shortly after in much the same style.

Now the man who was to transform the American landscape and establish the English villa garden in America was to appear on the scene. In matters of taste all the painters, writers, architects and patrons already under the spell of the Hudson were but demigods awaiting the great deity of the river, Andrew Jackson Downing. Dark and Spanish-looking, of an elegant and restrained manner, and with large expressive brown eyes, this son of Newburgh had spent his childhood and youth at the river's edge; in young manhood he and his brother established an orchard on land that was to become the fruit-growing center of the East. Then, in 1841, appeared a book that had the most astonishing success for one so turgidly written and so elaborately titled—A *Treatise on the Theory and Practice of Landscape Gardening, Adapted to North America: With a View to the Improvement of Country Residences*. It was shortly on every parlor table in the land, and at once Downing became the great publicist of the Romantic taste. Rejecting the old formal garden, the new art for him was "the beauty characterized by simple and flowing forms," or the American version of the English natural garden. He may also have been inspired by Edgar Allan Poe's *The Domain of Arnheim*, or *The Landscape Garden*, a paradise of bosky shrubberies and lily-fringed lakes with "a mass of semi-Gothic, and semi-Saracenic architecture sustaining itself as if by a miracle in mid-air."

Once the main points of a piece of ground were identified and the views discovered, Downing carefully placed trees

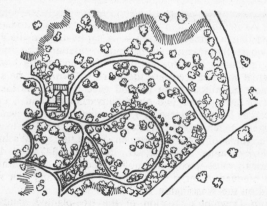

A villa garden designed by Andrew Jackson Downing.

A cottage in the Neo-Gothic, or Hudson River "Bracketed" Style,
popularized by Andrew Jackson Downing.

singly or in clumps to accent the points and the views. The
copper beech, the fir, the pine, the locust and the willow
were among his favorites. "Is it not, first of all, that such a
tree, standing where it can grow untouched and develop itself on all sides, is one of the finest pictures of symmetry and
proportion that the eye can anywhere meet with?" he asked;
and he compared nature's creation to the "Grecian Apollo itself." As for the contour of the grounds, "every gardener well
knows that no grassy surface is so captivating to the eye, as
one where those gentle swells and undulations rise and melt
away gradually into one another." The undulating lawn and
the great separate trees are the mark of Downing; he shaped
the now ubiquitous open lot and gave it form. As the focal
point of his gardens one almost invariably found a Gothic,
Tuscan or Moorish house by Davis which added an even more
Romantic touch to the landscape. He was called in to design
the grounds of the Smithsonian Institution in Washington
(built by James Renwick, Jr., between 1847 and 1855),
America's most important public building in the Gothic Revival manner. A large stone vase to his memory can still be
found on the Washington Mall.

With Downing's creation of the tree-planted, landscaped
lawn and the invention of the lawn mower, which replaced

the scythe in the 1850's, the pattern of the suburban plot, open and fenceless, became established. In fact, Downing saw the American way of life expressed in the modest house and garden. He found that with rare exceptions "our institutions, our habits, above all *the continual distribution of our fortunes* [authors' Italics], everything, in short, [taught] us so plainly the folly of improving large landed estates." He reasoned that "hence, the true philosophy of living in America, is to be found in moderate desires, a moderate establishment and moderate expenditures."

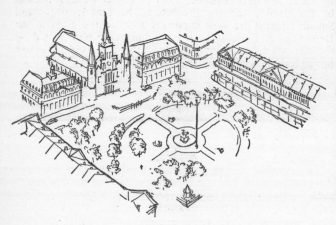

A view of Jackson Square, New Orleans, formerly the Place d'Armes, with the St. Louis Cathedral in the background.

Romantic taste, charming and naïve, paved the way for the more gauche conceits of the General Grant era and the entrance of the European-trained American architect. But before the triumph of the railroad, urban living, though more comfortable, was still simple, and only perhaps in New Orleans, the great transshipping point of the South which prospered more than any other American city in the 1830's, did the half-French, half-American population insist on making extravagance a part of life. In the Crescent City, the French Opera House, the theatres both French and American, the St. Louis Hotel, with the arcaded street designed to lead up to it, the stuccoed houses of the French Quarter and the tall Greek Revival houses in the beautiful Garden District offered perhaps the most eloquent testimony to the age in which so much that is important in our tradition originated. At the very end of the period a daughter of New Orleans, returning after an unhappy marriage and long years in Europe to her native city, gave to the Place d'Armes its present form. The Baroness Pontalba and her architect, Henry Howard, designed in 1848 the brick "apartments" that bear her name, later changing the goat pasture in the center of the square into a beautiful garden and subscribing to the equestrian figure of General Andrew Jackson which graces its center. Dominated by the three towers of the St. Louis Cathedral, which is flanked by the Cabildo and the Presbytère, the completed Jackson Square remains the most important architectural plaza in the United States. Since most of its buildings are now owned by the state of Louisiana, the square will be preserved forever for future generations to enjoy.

The memorial vase to Andrew Jackson
Downing. Designed by his partner, Calvert
Vaux, it stands neglected across the Mall
from the Smithsonian Institution
in Washington.

PART IV

The Age of Steam and Iron

1850-1880

THE MOST IMPORTANT EVENT of this age was the Civil War, which left its mark on the nation for more than a generation. One whole section of the country, the South, suffered financial eclipse, and its most famous cities—Charleston, Richmond, Savannah and New Orleans—languished. When the New York banker August Belmont wrote in 1861 to the London branch of the Rothschilds, then the most powerful financial firm in the world, that the North would inevitably win, his argument was based on the Union's much greater population, centered in large cities, and the wealth of its industries and farms. Another revelation was the power of the new Middle West, which gave the North its leading generals in the persons of Ulysses S. Grant and William Tecumseh Sherman. The new citizens of Ohio, Indiana, Michigan, Illinois and Wisconsin filled the ranks of the famous Midwestern regiments, confirming the solidarity of the states beyond the Alleghenies. Looming above all was the figure of Abraham Lincoln, son of pioneers, who came to the White House from a log cabin in southern Illinois.

The war proved a deterrent to industrial expansion in certain quarters, such as in shipbuilding, but in others, notably railroad rolling stock and farm machinery, it was a powerful incentive. Industry boomed in Chicago as the city furnished the reapers and harvesters needed to replace the farmhands gone off to war. New industries, like oil production and refining, joined in the expansion. Even railroad construction did not stop altogether; when the fratricidal battle came to an end in 1865, railroad building was ready to absorb the returning veterans and waves of new immigrants. By 1869 the continent had been spanned, and San Francisco was joined to the Union by rail.

The railroad is the great symbol of the Age of Steam and Iron. The scale has changed. A much more spreading city appears before our eyes, and it bulks larger in the center, because of the new business block with its cast-iron front and a general, though modest, increase in height. The early railroad terminals afford new entrances to the city; the homes of those newly made rich by the railroad, industry and merchandising begin to string along residential avenues, and rare colonies of commuters begin to cluster here and there at railroad stations near the larger cities. The tempo of the city is growing quicker; the age of finance capital is typified by Commodore Cornelius Vanderbilt, who started in the steamboat business and ended a railroad magnate. Millionaires have not yet begun to build palaces—wealth follows the fashions of the French Second Empire behind modest brownstone fronts under mansard roofs. Civic buildings also reflect the French taste. Tenements, in the modern sense of the term, have appeared in quantity, and the slum looms larger than ever before.

The city of the Picturesque Era is not a more beautiful city. Detail and ornament are coarser, erasing much of the visual pleasure of earlier street and villa architecture. There is a general heaviness in the somber buildings, which have taken on the darker hues of the new building materials, brownstone and pressed brick. The largest city remains New York, but Philadelphia and Chicago typify the age because of the railroads' activity in changing their earlier patterns.

1. *The Railroad*

Into Edgar Allan Poe's "Domain of Arnheim" puffed an iron horse. "They are cutting down all the trees in the beautiful valley on which I have looked so often with a loving eye," mourned the painter Thomas Cole over the Hudson River Valley, in a letter to his patron, the New York merchant Luman Reed. "Join with me in maledictions on all dollar-godded utilitarians." On the east bank of Downing's river enterprising capitalists were pushing the construction of the railroad between New York and Albany. Everywhere the new machine which had first appeared modestly was pre-empting the best sites, taking land once reserved for pleasure gardens and turning it into freight yards. Even L'Enfant's mall in Washington was to have tracks and a depot within its borders by 1870.

On other great rivers the railroad offered similar threats. The Pennsylvania Railroad reached Pittsburgh in 1852, and the Baltimore and Ohio arrived at Wheeling, West Virginia, in the same year with disastrous results for river traffic. "There is a perfect mania here for improvements," wrote a visitor to Pittsburgh a year later. "Every day somebody commences to tear down an old house and put up a new one with an iron front . . . One interest, however, is at a standstill, namely steamboating. Ten boats were burnt up and their wrecks lay at the wharf for a month, showing how little demand there is for wharf room."

The railroad was now everywhere in the East and in parts of the Middle West. In 1857 Abraham Lincoln, who obtained a substantial living as a railroad attorney, could reach every part of the Eighth Circuit of Illinois from Springfield by rail, a route he had formerly taken on horseback. In Europe, where the invention met an old civilization, it was forced to go more carefully, and much of the European city was spared; in America the railroad disregarded the scene and took whatever it pleased. To appreciate the power of the railroad of those days we need only look at the dominating role of the American highway in our own time. Both have taken over the urban periphery. The dominance of the railroad builder in the 1850's and for a generation or so to follow can only be matched by today's highway engineer. Old cemeteries, old houses, parks and waterfront sites fell to the railroad as they fall to the modern high-speed artery. Anthracite coal poured through Philadelphia to the docks on the Delaware over the lines of the Reading Railroad, and railroad tracks cut up Penn's city into a puzzle, forcing its expansion northward rather than more logically to the south or west. Chicago was transformed overnight from a canal town into a railroad city and laid claim to first place in the West. Only eight years after the first train entered its limits, the "City of the Wild Onion" was in 1856 the focus of ten trunk lines, and the railroad still dominates the physical scene there, despite a few terminal consolidations. In New York Trinity Church saw fit to sell what was left of St. John's Park to Commodore Vanderbilt for a freight yard in 1866. It was at this time that New York surrendered its harbor and rivers to the railroads as a giant belt line. Lighters and tugs were improved, and in 1866, the carfloat was invented to transfer whole trains from the New Jersey railheads to the docks and yards in Manhattan and Brooklyn. Inevitably the railroads guided the destiny of our great cities, just as they were to control the countryside.

Paralleling the triumph of the railroad came the widespread use of the fixed steam engine. Up to 1850 the main source of industrial power had been water; after 1850 it was steam, and steam power gobbled up coal. The grimy milltown of steam and coal was as much a part of this age as the clean waterpowered milltown of the previous one. Rebecca Harding Davis, mother of the famous journalist Richard Harding Davis, was one of the first American novelists to describe industrial conditions in fiction; her picture of pre-Civil-War Wheeling, West Virginia, down the Ohio from Pittsburgh, is scarcely inviting. "The idiosyncrasy of this town is smoke. It rolls sullenly in slow folds from the great chimneys of the iron foundries and settles down in black, slimy pools on the muddy streets. Smoke on the wharves, smoke on the dingy boats, on the yellow river,—clinging in a coating of greasy soot to the housefront, the two faded poplars, the faces of the passers-by. The long train of mules, dragging masses of pig-iron through the narrow street, have a foul vapour hanging to their reeking sides . . ." She goes on to tell a tragic story of Welsh puddlers, Cornish miners and Irish laborers working where "the mills for rolling iron are simply immense tent-like roofs, covering acres of ground, open on every side," while "beneath these roofs . . . [was] a city of fires." Such was the new industrial town of the 1850's.

What was true of Wheeling was equally true of St.-Etienne in France, Liége in Belgium, Essen in Germany and Birmingham in England. Railroad construction was molding all these cities. It provided markets for the produce of the iron mills, it carried coke and iron ore to the blast furnace and in America especially it freed the factory from dependence on water power by bringing in the coal to make steam. Americans can draw some solace from the fact that the newly created European town of the period was very little different from their own. The railroad was the great maw into which poured the produce of the new iron and machine works. When Chicago became the rail center of the West, its leading industries were car repair and car building shops, iron rail mills and boiler works. Cleveland and Toledo followed much the same course. Steubenville, Ohio, remained a prosperous river town until its first rolling mills, built in 1856, ushered in manufacturing. Altoona, Pennsylvania, was laid out as a market town speculation in 1849 but was soon changed into a milltown when the railroad reached it two years later. In 1854 the Pennsylvania Railroad chose Altoona for the site of its shops, and from the once quiet valley rose a cacophony of whistles and bells, the banging of freight cars and all the strident and melancholy noises of the new age. We tend to think of the Civil War as a dividing line between the idyllic pastoral America and its smoky urban aftermath, but in reality this great crisis only hastened an industrial process already well begun.

2. *New Towns on Prairie and Mountain*

Speculation continued to follow the frontier, which now moved farther and farther west, with the help of the railroad. What had been an initiation in President Jackson's day was now a well-worked formula. Everybody who staked a claim on the frontier thought in terms of a booming city. Frederick Law Olmsted, the landscape architect, has left us a description of "developments" along the Mississippi in the 1850's. "The villages having large names upon the map are really but a shanty or two . . ." he noted from a passing river steamer. "I had heard some ludicrous accounts of Cairo [the Eden of Charles Dickens' *Martin Chuzzlewit*] . . . at the mouth of the Ohio, but was fairly shocked with amusement to see it in all sober detail composed of item, one house leaning every way, uncertain of the softest spot to fall; item, one shanty, labeled 'Telegraph Office'; item, four flat boats, high and dry, labeled 'boarding,' 'milk' etc.; item, four ditto afloat, labeled 'postoffice,' 'milk,' . . ." All town names were appended with the word "city" in anticipation of the expected inhabitants, or at least a few gullible investors back East. Senator Ingalls of Kansas, when he first came west from Massachusetts in the same period, spent some time at Sumner, Territory of Kansas, and complained of the unfinished houses, the lack of order and the ever present mud. This boom-ridden town failed, and of the fourteen platted in Kansas on the banks of the Missouri in the 1850's indeed only three survived in 1867. When complaints are made today about the ugliness of many Midwestern towns, it is salutary to remember the condition of their founding and to ask ourselves why we should be naïve enough to expect anything more.

Together with the speculative towns of the prairie and the new industrial towns came the mining towns that sprang up in the North and the Far West. We have already seen a prototype of the 1830's in the Pennsylvania anthracite region. Had we made our way through partially settled Illinois in the same decade we would have come on the lead-mining town of Galena on the banks of the Mississippi. Copper was the next incentive. It was discovered on the Keweenaw Peninsula in northern Michigan in 1845. The first pits were sunk near Copper Harbor, and soon afterwards the companies (which were later consolidated in the Calumet and Hecla Mining Company, founded by Boston businessmen and source of many great Boston fortunes) built the towns of Hancock and Houghton. The boom has long since departed from the scarred peninsula but copper mining continues, a mile below the earth's surface.

All of these, of course, were forgotten when the cry of *Gold!* went up at Sutter's Fort in California in 1848. The mad rush was on, and it did not stop until the surface of the Western country had been thoroughly prospected for its hidden riches. First, modest cities of tents arose about the ore diggings, then wooden shelters and finally clapboard buildings, on which the ever present false front offered an impression of stability and height. Mark Twain, who worked as a journalist in the Nevada silver-mining towns during the Civil War, has left a description of the short life of the typical town:

> You will find it hard to believe that there stood at one time a fiercely flourishing city, of two thousand or three thousand souls, with its newspaper, fire company, brass-band, volunteer militia, bank, hotels, noisy Fourth-of-July processions and speeches, gambling-hells crammed with tobacco smoke, profanity, and rough-bearded men of all nations and colors, with tables heaped with gold dust . . . streets crowded and rife with business—town lots worth four hundred dollars a front foot—labor, laughter, music, dancing, swearing, fighting, shooting, stabbing . . . all the appointments and appurtenances of a thriving and prosperous and promising young city— and *now* nothing of it all but a lifeless, homeless solitude . . . In no other land, in modern times, have towns so absolutely died and disappeared, as in the mining town regions of California.

From the copper-mining to the silver-mining towns, from Placerville, California to Jerome, Arizona, named after Leonard W. Jerome, the American grandfather of Sir Winston Churchill, the story was repeated over and over again. Few of them exist except as ghost towns. Among those still flourishing are Lead, South Dakota, home of the Homestake Mining Company—which for a long time supported the free-spending William Randolph Hearst and his press—and, perhaps the most notorious, Butte, Montana, home of the Anaconda Copper Company.

Butte began as a city of tents in 1864 when gold was discovered; ten years later came the silver boom with shacks, frame buildings and refineries belching black smoke; only in 1883 did silver disappear, to be replaced by copper, and Butte's great days began. Then were fought the titanic battles for control of the richest hill in the world between the copper millionaires, William A. Clark, Marcus Daly and F. Augustus Heinze. No palaces were built here by the fighting millionaires; they chose New York and Washington for their social life. Instead they decreed that the city, which still produces one third of the copper mined in the country, should be born old and ugly and remain old and ugly until only a few years ago. "The barren, gray mine dumps with faded cottages in clusters at their feet; the huge steel and wooden gallows frames of the mines; the smoke-belching stacks; the crooked, crazy, dirty roads and crumbling sidewalks leading up the hill to the mines; the rickety, unpainted, bulging and leaning brick and frame buildings"—this was the scene in the 1930's. Not until the New Deal did the city get sewers, paved streets, parks, playgrounds and an art gallery. Since then business has continued the improvements, and Butte is beginning at last to leave behind it the Age of Steam and Iron.

The grimmer aspect of Butte is forgotten as we turn to the lost mining communities, once so prosperous and now abandoned. We are drawn to them as we are drawn to certain market towns, not so much because they are beautiful as because they recall a past era. In Virginia City, Nevada, Aspen, Colorado, Tombstone, Arizona, Placerville, California, and others the miners, often big spenders, built extravagantly for the pleasure of all; the weatherbeaten "opera houses" (pretentiously named small theatres), saloons and hotels still stand like aging beauties. Even Galena has remained untouched since the day Ulysses S. Grant made his home there before being called to the colors, and Jerome, crumbling on an Arizona mountainside today, tempts the passing motorist with "Visit Jerome, the Newest and Largest Ghost City in America."

While the mining centers of the West were entering their most ebullient phase, in western Pennsylvania occurred another boom with the drilling of the first oil well in the world at Titusville in 1859. Here, as on the Kansas prairie, frame houses were set along muddy streets to shelter the invading prospectors. Titusville was only one of many in the region. Of them all Pithole City, Pennsylvania, was the most astonishing. An oil well was drilled in January, 1865, on a lonely farm; by midsummer a town of 10,000 occupied the whole area.

It is a wooden town, not a brick or stone house in it [runs one description]. The streets are narrow with but a single plank for a sidewalk . . . The buildings on either side are of every size and shape imaginable, from a four-

False fronts on buildings in the silver-mining town
of Virginia City, Nevada.

story hotel to the diminutive stand of a gingerbread or
peanut merchant. The smell of new lumber, fresh paint
and the "crude" is everywhere discernible. Here may be
seen a building which is neither sided, floored nor finished
but the roof is up,—from the peak of which swings a
sign, informing the public that "Oil Leases" will there
be bought and sold . . .

Pithole City no longer exists.

Mining and oil booms gave rise to new industries along
the railroad sidings at the city's edge. With the iron mills
and the machine shops came the gold-, copper- and oil-refining
works. "The flat was crowded, odoriferous and smoky, with
lumber, oil and iron; but the oil predominated," Constance
Fenimore Woolson reported of the Cleveland Flats where
Rockefeller and other oil men were building new empires.
"Blue barrels met our eyes and a network of pipes, elevated
high in the air, ran hither and thither, while over, under, and
throughout all the pungent petroleum made itself felt in every
breath we drew. On we went," continued the author of the

beautiful but now neglected novel *East Angels,* "and the smoking chimneys grew into a forest, the railroad tracks on either side held long lines of singular boiler-shaped cars, and trestlework and tramways ran in every direction like arteries from the central steam engines." Such landscapes, strange in the 1870's, are common enough experience for today's motorist as he hurries by the oil-refining jungles of Bayonne, New Jersey, Whiting, Indiana, Marcus Hook, Pennsylvania, and San Pedro, California, or from a distance mistakes the cracking plants in the center of Texas City, Texas, for the expected skyscrapers.

3. *The City of the Civil War*

Unable to discover any confirmation of Emerson's prophecy that the industrial town and the railroad would eventually fuse into the American landscape, the mid-nineteenth-century traveler found as little evidence of cohesion in the larger cities, although plenty of human bustle and activity. Fancier carriages and larger drays greeted him on the city streets, and there was another form of transportation, the horsecar, which was replacing the earlier awkward omnibus. The new invention ran on rails and was already creating linear settlements running from the urban center. It had appeared first in New York in the 1830's when the city forbade locomotive-hauled trains in the middle of town, but as a street railroad proper the horsecar first operated in 1851. A year later a line was connecting Boston and Cambridge, which is described in Henry James's novel *The Bostonians.* Philadelphia had one in 1858 and in 1859 three lines opened in Chicago. "The roads are outrageous and everywhere cut up with the rails of the horse-cars," the Boston sculptor William Wetmore Story complained in 1865. "These horse-cars are the pest of the country, but you must take them or walk, unless you choose to pay a fortune away in carriages."

Cheap urban transportation was matched for the first time by an attempt to offer cheap lodging in the city. The real estate men and speculative builders had succeeded in meeting the demand for cheap houses with the invention of the balloon frame, but that was reserved for the newer cities and the outskirts of the older ones. Within the old centers nothing new was provided for the lower income groups until the 1850's. Until then, those who were denied the privileges of the boardinghouse found homes in slum dwellings, which were converted private houses, breweries, old warehouses or any structure with four walls and a roof in the older parts of our cities. Technically a slum is a residential neighborhood in which the houses are so run down, below standard and unhealthy that they are declared to be a menace to the occupants and to the community. They had existed since the eighteenth century in ever expanding numbers as immigration and population increased.

A New York physician has pictured the slum economy of the 1840's which paved the way for the construction of the new type of building, the tenement in our modern sense of the term. Dr. Joseph H. Griscom observed in 1845:

> *The system of tenantage* to which large numbers of the poor are subject, I think, must be regarded as one of the principal causes, of the helpless and noisome manner in which they live. The basis of these evils is the subjection of the tenantry to the merciless inflictions and extortions of the *sub-landlord*. A house, or a row, or court of houses is hired by some person of the owner, on a lease of several years, for a sum which yields a fair interest on the cost. The *owner* is then relieved of the great trouble incident to the changes of tenants, and the collection of rents . . .
>
> These slum properties [he went on to explain], in order to admit a greater number of families, are divided into small apartments, as numerous as decency will admit . . . These closets, for they deserve no other name, are then rented to the poor, from week to week, or month to month, the rent being almost invariably required in advance . . .

What is so striking about Dr. Griscom's analysis is that the system, with only slight variations, continues to this day in many slums, particularly those reserved for the Negro or Puerto Rican peoples.

Now came the tenement proper, which replaced the converted dwellings and others in the larger cities. (The word tenement has come to mean a slum dwelling rather than a multiple dwelling, as formerly.) There had been earlier tenements in New York, but the first large one appeared in 1850. "It is built with the design of supplying the laboring people with cheap lodgings, and will have many advantages over the cellars and other miserable abodes, which too many are forced to inhabit," noted the *Evening Post*. "The depth of the building is two hundred and forty feet, with a front of thirty-five feet. Each tenement consisting of two rooms and a hall, is nearly eighteen feet in width, and about twenty feet in length, giving twenty-four residences to each floor." This horror earned the encomium, "A praiseworthy enterprise and well worthy of imitation." Such a profitable "improvement" soon found imitators. Until the 1920's, an income of 7 to 10 per cent was considered standard for tenement property in New York. With perpetual overcrowding throughout the nineteenth century, the city evolved its own form of tenement building, usually double structures on a lot 25 × 100 feet, one facing the street, with the other in the rear and a tiny court between. Toilet facilities, if they can be so named, were in the cellar or under the sidewalk; they soon became cesspools. Windows looked out on black airshafts, and the corridors were never lighted and were so narrow that two people could just squeeze past one another. In one of these blocks 577 persons were confined in 96 rooms. As for playgrounds, theatres, pleasure gardens or other distractions, there were none; the children had the street and their elders the church, the saloon and the grogshop.

Some cities never developed a tenement building. Philadelphia continued to build row houses, although making them much smaller. The units here were sixteen feet wide and only two stories high, and into them would be packed half a dozen families. Most large cities, except New York and Philadelphia, turned to the wooden tenement, a multiple dwelling built around a balloon frame. Take those of Boston as an example. At one time the city had the worst slums in the country, made up of packed single-family houses. In one section of the city in the 1840's there was an average of thirty-seven persons per house. To absorb the swelling population of the 1840's and the 1850's the "Three-decker" was invented. Mention is made of one in Newark, New Jersey, in 1855, but its true home is New England, particularly in and around Boston. The name stems from the three wooden galleries, one above the other, at the rear of the four-story structure, which give the impression of three decks. "It is four stories high and has no entry or hall in it, every room opening by its one door on the four front piazzas which rise above each other," so Edward Everett Hale, author of *The Man Without a Country*, described an early version in 1869, which had

> in the rear, two closets only lighted from the doors, one of which may be eight feet square; the other is narrower. The front room, which opens on the piazza, is fifteen by thirteen perhaps. This is a suite for a family. And any day you pass you may see the children of forty such families disporting themselves on the piazzas. The reason why there are no windows in the back wall is that there

is another similar building, which has been squeezed in there in a space so narrow that it is not nine feet from the windows and doors to the wall opposite,—and, of that four or five must be given to the piazza . . .

The piazzas or "decks" have since migrated to the rear. The wooden tenements still survive in large numbers in New England; not until 1912, when the fireproofing of multiple dwellings became obligatory in Massachusetts, did they begin to disappear.

The appalling living conditions did not pass unnoticed, but the age did not have much time for reform. New York obtained its first tenement-house law from the state legislature in 1867, but it was carelessly enforced.

When the railroad came to the city, urban America was already wearing a stiff new dress, as if in welcome. The iron age was upon the country in another form: iron was being used in buildings. The metal had long been employed in the shape of bars to strengthen masonry; in England in the 1790's cast-iron beams and columns had been adapted to mill construction, a practice that eventually made its way to this country. Iron

"Three-decker" wooden tenements in South Boston.

was not used on façades until 1830, when John Haviland placed a complete cast-iron front on the fireproof Farmers' and Merchants' Bank of Pottsville, Pennsylvania. New Yorkers first saw the material on shop fronts in the 1840's. Finally, in 1848 a versatile watchmaker from Catskill-on-the-Hudson, James Bogardus, developed a complete structural system of cast iron with visible structural members in a building in downtown New York. One of his early efforts still remains on the northwest corner of Washington and Murray streets in that city. At once cast iron became the rage.

Easily made cast iron had the advantages that it could be bolted into a frame to stand any strain, that allowance could be made for expansion and contraction due to changes of temperature and that it could be fabricated in parts, shipped and then assembled. Whole buildings were sent in pieces around Cape Horn from the East coast. Baltimore fought with New York and Philadelphia to supply the western market; in 1870 a Baltimore company shipped an iron front for the Corbett Building in Portland, Oregon, which is yet standing. Many streets of iron fronts exist still. The wholesale drygoods district around Reade and Worth Streets in lower Manhattan has many such fronts, Market Street in Philadelphia offers excellent examples and until recently St. Louis could point to a whole section along its riverfront, where the Jefferson Memorial Park is now in process of development. In Washington cast iron forms the dome of the Capitol itself. The iron front was often skillfully made to simulate stone, and it is difficult to distinguish it under the thick layers of paint, except by tapping a pillar of an old building and discovering the metal by the hollow sound.

In a more leisurely fashion, iron made its appearance in another shape. There were horizontal rails for the railroad and horsecar line, and there were vertical rails for elevators. The first practical elevator with safety devices was the passenger elevator installed in 1857 by Elisha Otis in a building to be found on the corner of Broadway and Broome Street in New York. Two years later Otis installed the first passenger elevator in the Hotel Astor. With the invention of the geared hydraulic elevator in 1872, higher and larger buildings were made possible, and elevators were used more frequently.

Had there not been an expansion in the American business economy at this time large buildings would have been to no purpose, despite the presence of cast iron and the elevator. Although the individual businessman dominated this age of railroads, business organizations were becoming more and more elaborate. Factories were expanding in the milltown and

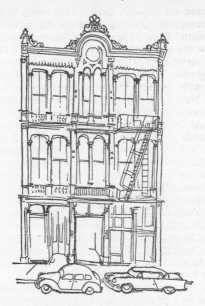

Cast-iron front of the Corbett
Building in Portland, Oregon.

office forces were enlarging in the company headquarters. New forms of business, such as life insurance and the department store, required more floor space.

In 1862 one of America's greatest drygoods merchants, Alexander T. Stewart, retained John Kellum to design a cast-iron palace, which stands at Broadway and 10th Street in Manhattan. Once the boast of the city, it became a branch of John Wanamaker. The Equitable Life Insurance Company built one of the first large office buildings in 1870 and, thanks to the new elevator, leased the top floor at a premium, something that had never been possible before. The art of crowding the lot had only begun: enterprising real estate men were preparing for a greater opportunity to come in the 1880's.

The large business office was not confined to the city. Typical of the commercial ambitions of the period was the "business block," to be found still in many small American towns. It took its place with the church, the bank and the railroad stations as one of the largest buildings in our communities.

These "blocks" of brick, cast iron or wood, often with a raised central feature framing the name and date, lend a flavor of an older time to the bustling main street of today's small town. Examples are to be found in Milford, Massachusetts, Red Wing, Minnesota, and Fort Smith, Arkansas, but they are so numerous in all parts of the country that one does not have to travel any distance to find good examples.

Just as cast iron was the innovation in larger buildings, pressed brick and brownstone were the new building materials in smaller structures. The use of wood continued, predominantly on the outskirts of cities; within cities, brick dominated —not the rough orange-pink brick of the first years of the century, but the dark ox-blood brick that we still see about us. The Industrial Revolution came to the brick industry in 1833, only to have the machines destroyed by the workers, who saw their livelihood threatened. Machine-made pressed brick was reintroduced in Philadelphia in the 1840's and by the 1850's was being used in all large cities, although the best kind came to be known as "Philadelphia pressed brick." An entirely different texture was given to buildings, dark and smooth instead of light and rough.

A definite change in taste favored the shift, for the dark brick was trimmed with brownstone. Limestone, marble and granite had served earlier, but they were pushed aside by the new material. It had long been in use in the Connecticut Valley, where large deposits are still found and had supplied the foundations for early houses in New Haven. The old library at Yale University, attributed to Henry Austin (1842), and the home of Skull and Bones (an undergraduate secret society) by Ithiel Town are examples of whole buildings built in brownstone. Charming though these two buildings may be, it is an indication of the period's taste that this stone, which was employed in the rear of the New York City Hall in the 1800's because it was cheap, came to veneer the fronts of the city's homes in the 1850's. Up to 1880, and to a lesser extent afterwards, row on row of brownstone or brownstone-and-pressed-brick houses were built in Manhattan and Brooklyn; the fashion spread over the country to Cincinnati, north to Troy and east to Boston.

Edith Wharton could not lightly pass over the gloom of New York in the 1860's and 1870's. "One of the most depressing impressions of my childhood is my recollection of the intolerable ugliness of New York, of its untouched streets and the narrow houses so lacking in external dignity, so crammed with smug and suffocating upholstery . . ." The author of *A Backward Glance* describes the city as "this low-

An elaborate brownstone house in New York
with stoop and mansard roof.

studded rectangular New York, cursed with its universal
chocolate-coloured coating of the most hideous stone ever
quarried [brownstone], this cramped horizontal gridiron of
a town without towers, porticoes, fountains or perspectives,
hide-bound in its deadly uniformity of mean ugliness."

In spite of the novelist's very justifiable picture, there were
certain planning schemes which showed that the Age of Steam
and Iron was not without some imagination. Real estate interests rediscovered the possibilities of filled land. Earlier
efforts were modest by comparison. Harrison Gray Otis had
leveled Beacon Hill and filled the flats along what is now
Charles Street in Boston, and in New York the waterfront
had been pushed out into the Hudson and East Rivers. The
Canton Company in Baltimore was created as early as 1828
to exploit 3000 acres of harbor frontage, but to become profitable the area had to await the full development of the railroad
in the 1850's. None of these could compare with the creation
of the South End and the Back Bay areas in Boston.

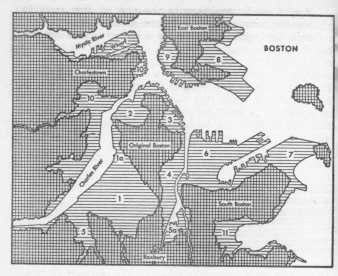

MAP OF MODERN BOSTON SHOWING FILLED LAND:

1. Back Bay, about 570 acres, mostly done after 1856 and continued to 1894.
1a. West Cove, about 80 acres, begun in 1803 and completed in 1863.
2. Mill Cove, about 70 acres, begun in 1804 and completed in 1835.
3. Great or East Cove, about 112 acres. 1823-74.
4. South Cove, about 86 acres. 1806-43.
5. Roxbury, about 322 acres; filling-in of which might be said to have started with that of the Back Bay, as it was a continuation of it, becoming quite active in 1878 and completed in the 1890's, excepting that part bordering on the South Bay which is in the section marked 5a.
5a. South Bay, amount 138 acres, begun in 1850, not yet completed.
6. South Boston, amount 714 acres, begun in 1836, still in process.
7. Marine Park, acquired in 1883, about 57 acres; bridge to Castle Island, July 1, 1891, included in South Boston filling.
8. Boston Air Port, authorized May 12, 1922, about 150 acres in 1928, opened on Sept. 8, 1923; part of the East Boston filling.
9. East Boston, amount 370 acres, begun in 1880, not yet completed.
10. Charlestown, amount 416 acres, begun in 1860, completed to present state about 1896.
11. Columbus Park with Strandway, amount about 265 acres, acquired 1890—1901; part of South Boston filling, as given above.

According to James L. Bruce, clerk of the Bostonian Society, the original area of Boston is accepted as having been 783 acres; filled land has since contributed from three to four times that amount to give the city its present shoreline.

(Map and data, courtesy of James L. Bruce.)

It has been estimated that over 3000 acres of modern Boston consist of made land. The city began quite early to spread out from the tadpole-shaped town of the seventeenth century, but the most important extensions occurred in the latter half of the nineteenth century. In a large speculative development between Tremont and Washington Streets, the city engineers, E. S. Chesbrough and William Parrott, laid out a plan between 1849 and 1853 that was based on the London pattern of a number of small squares. Worcester Square is the best surviving example. Unlike Louisburg Square, planned in 1826, where the houses were built by individuals, the South End squares have orderly rows of bow-fronted houses that were built by speculators. These rows give the whole district a quality which, despite the recent changes created by an extension of Massachusetts Avenue, still has great visual attraction.

The story of the Back Bay begins in 1814 with the construction of the eastern dike, now beneath Beacon Street, which cut off the tidal flats from the Charles River. After complicated negotiations with the Commonwealth of Massachusetts, a group of speculators in 1857 finally obtained the right to fill in the flats, then crossed by several dikes and railroad tracks. The architect Arthur Delavan Gilman is presumed to have drawn the plan the same year. It included Commonwealth Avenue, one of the early examples of the residential avenue. The actual filling did not begin until a year later, when 450 acres were covered at an average depth of fill of twenty feet. In 1879 the Fenway Park was designed by Frederick Law Olmsted to mark the boundary of the improvement. The fact that Back Bay does not have residential squares is compensated for by its well-built streets of houses, strictly regulated as to height and setbacks, and by its usually handsome, urbane architecture.

On an even greater scale, and often tied to large real estate developments, were the great bridges that began to span American rivers and harbors, their towers rising for the first time into the skyline. The Eads Bridge (1867–71) in St. Louis was one of the first, a monument to Captain James B. Eads's success in throwing a single span of steel across the Mississippi. His efforts were eclipsed by the Brooklyn Bridge (1869–83), designed by John A. Roebling and built by his son, Washington. The construction itself had something of the epic to it: the father died shortly after completing the design, and the son, half paralyzed from the aftereffects of the "bends," suffered while working on the caissons, supervised the construction from a bed in a room on Brooklyn Heights.

Other bridges may rise higher or cross wider spaces—the Transbay Bridge and the Golden Gate Bridge in San Francisco, the Mystic River Bridge in Boston, or the more recent Delaware River and Chesapeake Bay Bridges—but none can compare with the work of the Roeblings. Although engineers, they were not afraid to seek the help of art; by using the Gothic arch in the towers they gave the bridge an esthetic attraction that has been celebrated by poets and painters ever since.

Of far more significance to everyday life in the city was the introduction of our first great urban parks and of the residential avenue. To compensate for the spreading ugliness and misery brought on by chaotic industrialization, many felt the need for creating great public pleasure areas. Small public promenades, such as the Battery, of both Charleston and New York, or the Boston Common, had existed for some time, and private pleasure grounds thrown open to the public by their generous owners, formed other oases. Such a one was the park of "Belvedere," the estate of John Eager Howard, the name of which lingers on in Baltimore's largest hotel. New Yorkers took the ferryboat across the Hudson to Hoboken, where John Stevens, pioneer railroad builder, bade them welcome to his "Elysian Fields." Although the Stevens Institute of Technology occupies most of the estate, we can savor to this day the delight that the public obtained from the view of the river and the city before them.

Otherwise people longed in vain for promenades and parks that the commissioners of the 1811 plan for Manhattan had omitted to provide. "Certainly, if the City of New York were destined to stand on the side of a small stream, such as the Seine or the Thames, a great number of ample spaces might be needful," they had told the hapless citizens, "but those large arms of the sea which embrace Manhattan Island render its situation in regard to health and pleasure, as well as to convenience of commerce, peculiarly felicitous." New York had to wait fifty years for the crusading of the poet William Cullen Bryant and the landscape designer Andrew Jackson Downing to spur the creation of its Central Park.

To Philadelphia goes the honor of having in 1855 the first public park of any size, and today Fairmount Park, 3845 acres in area, is the largest park within the limits of any city in the country. The fact that the city drew its water from the Schuylkill made it almost obligatory that the banks of the river be protected. In 1812 the first five acres were purchased for the water-works pumping station. Slowly additional land was obtained, until by the 1870's the park had close to 2000 acres. The creation in 1867 of the Fairmount Park Commission, part public and part private, and the Fairmount Park Art Association in 1872 helped to turn the vast acreage into the beautiful scene we know today.

If Philadelphia took the lead in size, New York triumphed in the matter of art. The milestone in the history of American parks and of American landscaping was, of course, the creation of the already mentioned Central Park. In 1858 a competition was held for its design, and Connecticut-born Frederick Law Olmsted and Calvert Vaux, the English architect who had been associated with Downing, took the prize. In the center of Manhattan Island. Downing's sinuous line and undulating lawn were skillfully adapted to the exigencies of a public pleasure ground. The two artists added their own contribution by taking advantage of the topography and using such inventions as sunken roadways to rid the park of the traffic nuisance, a practice that could well be imitated by modern highway engineers. Calvert Vaux designed many of the small buildings scattered through this great park. "You may . . . often see vast numbers of persons brought closely together," Olmsted told the American Social Science Association in 1870, "poor and rich, young and old, Jew and Gentile. I have seen a hundred thousand thus congregated . . . and I have looked vainly among them for a single face completely unsympathetic with the prevailing expression of good-nature and light-heartedness. Is it doubtful that it does men good to come together in this way in pure air and under the light of heaven?"

For Olmsted this was the beginning of a great career. Interrupted by the Civil War, when he became secretary of the United States Sanitary Commission, predecessor of the American Red Cross, his great work was launched when he turned to landscaping as a profession. After 1865 we find him everywhere, in Buffalo (Delaware Park), Brooklyn (Prospect Park), Detroit (Belle Isle Park), Montreal (Mount Royal Park), Washington (the grounds of the United States Capitol) and Boston (the Boston Park System). Despite all this Olmsted had sufficient time to battle, together with Charles Eliot Norton, the eminent art historian, for the preservation of the area around Niagara Falls. Olmsted was to gain other honors in the city of the American Renaissance, but his masterworks belong to the Civil War era.

One of Olmsted's ideas for Central Park had been to connect it to all parts of the city with green thoroughfares. Although this was never carried out, the green boulevard soon appeared in other parts of the country. The residential avenue has received no attention as a city planning phenomenon, but it was inevitable that the innovations of Baron Haussmann in Paris would be experimented with in America. Certain streets, like lower Broadway in New York or the Battery in Charleston, had been reserved for the more fashionable residences in the 1800's, but the exclusive street had come about by accumulated tradition rather than by design. One conspicuous exception existed in Hillhouse Avenue in New Haven, laid out as early as 1792. Despite the destruction of some of its houses, it remains one of the most beautiful streets in the country. Mansions in the Tuscan and Greek Revival manners by Ithiel Town, Alexander Jackson Davis and Henry Austin still give it a cachet unrivaled elsewhere. There was, of course, Commonwealth Avenue in Boston, but that did not obtain its architectural frame until the late 1870's and the 1880's.

In the rising cities of the Middle West the residential avenue came into its own. Euclid Avenue in Cleveland blossomed in the decades following the Civil War, as the new millionaires, whose fortunes came from the smelly flats below the city, raised large mansions on the wide thoroughfare. A double row of trees formed two leafy bowers unbroken by cross streets for a half mile or more, and on either side lawn and garden repeated a seemingly endless vista of beauty. Known as Prosperity Street and Millionaire's Row, it was declared America's most beautiful avenue and compared favorably with the Nevsky Prospekt in St. Petersburg. In Chicago, as part of the park system favored by real estate developers, Drexel Boulevard was laid out in imitation of the Avenue de l'Impératrice in Paris, 200 feet wide with a forty-foot building line on either side; down the center were set rows of trees. Others were the curving Summit Avenue in St. Paul, Minnesota, where F. Scott Fitzgerald was later to pass his boyhood in a New York-style brownstone house, and Prospect Avenue in Milwaukee. In St. Louis, Missouri, the residential avenue became a large private street with gates at each end to ensure privacy. Benton Place, the first of these, dates from 1867, and Vandeventer Place from 1870. The latter had a long list of restrictions—stone steps had to be scrubbed twice weekly and each window had to have three sets of curtains. Westmoreland Place, today the best kept up, followed in 1899.

The residential avenue was part of the fashion for the Second Empire. Like their Parisian counterparts the American rich built ample houses, where they could entertain, and laid out long avenues where they could parade up and down in their carriages. With the flight of the millionaires to the distant suburb, this pattern has completely changed, and to drive along Euclid avenue is to be rewarded by vistas of blight: gas stations and gaping holes where the mansions of the Age of Steam and Iron have been torn down and the ornate balconies and copper roofs sold off for scrap.

4. The Fashion for the Picturesque

In the Romantic Era Americans had discovered that there was another side to nature than the menacing wilderness. The pastoral image became an inspiration and even influenced the architecture of cities. With the spread of the railroad the image began to fade, and taste forsook the country to return to an urban home, much as landscape architecture, formerly reserved for country villas, came to be found in city parks under the magic of Olmsted.

"From the moment that railways were introduced, life took on extravagance," was the opinion of Henry Adams. For the newly rich whose fortunes derived from the railroad and everything it had made possible, it was far more diverting to be extravagant in the city, where there was an audience. Inevitably Paris, the Paris of the Second Empire, became the ideal and model for all. The French capital had dictated women's fashions in America since the end of the Napoleonic Wars, and from the 1840's Americans sought out French mirrors, clocks, window hangings, furniture and gewgaws. The R. S. Morse house (1859) in Portland, Maine, by Henry Austin, the New Haven architect, is furnished in the highest French style of the 1850's. So too the Harral house (1846 by Alexander Jackson Davis) in Bridgeport. Soon John Henry Belter, last of the great New York furniture makers, would turn out furniture and other objects in the Second Empire version of the Louis XV Style.

The coming to power of Napoleon III and his marriage to the beautiful Eugénie made Paris the mecca for all Americans. It was during the Second Empire that Americans settled there in such numbers that they formed a permanent colony. The music of Offenbach joined with the airs of Stephen Foster, and Americans at home indulged a passion for marching in highly colored uniforms imitating those of the French Zouave troops. The Northern infantryman even wore the kepi (military cap) of the Imperial troops. Congressmen, caught in the swirl of fashion, favored tearoses in their lapels in the manner of the French statesman and half brother of the emperor, the Duc de Morny. The elegant spiky Imperial competed with the full beard of an earlier generation.

In cities and towns a variety of architectural taste flourished—the Second Empire, several forms of the Gothic Revival, the Queen Anne and the Richardsonian Romanesque. There was no guiding "school" as in the days of Jefferson; that had been replaced by the search for variety on the part of the Romantics. Even more than in the previous generation, emphasis was on the unusual, the original or the piquant, rather than on the beautiful or the sublime. For that reason the menagerie of styles may properly be called Picturesque, a fashion culminating in the strange Megalithic work of Henry Hobson Richardson. The mansard, a steep roof invented in Paris to by-pass the height restrictions, can be found almost everywhere in the country, atop a Cape Cod house or crowning a mining-town hotel. New York is presumed to have had the first in 1850; it capped a house on Fifth Avenue by Detlef Lienau, an architect of German extraction but trained in Paris. Every city and town could boast of the mansard shortly. The Union League Club of Philadelphia, founded by an association of business and professional men to further the Union effort in the Civil War, has its home in a pressed brick and brownstone building (1865) with a noticeable mansard. A high French roof distinguishes the Western Penitentiary outside Pittsburgh. Another outstanding example is on the great Harmony Mill Number Three (1866) in Cohoes, New York. In this American vision of a Parisian palace, the Empress Eugénie herself might have safely walked in galleries where, as the poet Erasmus Darwin apostrophized:

> *With wiry teeth revolving cards release*
> *The tangled knots, and smooth the ravell'd fleece;*
> *Next moves the iron hand with fingers fine,*
> *Combs the wide card, and forms the eternal line;*
> *Slow, with soft lips, the whirling can acquires*
> *The tender skeins, and wraps in rising spires;*
> *With quicken'd pace successive rollers move,*
> *And these retain, and those extend the rove;*
> *Then fly the spoles, the rapid axles glow,*
> *And slowly circumvolves the labouring wheel below.*

The Tuileries Palace in Paris, home of the emperor of the French, was the great model. Here order was piled on order in an elaborate fashion ending in a high roof. So official a style, well within the classical tradition, was automatically taken over in American government buildings. The Department of State in Washington is housed in a tall structure (1871) by A. B. Mullet, the Capital's main sample of the

Paul Revere Mall in Boston. The White Fund financed the planning of this open space at the suggestion of Mayor James M. Curley. It was designed by the landscape architect and city planner Arthur A. Shurcliff, assisted by the architect Henry R. Shepley. The statue of Paul Revere is by Cyrus Dallin. The Old North Church (Episcopal), which had the first steeple in America, stands in the background. *Arthur Griffin. Reprinted by special permission from* Holiday, *copyright, 1947, by the Curtis Publishing Company.*

THE COLONIAL PATTERN

Reconstructed house (ca. 1676), once the home of Paul Revere, North Square, Boston. The house of the famous silversmith, engraver and patriot was restored in the 1920's by the architect Joseph E. Chandler. An echo of the Medieval Style in American architecture.

Arthur Griffin. Reprinted by special permission from Holiday, *copyright, 1947, by the Curtis Publishing Company.*

View of the Governor's Palace in reconstructed Williamsburg, seen through elaborate wrought-iron gates. It was probably the finest residence in the colonies. The main portion was begun in 1706 and finished in 1720. The Ballroom Wing, the work of Richard Taliaferro (ca. 1749-51), is shown to the left, beyond the formal garden of elaborate bedding and trimmed hedges.

Thomas L. Williams; courtesy of Colonial Williamsburg.

Courthouse (early 18th century) and square at King William, Virginia. The clerk's office and jail were built after 1885 in the spirit of the original. A typical Civil War statue can be seen in the center.

Virginia State Chamber of Commerce.

The New Haven Green, laid out in 1638, showing the fourth meeting house (Congregational), built in 1813-18, by the architect Asher Benjamin and occupying approximately the original site. A late example of the American Baroque Style. This green served as a prototype for later rectangular greens in the Ohio country and throughout the Midwest.

Dieter Hammerschlag.

View of the grass terraces in the gardens of Middleton Place on the Ashley River near Charleston, S. C. One of the few colonial gardens which have come down to us in the spirit of the original.
F. S. Lincoln.

Independence Hall, Philadelphia. The first civic center in a great city in the United States. The central portion was built from 1731 to 1753, the wings from 1736 to 1739. The steeple, constructed in 1828, is the work of the architect William Strickland. Originally the State House for the Province of Pennsylvania, it was here that the Second Continental Congress met and voted the Declaration of Independence in 1776.

National Park Service.

(*Right*) University of Virginia campus in Charlottesville (1817), Thomas Jefferson, architect. A one-time library, modeled on the Pantheon in Rome, forms the center of this design in the grand manner for an "academical village." The buildings at the south end of the Lawn, which now close the vista, were designed by the firm of McKim, Mead and White in 1898.

Ralph R. Thompson; courtesy of the University of Virginia.

State Capitol, Richmond, Virginia. The first monumental building in the United States (1785-98), by Thomas Jefferson. Its American Roman scale stands out in sharp contrast to the American Baroque of Independence Hall.

Virginia State Chamber of Commerce.

THE YOUNG REPUBLIC

Approach to Mount Vernon Place, Baltimore. The Washington Monument, designed by Robert Mills in 1815, an example of the American Roman manner, actually completed in 1829. The Peabody Institute (1861-78) is on the right with the Mount Vernon Place Methodist Church (1872) beyond. The equestrian statue is that of the Marquis de Lafayette by the sculptor Andrew O'Connor.

A. Aubrey Bodine. Reprinted by special permission from Holiday, copyright, 1947, by the Curtis Publishing Company.

Entrance to Fort Jay (1801), Governor's Island, New York City. A rare example of embellishment of military installations in the United States. It is still standing, although the Cap of Liberty no longer appears above the clustered trophies.

Courtesy of the New York Historical Society.

Merchants' Exchange (1831-34) by the architect William Strickland, showing the Greek Revival influence. Still standing on Third and Dock Streets in Philadelphia, it is being cleaned and restored as part of the Independence National Historical Park Project of the National Park Service.

H. H. Reed.

THE ROMANTIC ERA

"Pirates' Alley" in New Orleans, a city that reached its greatest importance in the Romantic Era.

Sawders from Charles Phelps Cushing.

"Sunnyside," home of Washington Irving in Tarrytown, New York. The author of "Rip Van Winkle" turned to a Romantic Revival style, part Gothic and part Dutch vernacular. Designed in 1836 by the painter George Harvey, it has lately been restored and opened to the public through the interest of John D. Rockefeller, Jr.

Wayne Andrews.

Interior of the Roman Catholic Cathedral of SS. Peter and Paul (1846-64) on Logan Circle, Philadelphia, by the architect Napoleon Le Brun. A late example of the American Roman Style, it contains murals by Constantino Brumidi, who also decorated the United States Capitol.

Standard Photo Service Co.; courtesy of the Diocesan Office of the Roman Catholic Church in Philadelphia.

Mural in the dome of the Capitol, Washington. "The Apotheosis of Washington" by Constantino Brumidi, begun in 1862 and completed three years later. This is a false ceiling below the cast-iron interior dome of the Capitol building. *Courtesy of the Office of the Architect of the Capitol, Washington, D. C.*

THE AGE OF STEAM AND IRON

Central Park (1858), New York City, by Frederick Law Olmsted and Calvert Vaux. America's pre-eminent contribution to city planning and the art of landscape design in the Age of Steam and Iron. *Gottscho-Schleisner.*

A monumental interior space in America: the main waiting room of Pennsylvania Station (1906), New York City, by McKim, Mead and White, which rivals in scale the Baths of Caracalla in Rome.

A. F. Sozio; courtesy of the Pennsylvania Railroad Company.

THE CITY BEAUTIFUL

America's first great private palace, the mansion of William K. Vanderbilt, which formerly stood on the corner of 52nd Street and Fifth Avenue in New York City. Designed by Richard Morris Hunt in 1879, it announced the American Renaissance Style.

Brown Brothers.

The World's Columbian Exposition of 1893, Chicago. Daniel H. Burnham, Richard Morris Hunt, Frederick Law Olmsted, Augustus Saint-Gaudens and other leading artists collaborated in this grand design which initiated the City Beautiful Movement. The giant statue of the Republic in the foreground was the work of Daniel Chester French; Hunt designed the domed Administration Building at the end of the vista.

Courtesy of the American Institute of Architects,
Richard Morris Hunt Collection.

View of the Capitol, the Mall and the Washington Monument from the roof of the Library of Congress. Major L'Enfant made the Mall the center of his famous plan for the federal city in 1791 and one hundred and ten years later Daniel H. Burnham, at the head of a committee of artists, carried his design to completion. The white low-domed structure just beyond the Capitol is the National Gallery of Art (1939), by the architect John Russell Pope and Eggers & Higgins, consultants.
Horydczak.

The Detroit Public Library (1923) in the Automobile City. One of the many splendid public libraries in America, it is the work of Cass Gilbert, the architect of New York's Woolworth Tower, and an example of the Age of Taste in the Midwest. *Carl Wienke; courtesy of* The Detroit News.

THE CITY OF TOWERS

In San Francisco a handsome dome, symbol of democracy, crowns the city hall (1915) by John Bakewell, Jr., and Arthur Brown, Jr. It stands at the focal point of America's most generously planned civic center. The building beyond, on the left, is the municipally owned opera house (1932) by Arthur Brown, Jr., and G. Albert Lansburgh. *Moulin Studios.*

The Clarence Buckingham Fountain rising against
the skyscrapers on Michigan Avenue in Chicago. The
largest fountain in the world (its closest competitor
being the Latona Fountain in the gardens of Versailles) was designed by Bennett, Parsons & Frost of
Chicago and Jacques Lambert of Paris in 1927. The
sculpture is by Marcel Loyau, also of Paris.

Chicago Park District.

The skyline that still astonishes the world; an airview of downtown Manhattan in New York City. The magnificent chaos of towers rises sharply above the busy waterfront, creating America's most spectacular contribution to the history of urban architecture.

Ewing Galloway.

The skyline of Miami at night. The importance of this American city dates from the Florida real-estate boom of the 1920's.

City of Miami News Bureau.

The San Antonio River Park in downtown San Antonio, Texas. Financed by the city and the Works Progress Administration, the park was created along the river banks in 1939.

Sawders from Charles Phelps Cushing.

Fireworks over the White House on the Fourth of July in Washington. The White House is in the foreground, the Washington Monument in the center and beyond can be seen the Jefferson Memorial.

Lawrence S. Williams. Reprinted by special permission from Holiday, *copyright, 1950, by the Curtis Publishing Company.*

Second Empire Style. The city halls of Boston, Detroit and Philadelphia are other conspicuous examples. These public buildings, particularly the Philadelphia City Hall (1871–81) by John McArthur, Jr., and Thomas U. Walter, still command attention and are not without a certain majesty. The main building at Vassar College, built in 1865 by James Renwick, Jr., needs only the French tricolor to take us in our imagination to Paris and the court of the empress.

Alexander Jackson Davis and Richard Upjohn continued to work in the Gothic manner in the 1850's, although of this period no outstanding examples of their work remain. Upjohn scattered small churches, mostly Episcopal, throughout New York State and Massachusetts, the best being St. Peter's in Albany. The Civil War reduced the practice of both, but their style was carried on by James Renwick, Jr. To him we owe St. Patrick's Cathedral (1858–87) in New York City. Another form of the Gothic appeared from England in the late fifties, inspired by the writings of John Ruskin, the great Victorian critic. The evangelical prose style of this latter-day prophet could not fail to touch an audience in America, and he won a public here equal to his English one. Memorial Hall (1874) by Ware and Van Brunt, erected by Harvard University to its Civil War dead, proclaimed his influence in New England, and traces of Ruskinian Gothic (as in the New Haven City Hall done in 1871 by Austin), mark a good many American communities.

Still another Gothic style was to appear, this time from France. The most powerful figure in nineteenth-century architecture, both in this country and Europe, a figure no less influential today because of his emphasis on construction in design, was Eugène Emmanuel Viollet-le-Duc. The restorer of half the medieval cathedrals and castles of France had turned from his archaeological labors to write architectural dictionaries, heavily illustrated, and so many other works between 1854 and 1878 that the world of art was inundated by the torrent. American architects like Richard Morris Hunt, Bruce Price, Frank Furness and the Hewitt brothers felt his power directly. In America his hand can be seen not so much in church architecture as in commercial and domestic work. Several banks still standing on Chestnut Street in Philadelphia bespeak the man, and in designing the Pennsylvania Academy of Fine Arts (1871–76) in the same city Furness and Hewitt were obeying the dictates of the French restorer.

Even the drawing room could not escape the energetic Frenchman, thanks to the wide popularity of *Hints on Household Taste in Furniture, Upholstery, and Other Details* by the English art critic, Charles L. Eastlake. A new taste in interior decoration and furniture came from Eastlake's *Hints*, lifted almost wholly from Viollet-le-Duc. "In the sphere of what is called industrial art, use and beauty are, in theory at least, closely associated for not only has the humblest article of manufacture, when honestly designed, a picturesque interest of its own, but no decorative feature can legitimately claim our admiration without revealing by its very nature the purpose of the object which it adorns," the book assures us, and "one of the chief merits of the Pointed [Gothic] Style is that the origin of every decorative feature may be traced to a constructive purpose." The Eastlake message is echoed today in the literature of the Functionalist school, although the designs that he invented bear no relation to the contemporary "International Style." The first English edition of Eastlake appeared in 1868, the first American in 1872, and by 1881 it had gone through six editions in this country alone. The Eastlake Style emphasized "honesty" rather than pleasure and the straight line instead of the curve; the voluptuous lines of the Second Empire were gone by the end of the Age of Steam and Iron.

Somewhat later, the tradition started by Eastlake and another Englishman, William Morris, was carried on by Elbert Hubbard, soap salesman extraordinary and pioneer advertising man, at East Aurora, New York. Hubbard, who established successful craft shops for printing, furniture making and leather working, publicized and supported his venture by lecture tours and his magazine, *The Philistine*. (His best-known literary effort was the famous *A Message to Garcia*, written in 1899.) His furniture, which includes features foreshadowing the "Mission Style," later popularized by the craftsman Gustav Stickley, followed the precepts of Viollet-le-Duc and Eastlake by revealing all its construction. Hubbard's link with today was his friendship with the then youthful Frank Lloyd Wright. Hubbard announced to Wright in the 1890's: "Modesty being egotism turned wrong side out, let me say here that I am an orator, a great orator! I have health, gesture, imagination, voice, vocabulary, taste, ideas—I acknowledge it myself. What I lack in shape I make up in nerve . . ." To which Wright replied: "Not only do I intend to be the greatest architect who has yet lived, but the greatest who will ever live. Yes, I intend to be the greatest architect of all time . . ."

It was common at one time to lump most of the nineteenth-century styles under the term Victorian. Now we generally recognize them as stemming from individual French or English influences. In much the same fashion we once termed a certain wooden architecture as "General Grant," because it appeared during his term of office as president. Actually this style derives largely from Richard Norman Shaw, another Englishman who had studied the dictionaries of Viollet-le-Duc. Gothic dormers, bays and overhanging eaves were part of his offering, as well as new shingle patterns that can be traced to the article on "Slate" in the *Dictionnaire raisonné de l'architecture française du XI° au XVI° siècle*. To these Shaw added freely treated classical detail, giving birth to the style called "Queen Anne" in England, although it bore no relation to the architecture of the gouty monarch's reign.

Much of the Picturesque wooden architecture exists still. It is to be found in early suburbs, which began to appear more frequently on the outskirts of our cities. Today these same cities are swallowing up what remains of them. One or two of these suburbs stand apart from the general run; an example is Lewellyn Park in New Jersey, designed in 1852 by Davis. Although nearly all of the buildings designed by him have gone, there are samples of the General Grand Style. Another Picturesque suburb is Riverside (1869), created by Olmsted and Vaux on the outskirts of Chicago. Shaw would have been much at home among its early wooden houses. Apart from the nascent suburbs of the time, the blossoming summer colonies offer handsome specimens of the Picturesque. With the improved rail service after the Civil War, more and more people began to desert the city for the mountains and the seashore; becoming impatient with the big wooden hotels, they built their own cottages by the sea. General Grant himself, when President, had his summer house at Long Branch, New Jersey, not far from New York City. Newport, too, before the coming of its seaside Renaissance palaces, had many wooden houses with comfortable piazzas in the new style. New York matrons with their families sought refuge here in the summer and attended the famous champagne picnics of Ward McAllister while their husbands worked away in the city.

Among the best summer houses built in the 1870's were those of a Boston architect, then coming into prominence, Henry Hobson Richardson. One of the first American architects trained in France, he came under the spell of Viollet-le-Duc, but unlike others he evolved his own very special style. Viollet-le-Duc had rediscovered the French Romanesque, the architecture of Europe between the Roman period and the Gothic, and this Richardson took and made American. His appearance on the architectural scene was like a bumblebee among moths, for he scattered all about him. From 1875 to 1890 he was to enjoy a most extraordinary vogue. His careful

Trinity Church in Boston, designed by
Henry Hobson Richardson in 1876.

use of materials, the solid, almost fortress-like quality of his
buildings, his fondness for asymmetry and the thoroughness
of his approach proclaimed the first of the Picturesque Seces-
sionists, a tradition lingering today in the work of Frank Lloyd
Wright. (Picturesque Secessionism, the term used by the late
Sir Charles Herbert Reilly, distinguished British architect and
critic, is an architectural movement that has seceded from the
classical tradition and turned to the Picturesque effect, with
heavy emphasis on the mechanics of construction as an esthetic
goal. The movement today, usually called "Modern" or
"Organic," also places a premium on originality as a goal,
originality taking the place of beauty, the traditional aim of the
architect.) Shepley, Rutan and Coolidge (now called Shepley,
Bulfinch, Richardson and Abbott) in Boston, the Potter
Brothers in New York, John Wellborn Root and Louis Sullivan in Chicago and Leroy S. Buffington in Minneapolis were
Richardson's most eager immediate followers. The newer
homes on the residential avenues of the Middle West were
stamped by his style, but especially the church architecture of
the period shows his influence. Trinity Church (1876) in
Boston, where he commanded the services of John La Farge,
Augustus Saint-Gaudens and Stanford White, was his proud-

est monument, and it set the standard. A whole group of buildings, public and private, by this Bostonian architect may be seen in North Easton, Massachusetts, a Picturesque company town built by Oakes and Oliver Ames, leading shovel manufacturers and railroad speculators. Impressive as Richardson's work proved to be amid the Battle of Styles, he was shortly forgotten when Picturesque Secessionism was swept aside and overwhelmed by the American Renaissance.

The Battle of the Picturesque Styles inevitably exhausted the public with its variety and its efforts at originality. In the end it left them alienated. When once the classical tradition of the American Roman was re-established, when the American Renaissance had demonstrated its worth, Americans then knew where to turn. In the early 1880's a Boston architectural magazine polled its subscribers to discover their favorite building. Richardson's Trinity Church came first with a big majority. Fifteen years later another publication took a similar poll. This time the readers' choice fell on the national Capitol. The Picturesque Age was gradually being forgotten.

PART V

The City as a Way of Life: The Expanding City I

1880-1910

A GREAT DEPRESSION from 1873 to 1879 marked the end of the Age of Steam and Iron. When the nation emerged from its economic slough, transportation, industrialization and corporate organization leaped ahead. The expansion placed more and more reliance on individual enterprise as Americans embraced the philosophy of Herbert Spencer. Individual initiative, industry and self-discipline had been the message of Emerson in the 1840's; Spencer placed the message in the context of scientific progress. In the 1860's the English philosopher applied Darwin's biological concept of the survival of the fittest to Man and created a science of society. "Light came as in a flood and all was clear," exclaimed Andrew Carnegie on first reading Spencer's work. Americans in all walks of life—clergymen, clerks, professors, laborers, lawyers, statesmen and businessmen—wholeheartedly accepted the notion that free and even violent competition among individuals was essential to the natural rise of the fittest who were destined to lead America. Only a few found any contradiction in the fact that these business leaders, in the name of economic freedom, were organizing the national economy into giant combines, monopolies and trusts. "This movement was the origin of the whole system of modern economic administration," John D. Rockefeller remarked once, looking back on his own career. "It has revolutionized the way of doing business all over the world. The time was ripe for it. It had to come, though all we saw at the moment was the need to save ourselves from wasteful conditions . . . The day of combination is here to stay. Individualism has gone, never to return." Americans embraced the ideal of "bigness" as they embraced the ideals of free competition and the survival of the fittest—in the corporation, in wealth, in the labor force, in social problems and in their cities. Little wonder that they created hideous industrial towns and giant jungle cities, instruments at once of pride and

118

despair. Migration to America was encouraged on a scale never seen before: over five million immigrants arrived in the decade after 1880. In 1880 the census takers discovered that New York was the first city to amass a population of over a million people. Chicago achieved the same ambition by 1890. From this time on, the city had to be counted as the dominating factor in American life.

1. *The Technological Wave*

The new city would never have been possible without the aid of new inventions, new machinery, new techniques and new forms of production and distribution. Certainly the most blessed of these was electric light. Edison invented his lamp in 1879 and two years later, with the financial backing of J. P. Morgan, he built the world's first power station on Pearl Street in downtown New York. By 1900 electricity was commonplace; the "Great White Way," or Broadway as we know it, exerted its magic on the public a few years later. For color at night, American cities had to wait until 1923, when the neon tube was perfected by the French inventor Georges Claude and installed over a movie marquee on Times Square.

The telephone was no longer a toy. New Haven had the first commercial switchboard in 1878, and telephone wires soon joined the earlier telegraph wires above the city street in what was possibly the worst form of urban decoration ever devised. The wires and poles, which still curse large areas of our cities, disappeared from urban centers in the early 1890's, not out of a desire to make the city more beautiful, but to remedy a nuisance: the wires had snapped and the poles had collapsed under the weight of winter snow and ice, as any photograph of the famous blizzard of '88 will testify.

The application of electricity to transportation was very much part of the age. The horsecar remained the main form of cheap transportation until the 1890's, although the cable-car, first used in San Francisco in 1873, nudged it off the main lines. The notorious Charles T. Yerkes, Theodore Dreiser's model for the hero of *The Financer, The Titan* and *The Stoic,* introduced the system to Chicago in 1883. This underground moving cable and its cable house were only an interlude before electric traction. Richmond, Virginia, saw the first practical trolley bounce along its streets in 1888. Shortly afterwards the trolley was taken up by enterprising businessmen, among them William C. Whitney, Joseph Widener, Harry Elkins, Thomas Fortune Ryan and other associates, more familiarly known as the "Traction Ring," who became interested in consolidating the old horsecar and cablecar lines. In the process of converting them to electricity, these financiers built paper corporations of questionable necessity and disposed of the shares to the public at enormous profit.

Rapid transit progressed in equally spectacular fashion. That wonder of the urban scene, the elevated railroad, was first put to use in New York in 1869, but it took ten years for New Yorkers to become accustomed to the noise and smoke of the small steam locomotives, and then the "El," on the initiative of Cyrus W. Field, promoter of the Atlantic cable, spread in all directions on Manhattan. Most of the lines on Manhattan Island were put up between 1878 and 1881, in part extending across still open fields to attract investment. In the next decade they invaded Brooklyn and part of the Bronx. In 1892 Chicago made acquaintance with the El, and five years later it had twisted around the downtown section in such a fashion as to form "The Loop," the name given to the financial, hotel and shopping district. Boston and Philadelphia obtained their systems too. Happily, the monster was confined to the larger cities, which are ridding themselves of the nuisance only today.

Often the older methods of transportation were too well entrenched to be dislodged quickly; often, too, the Traction Ring played with securities instead of trying to improve the systems. The El was not electrified until the turn of the century and horsecars continued to operate in New York in the 1900's. "But the horsecars run even under the elevated tracks," complained the visiting Bostonian, William Dean Howells, in 1896. "At some corner two cars encounter on the parallel tracks below, while two trains roar and shriek and hiss on the rails overhead, and a turmoil of rattling express-wagons, heavy drays and trucks, carts, hacks, carriages, and huge vans rolls itself between and beneath the prime agents of the uproar." Cobblestone thoroughfares, still to be found in many cities, recall these nightmare traffic scenes. Smooth asphalt streets, in use in Paris as early as 1854, were not seen in any quantity until the eighties and the nineties, when bicycle enthusiasts forced the improvement.

The turn of the century found a solution of rapid transit in the subway. London (1886) and Budapest (1893) had their "undergrounds" before a trolley-car line was placed under Boston streets and the first section opened to public travel in 1897. A branch under the harbor by way of a tunnel was opened not long afterwards. August Belmont II, banker, and John B. McDonald, engineer, built the first line in New York in 1904 and a few years later they had tunneled through to

Brooklyn and had gone over a bridge into the Bronx. Belmont was to lose his fortune in a struggle with the Traction Ring, but by then the lines were transforming the city, spreading it out and making it the modern metropolis that it is today.

The many new forms of communication and transportation encouraged a phenomenal rise in real estate values. Speculation boiled over, underlining the importance Henry George had given to land value by the theory of the single tax in his *Progress and Poverty* (1879). In Manhattan, where the upper part of the island had remained in the same hands since the Revolution, parcels of old farms were sold off at auction. There had been an early sale lasting from 1869 to 1871, that of the Dyckman homestead, but the city, caught in the depression of 1873, did not have another large sale until 1880. One after the other estates came on the market: the Carman sale in 1880, the Jumel sale (the mansion remains) in 1882, the Jones sale in 1889, and the Morgenthau sale in 1891. This last was very successful. Purchasing a big parcel at 181st Street from Levi P. Morton, then vice-president of the United States, Henry Morgenthau, Sr., and his associates proceeded to make a profit of $480,000 in a month or so on an initial investment of $300,000. The west side of Manhattan, bare fields in the 1870's, became filled with homes, churches, tenements and apartment houses. The still unfinished Cathedral of St. John the Divine was begun in 1892 on Morningside Heights, and Columbia University moved to its present site nearby in 1897. After 1905 Morgenthau, who was to become an elder statesman in Wilson's administration as well as one of New York's great patrons of music, organized the "subway boom" in the Bronx. On the land opened up by the new transit lines, he assembled 2500 lots which he disposed of for $9,000,000, an extraordinary real estate operation even for our own time.

Chicago was not to be outdone by New York in real estate speculation, which was part and parcel of the Midwestern tradition. From 1886 to 1894 Chicago enjoyed a land boom, thanks in part to the arrival of operators from deflated booms in Kansas City, Minneapolis and Omaha. The combination of a rapidly increasing population—great numbers of Italians, Poles and Russian Jews arrived after 1880—and improved transportation touched off the explosion, and the cry was "Everyone is a bull in real estate." The comment of the Chicago novelist Henry B. Fuller was appropriate:

The city was emphatically still in the "real estate" stage. Anybody arriving without profession or training straightway began to sell lots. Nothing lay more openly abundant

than land; the town had but to propagate itself automatically over the wide prairies. The wild flowers waved
only to welcome the surveyor's gang, and new home-
seekers—in the jargon of the trade—were ever hurrying
to rasp themselves upon the ragged edges of the outskirts.

2. *The Apartment House and the Tall Office Building*

In the old parts of the city the real estate developer now
discovered a new instrument for improvement, the apartment
house. It is strange that the American who prides himself on
meeting problems empirically, and often succeeds in so doing, should have failed in this instance to develop a new form
of dwelling for the well-to-do until such a late date. The tenement for the poor, after all, had evolved thirty years before.
In 1880 the one-family dwelling remained standard for the
middle class. "You know that no American who is at all comfortable in life will share his dwelling with another," Cooper
had said when the city was still young. The American real
estate operator continued to satisfy this vanity long after the
illusion of it was clear; the result, as we have seen, was the
omnipresent boardinghouse.

That Parisians had been accustomed to apartment-house living for a hundred years and more made little difference to the
wealthy New Yorker or Bostonian. The modern apartment
house is an innovation of the French eighteenth century; descriptions and illustrations of Paris examples can be found in
the books of J. F. Blondel. Only the influence of Paris in the
1850's found architects in America like Calvert Vaux talking
of "buildings, several stories high . . . with all the rooms required for a family grouped together on one-level . . . and
these approached through one hall-door from the public staircase." New Orleans often lays claim to the first apartment
houses in America, the Pontalba Buildings on Jackson Square,
but they are actually a sophisticated form of the row house,
with shops on the ground floor. Mention is made of an early
apartment building in Boston designed by Arthur Delavan
Gilman of Back Bay fame, an uncertain attribution. By the
1860's there was plenty of discussion of "French flats," as
they were first called. To Richard Morris Hunt, brother of
the painter William Morris Hunt, goes the honor of designing
in 1869 the first definitive apartment building, the Stuyvesant,
still standing at number 142 East 18th Street in New York.

It was no easy matter for the French-trained Hunt, who also
built the first studio building in the country (51 West 10th
Street), to persuade respectable New Yorkers to take advan-

The Dakota Apartment House
by Henry Janeway Hardenbergh, 1879.

tage of the apartment house. They were as provincial as the rest of the country at the time and were convinced that the "French flat" would lead to a breakdown of the American family. The name itself suggested a dangerous and racy way of life. The well-traveled, who saw a threat of the highhanded Paris concierge being introduced to New York, hesitated at the idea. The much abused custodian of the Paris apartment houses, who takes care of messages, mail and deliveries and answers the night bell, was considered a possible foreign menace. The "moral" threat in sharing a building with so many other people and the promiscuity encouraged by several families living on the same floor raised further objections from many New Yorkers. Although Hunt provided a room near the entrance for a concierge, the Stuyvesant Apartments proved extremely popular. By 1880 the new form of dwelling was being built by the hundreds.

The first apartment houses were relatively simple affairs, often converted brownstones. Some of them, however, took ideas from the hotel, such as the common kitchen and common laundry, but this experimentation did not last long. One of the first fireproof apartment houses in New York still stands at 21 East 21st Street on a narrow twenty-five-foot lot, designed by Bruce Price, the architect who laid out the sporting suburb of Tuxedo Park. The first apartment house on a lavish scale was the Dakota, which overlooks the western rim of Central Park at the corner of 72nd Street. Here in 1879 Edward Clark, president of the Singer Sewing Machine Company and founder of one of our great financial dynasties (the Clark family underwrites the well-known Farmers' Museum in Cooperstown, New York, and owns a large collection of contemporary art), purchased a number of lots and retained Henry J. Hardenbergh, architect of the Plaza Hotel, to design one of the city's handsomest apartment buildings. It is a large square block of dark yellow brick and dark stone, heavily ornamented and boasting such innovations for the time as the servants' entrance, special service stairways and service elevators.

The improvement in the hydraulic elevator made apartments more convenient and more popular. "We were talking about your apartment, Mrs. Roberts. It's charming," remarks a guest in the Howells play, *The Elevator*. "It *is* nice," her hostess replies. "It's the ideal way of living. All on one floor. No stairs. Nothing." There are exclamations at the notion of the elevator; the farce revolves about the accident of the contraption being stuck between two floors. "It's the only thing that makes life worth living in a flat," the hostess patters on. "All these apartment hotels have them." In Boston alone there were over two thousand elevators in a variety of buildings by the year 1884, when the play was written, and many more in New York. The apartment house had been accepted, and even Chicago had a "flat fever" in its construction boom.

Paralleling the arrival of the apartment house was the coming of the tall office building. One of the innovations of the 1860's had been the large office block built to meet the changes in our business economy, but the "cloud scrapers," designed to house even larger business organizations, were to bring about a revolution in the skyline; temples to commerce were shortly to eclipse the temples of God. In 1873 several buildings were built in New York which could properly be termed the first skyscrapers. One of them, the tower of the New York Tribune building by Hunt, still looks down on the City Hall from the old "Newspaper Row." The depression killed off any incentive to build others, but in the 1880's they began to rise again.

The early efforts faced a limitation in their method of construction which was still entirely of masonry. To support the new heights, walls had to be given extraordinary thickness. In Chicago the Monadnock Building (by Burnham and Root in 1891), one of the last of the tall buildings built solely of masonry, carries sixteen stories on walls fifteen feet thick at their base. Obviously another method had to be found to fashion the skyscraper. William Le Baron Jenney, the Chicago architect and graduate with high honors of the Ecole Centrale des Arts et Manufactures in Paris, developed a skeleton construction of iron and steel in 1884 which carried the building and left the walls as "curtains." (The Minneapolis architect Leroy S. Buffington later laid claim to the invention of the steel frame, insisting that he obtained the idea from an essay by Viollet-le-Duc.) New York did not obtain its first steel construction until five years later, and the race was on between the two cities for the biggest building, as real estate men and corporation executives put higher and higher structures on small lots. The Tacoma Building by Holabird and Roche in 1888, with its emphasis on glass in its façade, and the Auditorium Building of a year later, in which Adler and Sullivan favored Megalithic originality, were examples of the new type in Chicago. New York clung to the more conventional forms in the Saint Paul Building (1899), by George B. Post, with its crouching stone giants, and the Metropolitan Life home office (1893) by Napoleon Le Brun and Sons, inspired by the French Renaissance. (This last is now being stripped of its old walls, to be replaced with the contemporary cliché of flat limestone and glass.)

As Fuller's novel *The Cliff-Dwellers* explains, the new buildings were cities unto themselves. A tenant could eat, drink, have a haircut, obtain legal advice or consult a real estate broker without leaving the building. It was not unusual for the head office of a corporation to be housed in one skyscraper, as in the instance of the Metropolitan Life. Life insurance companies, which were then growing rapidly, were the leaders in this practice of assembling their large clerical forces into one building. The handsome New York Life building (1890) in Kansas City by McKim, Mead and White and the equally handsome Prudential Building (1894) in Buffalo by Louis Sullivan were typical. With these as a beginning America was later to make its most spectacular contribution to world architecture and to the urban scene in the age of the City of Towers.

3. *Railroad Towns and Industrial Suburbs*

Beyond the range of the city and its teeming multitudes, urbanization proceeded apace. The railroads, which had already crisscrossed the American landscape, continued to shape the country as forcibly as in the previous generation. In addition to joining existing cities and towns, the railroad corporations now promoted new communities and laid out new towns. The picture is not a pretty one, but the towns created are part of the American tradition and are so numerous as to deserve more attention than they usually receive.

Some railroad corporations were extremely highhanded with the power delegated them by the people. Frank Norris, in his famous novel *The Octopus,* described the hold of the railroad over the California wheat farmers in the San Joaquin Valley. Just as revealing on the blackmailing tactics of the Central Pacific was a member of the California Constitutional Convention of 1879. He explained in a verbatim transcript:

> They start out their railway track and survey their line near a thriving village. They go to the most prominent citizens of that village and say, "If you will give us so many thousand dollars we will run through here; if you do not we will run by," and in every instance where the subsidy was not granted, that course was taken. Here was the town of Paradise in Stanislaus County; because they did not get what they wanted, they established another town four miles from there. In every instance where they were refused a subsidy, in money, unless their terms were acceded to, they have established a depot near the place and always have frozen them out.

Many were the Paradises that were passed by and left to bleach like the bones of dead cattle on the prairie or in the valleys of the West.

Not all railroad men were as ruthless as the Big Four of California—Huntington, Hopkins, Crocker and Stanford— the owners of the Central Pacific. The Chicago, Burlington and Quincy, a latecomer that crossed the plains west from Chicago, showed instead a mixture of generosity and common sense. A railroad was of little value in a land without people, and the Burlington, not having the through traffic of the competing Union Pacific, had to create its traffic by encouraging settlement. Given 2,720,000 acres of public land by the government in Iowa and Nebraska, it formed a town-development project. A real estate corporation made up of company officers would buy land wherever stations were planned, in order to keep off speculators. Once the station stop was announced, they plotted a town, financed a warehouse and a dwelling for their agent, often before the rails reached the future settlement; they would then offer two lots and a cash subsidy to the first congregation for building a church. They were often equally generous to other congregations, recognizing the ancient role of religion in cementing communities. The promoters made a modest profit and, to be sure, gave the towns uninteresting plans, only relieved by an occasional green railroad plaza, but they assured orderly development and they spared the settlers high land costs. West of Lincoln, Nebraska, it was their whim to create the so-called alphabetical stations: Crete, Dorchester, Exeter, Fairmount, Grafton, and so on. A local newspaper, not always in favor of the Burlington, grudgingly admitted that the land company had been exploiting its property "not for the purpose of getting speculative figures for lots, but to induce settlement." The true heroes of this new pioneering remained the firstcomers, who spent the early years in box cars on sidings while their houses, stores, offices and churches were under construction.

A wave of milltown building also followed the second spurt in rail construction. In the West the railroads built the rural trading centers; in the Middle West and East they were responsible, in many instances indirectly, for new factory towns. A spectacular development took place in the 1880's and 1890's when, from West Virginia, one railroad raced the other to the harbors on the Eastern seaboard or north to the Ohio and the Great Lakes in an attempt to gain control of the bituminous coal-carrying trade. The Chesapeake and Ohio came out of a reorganization in 1878, fresh and ready for competition. The Norfolk and Western, a combination of smaller lines, was organized in 1881 and reached the rich deposits of the Pocahontas coal fields of West Virginia in 1883. Between 1881 and 1910 the Baltimore and Ohio built nine branch lines into the coal fields. The work of construction engineers, new towns created as a result of this enterprise were conspicuous for their uniform lack of distinction. This was true also of the iron and coal towns around Birmingham, Alabama, where real estate speculators enticed unwary investors by building blast furnaces and steel mills, not with the object of making iron and steel, but only to sell town lots!

Outside the older cities, new towns, which may more properly be called industrial suburbs, developed along the many belt lines and branch lines built at this time. This was the era of bigness in the size of manufacturing plants, just as it was in the size of the corporations that owned them. Formerly the manufacturing processes of most industries had been scattered in numerous small plants, often within a city; now they were consolidated and built on the urban periphery. The demand for steel, chemicals and other products was a further incentive to large-scale production. Typical of the move from the central city was the concentration of steel production by Andrew Carnegie at his Bessemer plant in Homestead, built in 1881, seven miles up the Monongahela from Pittsburgh. Carnegie, one of the pioneers in bringing the process of production under one management, from the extraction of raw materials to the finished goods, concentrated on fewer and larger mills. He and his imitators developed the towns of Duquesne, McKeesport, Aliquippa, and Ambridge near Pittsburgh, Granite City, Alton and East St. Louis near St. Louis, Garfield, Lodi and Kearny near New York and the "Cities of the Calumet" near Chicago.

The pattern is a familiar one. Along the railroad siding stood the giant mill and the space for piles of raw material while beyond the mill gate stretched the checkerboard of small frame or brick houses of the employees, many of them company owned. Scattered among these were churches, schools, an occasional library, one street reserved for commerce and one for saloons. Mills that consumed large quantities of water were situated next to a stream or a river, which rapidly became an industrial sewer. In Homestead, as in the others, the great mill stood next to the river and the tracks, while on its other side the gridiron marched up and down the nearby hills. Two-story frame houses on twenty- or twenty-five-foot lots faced the street, and behind them stood smaller houses. Nothing relieved the drabness of the town, not even the trees. In order to know the full horror of Homestead, it had to be seen in winter. Only as one moved away from the mill did one come on larger houses, healthy trees, thanks to the fresher air, a park or two and the ever present library, which Carnegie had endowed. In Homestead the library offered more than books; it had baths, bowling alleys and recreation halls. These amenities were of little use to men coming off a twelvehour shift, too exhausted for anything except food, drink and sleep. A commercial street and the inevitable saloons offered less pretentious relaxation. The electric trolley provided cheap transportation to Pittsburgh and to a picnic ground or "trolley park" out in the country at the end of the line. This was the scene in the 1890's. The town has changed much since then. In our time the steelworker is no longer tied close to the mills; he has his automobile and his home in a nearby development. Above all he has the bargaining power of his trade union, and time and money, none of which he had forty years ago.

Accompanying the expansion of the steel towns was a kind of industrial village, the "coal patch." Visiting the coal mining region of western Pennsylvania and West Virginia, the traveler is greeted by a desolate countryside and by small groups of bleak gray wooden frame houses zigzagging up and down the hilly countryside or nestling grimly in a hollow. Fifty to a hundred houses, all alike and placed apart from each other, with outdoor toilets, all company built and once company owned, stand along a dusty treeless street where the sidewalks are of coke ashes or slate from the mines. Until 1933 these ugly communities of bituminous-coal miners were ruled by the famous "coal and iron police" of the great steel and coal corporations, and no one from the outside world was allowed in, except the doctor and the undertaker. All has changed since; the miners have achieved a measure of security, while the beehive oven, once the main source of coke,

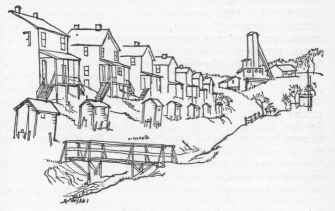

A "coal-patch" village in western Pennsylvania.

has been replaced by the cleaner and far more efficient by-product coke oven; even the scarred landscape is beginning to take on a covering of green.

Manufacturing now began to initiate the building of industrial suburbs. Granite City, outside St. Louis, was founded in 1893 by the Niedringhaus brothers, granite-ware manufacturers, and Gary, Indiana, in 1905, was created by the United States Steel Corporation. Real estate developers were no less enterprising. Barberton, an industrial suburb on the outskirts of Akron, Ohio, is an example. It sprang from an industrial real estate project of Columbus Ohio Barber, the "Match King" who founded the Diamond Match Company. To lay out the town that took his name, he retained M. J. Alexander, an engineer who had been responsible for many of the new towns built along the right of way of the Norfolk and Western. Barber and Alexander, not too successful at first, finally persuaded the Pittsburgh Plate Glass Company to build a plant there in 1898, and Barberton is today a prosperous adjunct of Akron.

An interesting experiment of the age was the model company town, a rarity by comparison with the milltown and the industrial suburb. Here we find attempts at planning, design and distinctive architecture, although not equal to that of the First Industrial Age. It was not from the earlier American tradition of model town-building in Lowell and Dalton, Massachusetts, or in South Manchester, Connecticut, that George M. Pullman drew his inspiration for the town he named for

A view of Pullman, Illinois.

himself, Pullman, Illinois. The founder of the most spectacular company town in the country looked to the industrial cities of the Ruhr, and particularly to the Krupp Works of Essen. In 1884 he purchased a block of land on the shores of Lake Calumet, at present a part of Chicago's far South Side, and commissioned Solon S. Beman to design a model town of brick and stone, noteworthy for its porticoed square, its town hall, its landscaped parks, its library and its solid houses. For the first time in the country's history, a whole town had been designed by an architect. Although the dark red brick is not the current taste and the style definitely Viollet-le-Duc Gothic, it is nonetheless unusual for its uniformity and the general order. But Pullman, for all its architectural ingenuity, was no paradise; as a result of his low wage and high rent policies the manufacturer of the railway "palace car" in 1894 set off one of the bitterest strikes of the time, which spread to Chicago and the railroads. It was the fate of more than one company town to be the scene of bloody labor battles, notably that of the Colorado Fuel and Iron Company at Ludlow from 1912 to 1914.

The Pullman strike proved a great deterrent to model-town building in the region of the big cities. The Niedringhauses left out all amenities at Granite City except a neglected park, and the builders of Gary confined their efforts to platting and easy home-financing. This was to be regretted. A less intransigeant attitude on the part of the entrepreneur, a proper system of home-financing and an opportunity for other industries to enter Pullman would have increased the variety and number of jobs; such care might have ended in success. City planning and unified architectural design were lost to these new communities by the obduracy of George M. Pullman, who died so fearful of human nature that he asked to be buried twenty feet underground in a coffin encased in steel and asphalt.

4. *The Dormitory Suburb*

In the East and Middle West most industrialists thereafter neglected the chance to demonstrate that the mechanical monsters of their creation could be made an integral part of the community. Instead they began to divorce the factory from the ideal of comfortable living. Although they still kept their place of business in the city, a few people were getting as far away from the industrialized city as they could. Jumping the outer ring of smoky factories, the industrial or banking rich who favored the country, with its opportunities for the newly fashionable sports and pastimes like golf, tennis and riding to hounds, created prototypes of the modern dormitory suburb.

The sporadic attempts at suburban living in the previous generation had not been altogether successful because of inadequate transportation facilities. The dormitory suburb demanded good rail service. This did not come until the 1880's, by which time even sedate, respectable Brookline, outside Boston, was being termed a "bedroom." One after the other, old market towns and summer resorts near growing cities became suburbs, or new elysiums like Tuxedo Park outside of New York were created. The story of Old Greenwich, Connecticut, today three quarters of an hour from New York, is typical. Shipping, shipbuilding and potato growing sustained the town in 1800; the summer colonists came in the 1830's. Twenty years later, after the railroad to New York was double-tracked, a dozen men took the hour-and-a-half ride daily to town. On their return these pioneer commuters would jump the train as it slowed down to a stop before crossing the drawbridge of Indian Harbor. Finally in the 1880's their growing band, impatient with acrobatics, agreed with the railroad to build a station, maintain it and retain a station agent. Today Greenwich is synonymous with the word "suburb." Chestnut Hill in Philadelphia, based on a branch line of the Pennsylvania Railroad, came in 1884, and Lake Forest, outside Chicago, was transformed at about the same time into a year-round community with fast rail service for businessmen.

One distinction of these select arcadias, the binding element of the society, was the country club. There had been clubs downtown for social and business reasons, nearly all reserved for the men; there were clubs and associations for riding and shooting, again reserved for men. The country club with its elaborate clubhouse and grounds for numerous sports was open to members' families, where people of both sexes and all ages had some form of amusement. "The restaurant and ladies' parlor shall always be open to the ladies and children of any member's family and to other ladies and children when accompanied by a member . . ." announced a bylaw of The Country Club, founded in Brookline in 1882; it is presumed to have been the first example of this American phenomenon. Originally formed for drives and race meetings reserved for well-to-do Bostonians and residents of Brookline, it soon branched out to sponsor all kinds of sports, including curling.

The fashion spread rapidly, until there was the Green Spring Valley Country Club for Green Spring Valley outside of Baltimore, the Piping Rock on the North Shore of Long Island, the Burlingame Country Club for Burlingame outside of San Francisco, names familiar to the devotees of the Society Page from coast to coast. Tuxedo Park, still one of the most elaborate of the suburban havens—the architect Bruce Price spent some $2,000,000 for Pierre Lorillard III, tobacco millionaire, in creating it—has a country club in which membership is obligatory for admission to the community. The new amenity gave its name to a whole suburban development, the Country Club District of Kansas City. The country club, to Henry James viewing his native land in 1905, stood for "the apotheosis of the Family" in America.

5. *The Tenement and the Urban Reform Movement*

Only the few who could afford such luxury were forsaking the city for the suburb. The less fortunate could not live beyond the end of the trolley line. Wretched slums continued as new waves of immigration flowed into the country. New York was the leader in tenement house "reform"—it could hardly be termed progress. A prize-winning design in a plumbing magazine for 1879 served as the prototype for the "Dumbbell" tenement, also known as the "Old Law" tenement because its plan was made standard by law in that year. With the lot coverage limited to 65 per cent and two out of three rooms of each apartment looking out on narrow airshafts, it was little improvement on the former "Railroad" tenement. Richard Morris Hunt, in his critique of the architectural exhibit of the Centennial Exposition of 1876, complained that the "important problem, viz, the amelioration of dwellings for the laboring and industrial classes, has been almost entirely ignored . . ." but his appeal for better housing passed unnoticed. A rare exception was the work of Alfred Treadway White and the Improved Dwellings Association, through whose incentive decent housing was built in Brooklyn and in Manhattan between 1878 and 1880. (The Brooklyn example is to be found at the corner of Hicks and Baltic Streets and the Manhattan at First Avenue and 72nd Street.) Only with the "New Law" of 1901, which encouraged the use of wider lots, was a remedy found, but by then the Dumbbells had spread over Manhattan Island like a scab.

Better conditions were not obtained without a long and tiring struggle. The urban slums had for some time received the attentions of the churches and charitable organizations; many had missions to bring help and consolation to the poor and the miserable. On the whole they were tiny oases in the middle of great squalor; neither legislation nor good works could do more in the face of the thousands crowding into the city, the criminal working conditions and the negligence of the business community that lasted to the turn of the century. A more effective form of help appeared in the late 1870's, when many Americans began to hear of the work of Octavia Hill and Canon Samuel A. Barnett in London's notorious Whitechapel. Their most famous American disciple was Jane Addams, who in 1889 created Hull House, bringing hope to Chicago's teeming South Side. The help that Miss Addams and her co-workers offered went far beyond medical assistance or counsel; in the first building erected for Hull House she included an art gallery and an art school with night classes. This was the first of its kind to be established in a workingman's community in America, a recognition of the hunger of all men for beauty. The role of the settlement house in music and especially in the dramatic arts has long been important in America; more than one world-famous actor first discovered his vocation in the humble theatre of the settlement building.

Another significant development of the 1880's was the coming of the "social church," which began to take on larger responsibilities by meeting some of the demands of parishioners for recreation, education and general welfare. Dr. William S. Rainsford, of the Episcopal St. George's Church on Stuyvesant Square in New York, was among the first to broaden the activities of the parish. This work resulted in a change in church design; instead of restricting the buildings to the church edifice and a simple parish house, schools, clinics, and a recreation building were often appended. All denominations began to assert once again a position in the community which they had lost with the coming of the Industrial Revolution, and incidentally began to shape a church building pattern that is especially American.

Reform was very much in the air in the 1880's, as Americans began to wonder what form of life their sprawling swarming cities were breeding. The self-satisfaction of the earlier generation was giving way to the feeling that something out of the ordinary had to be done, especially in the area of political reform. The comments of foreign visitors were no longer dismissed in provincial anger. In this atmosphere of self-questioning appeared the famous work of Viscount Bryce, *The American Commonwealth.* The inquisitive British historian praised and damned so engagingly and so searchingly that many Americans began to look at themselves for the first time. If, in his scales, our Constitution stood high, it was balanced by his outright condemnation of our municipalities. "There is no denying that the government of cities is the one conspicuous failure of the United States," was his comment in 1888. Americans were aware of the wretchedness of their local governments, but no one of such authority had hitherto sentenced them quite as sharply.

There had been "cleanup" administrations from 1800 on, but every one of them had been short-lived. With the city growing in what appeared to be hopeless disorder, the boss and his political machine were accepted as part of the pattern. Although identified too often as a post-Civil-War phenomenon, the system had existed for a long time, but after 1865 the cities had grown more rapidly than ever and with their growth, the scale of corruption. The most scandalous of all cities was the biggest; in Boss Tweed New York could boast that it outpaced all others with corruption as well as with population. But no city escaped the menace. A reform government would be voted into office by an outraged citizenry, only to face defeat after two discouraging years of power. The fault lay too deep for simple political "cleaning up"; as a people we had no idea, until the 1880's, of the nature of a city and what a city stood for. As late as the 1900's, no administrative distinction was made between government and business. "Ever heard that business is business?" Tammany Boss Richard Croker announced to Lincoln Steffens. "Well, so is politics business, and reporting—journalism, doctoring —all professions, arts, sports—everything is business." And especially was this true of the administration of cities— those in office were there only to make money. The nominal political power that existed in the city was vested in a bicameral council; a strong executive was unheard of. Some one individual had to run the city under such conditions, and the political boss filled the vacuum. Brooklyn, then a city in its own right, obtained in 1882 the first "strong mayor" of the country in the person of Seth Low, later mayor of New York and president of Columbia University.

The pace for administrative reform, and it was a very gentle one, was set by the federal government with the Pendleton Civil Service Act in 1883 signed by President Chester A. Arthur. Modern methods of budget-keeping and financial control did not exist prior to 1900; even the best of mayors was hampered with wretchedly outdated methods. One sign of change was the creation of the National Municipal League in 1894 for the express purpose of improving city departments and clarification of the city government's power. Such humble responsibilities as garbage collecting, sewage and water supply had to be understood and studied before they were properly organized. The triumph of Andrew Haswell Green in bringing about the consolidation of Greater New York in 1898 is one of the landmarks in American urban history. The first municipal program of the National Municipal League, announced a year later, called for more home rule, a strong mayor and council, the short ballot and the merit system for city employees. At last, in the wave of reform that came in the Progressive era, many improvements made headway. "Golden Rule" Jones, elected mayor of Toledo, Ohio, in 1897, introduced free kindergartens in public schools, built playgrounds and granted the eight-hour day to city employees. Shortly afterwards Tom Johnson was chosen mayor of Cleveland; among his many reforms the famous mayor numbered the introduction of city planning. The trend to improvement gained momentum with time, and with the coming of the City Beautiful movement, far more was done to alleviate the sorrier side of city life.

PART VI

The City Beautiful:
The Expanding City II

1880-1910

A FRESH CURRENT flowed through the American urban scene in this generation; not all was dedicated to mere expansion. Many Americans became impatient of the chaos and saw, as did the philosopher Charles Peirce, that the community must control unbridled individualism. Slowly it dawned that there was danger in urban disorder and that America was not to be measured by bigness alone—art too must have its role. With much the same spirit and energy that they devoted to their business, Americans made amends for past errors. The City Beautiful movement was their offering. Without it we would not have had our great libraries, museums, terminals and civic centers, which captured the public imagination both here and abroad. It was the age in which the businessman made his greatest contribution to American culture and the government followed his lead.

1. *Palace and Monument*

The new American millionaires may have been bold as brass in their titanic battles for control of business empires, but at first they were as timid of innovation as the less affluent when it came to adopting new forms of dwellings. True, the Potter Palmers built a stone turreted castle in Chicago which Boni de Castellane, the French dandy, called "sumptuous and abominable"; but when Marshall Field, the Chicago drygoods merchant, built himself a home on Prairie Avenue, a solid mansion of pressed brick and brownstone with a mansard roof, there was nothing in the building to show that Field was one of the wealthiest and most powerful men in the city.

Alexander T. Stewart, his New York counterpart, had a larger mansion on Fifth Avenue, equally undistinguished. The standard was at last set by William Kissam Vanderbilt, grandson of the famous Commodore, who spent $3,000,000 between 1879 and 1881 on a house that once stood on the corner of 52nd Street and Fifth Avenue. Designed by Richard Morris Hunt, this building heralded the arrival of the private "palace."

> How gay were the gala evenings when the house was ablaze with lights and Willie and I, crouching on hands and knees behind the balustrade of the musicians' gallery, looked on a festive scene below—the long dinner table covered with a damask cloth, a gold service and red roses, the lovely crystal and china, the grownups in their fine clothes [recalls Consuelo Vanderbilt Balsan, who, as Duchess of Marlborough, was afterwards to be the mistress of an older English palace]. The dining room was enormous and had at one end twin Renaissance mantel-pieces and on one side a huge stained-glass window, depicting the Field of the Cloth of Gold on which the kings of England and France were surrounded with their knights, all not more magnificently arrayed than the ladies a-glitter with jewels seated in high-backed tapestry chairs behind which stood footmen in knee breeches. Next to this big dining room was a small breakfast room adorned with Flemish tapestries and Rembrandt's portrait of the Turkish Chief. Then came a white drawing room hung with a fine set of Boucher tapestries; here were the beautiful lacquer *secrétaire* and commode, with bronzes chiseled by Gouthière, made for Marie Antoinette. Next door our living room, a paneled Renaissance salon, looked out on Fifth Avenue.

Despite the hours of tedium which must have passed in these rooms, where uneasy formality rivaled Spanish etiquette in its severity, what pleasure they gave to the innocent beholder and how significant was the patronage extended to the arts!

It is recorded in George Harvey's life of Henry Clay Frick that the Pittsburgher, already a Carnegie partner at the age of thirty-one, walking one day on Fifth Avenue with Andrew Mellon, the future Secretary of the Treasury, paused before Hunt's great mansion, still in process of construction, and speculated on the cost of its maintenance. This was in 1880, twenty-five years before Frick, having sold his holdings to United States Steel, himself moved to New York and rented one of the Vanderbilt mansions.

In 1914 Frick moved into his own palace, built for him by Carrère and Hastings at a cost of $5,400,000. This mansion, one of the last left on the avenue, now houses, as its builder planned, one of the world's most magnificent art collections, which Frick assembled and left to the public as a museum. We can be thankful for this indulgence on the part of our millionaires, who were abetted by the architects and artists of the period. Witness the Havemeyer collection, now in the Metropolitan Museum of Art, assembled on the advice of Mary Cassatt, and Mrs. Jack Gardner's Italian palace on the Fenway in Boston, which John Singer Sargent and Bernard Berenson helped to fill with treasures.

Palace after palace rose on the great avenue, until by the 1900's it had become one of the sights of the nation, exciting the envy and admiration of all, and attacks on its extravagance from the nation's pulpits only served to make it seem more fascinating. For many a rising businessman and his wife it became an aim in life to have a Fifth Avenue address.

Limestone was the chief material of the Palace Era, varied occasionally by marble and travertine. Ornament was very carefully applied, both inside and out, and the taste of the furnishings was far superior to those of the houses built before 1880, more attention being given to the quality of the furniture and particularly painting. Sometimes artists like Augustus Saint-Gaudens and John La Farge were called in to contribute their skill. Hunt's palace style followed the style of the Francis I period in France, and it remained the fashion for a while, until in the late 1890's taste turned to the French Classic of Louis XV and Louis XVI.

Only a few examples of the private palace can be seen in New York today, but many are still to be found in Newport, Rhode Island, where rich New Yorkers summered in large numbers. It was the heyday of the resort. Here Hunt built "Ochre Court" in 1888 for Ogden Goelet, whose fortune in New York City real estate permitted him this extravagance. Hunt also designed the classical "Marble House" for William Kissam Vanderbilt in 1892 and, three years later, the famous "Breakers" for Cornelius Vanderbilt II, today opened to the public for the benefit of the Newport Preservation Society by his daughter, the Countess Lâszló Széchényi. Horace Trumbauer, the Philadelphia architect, designed "The Elms" for the coal millionaire Edwin Berwind, a magnificent house in the Louis XV manner with sumptuous French interiors and gardens.

An error is often made today in believing that this love of splendor was confined to our millionaires, while the American

Garden front of "Marble House," a seaside villa in Newport, Rhode Island, designed by Richard Morris Hunt for William Kissam Vanderbilt in 1892.

people shunned displays of luxury. In many ways we are an extravagant people, although our extravagance may find its outlet in sports and clothes and all too rarely in the arts and the embellishing of our cities. The building of private palaces by the American rich was only one expression of the period. Hunt's design for the Vanderbilt house was the first signal of the change, but it was soon followed by others. McKim, Mead and White between 1886 and 1896, built the great public library in Boston, a building inspired by the work of Leon Battista Alberti and of Henri Labrouste. With its murals by Puvis de Chavannes and its handsome marble hall and stairs it is one of the great buildings of the country.

These were signs of a new taste, to be sure, although the public was not fully aware of it. Other monuments stirred America's heart. On a bitter December day in 1884, President Chester A. Arthur watched the aluminum cap raised to the top of the Washington Monument, an event announcing its completion after thirty years and more of work. In the beautiful classical shaft America raised the highest masonry structure ever built by man. Two years later the Statue of Liberty by Bartholdi, with its base by Hunt, lifted high her torch beside "the golden door" of New York Harbor. "We shall not forget that liberty has here made her home," was President

Soldiers' and Sailors' Monument in Indianapolis, designed in 1887 by the
German architect Bruno Schmitz and
completed in 1902.

Cleveland's welcome to the munificent gift of the French
people to America, "nor shall her chosen altar be neglected."
Emma Lazarus sang her beautiful song to the New Colossus:
"Give me your tired, your poor, Your huddled masses yearning to breathe free . . ." Americans now had two spectacular
monuments, which could only find comparison far back in
history in the days of Hellenistic Greece and Imperial Rome.

A third appeared in 1889, on the centenary of Washington's
inauguration in New York. In homage, President Harrison,
imitating the first President, went by boat from Elizabethport,
New Jersey, to the foot of Wall Street across a harbor where
"small boats with double-reefed sails and beer ballast were
under your bow every moment" and "ferryboats, river boats,
tugs, yachts and launches were stepping on each other's heels,
climbing each other's backs and kicking each other's el-
bows . . ." On the edge of Washington Square the president
was greeted by a large temporary arch by Stanford White. the

first elaborate arch since those built for Lafayette sixty-five years before. New Yorkers were so enthusiastic about White's creation that they subscribed to build a permanent one, the stone arch now standing in the square at the end of Fifth Avenue, the first permanent arch of triumph in America. The Washington Monument, the Statue of Liberty and the Washington Arch were symbols of a new power and a new yearning on the part of the American people.

In the Statue of Liberty could be seen more than the figure of Liberty holding high her light of Freedom, more than the symbol of friendship between the two great republics. The new colossus stood for the joining of the two nations in the classical tradition. American artists and architects had now begun to study in France. The only architectural school of any tradition and distinction in the world at the time was in Paris. To the Ecole Nationale Supérieure des Beaux-Arts streamed the students, who, at the expense of the French government, for there was no tuition fee, obtained a first-class education. After three or four years abroad, they were at home in at least one foreign language and they had at their fingertips the great examples of world art from Edinburgh to Istanbul. Louis Sullivan, although he spent a good part of his life battling the classical tradition, freely acknowledged his debt to France. The Ecole opened his eyes, he wrote in *The Autobiography of an Idea,* "to the quality and reach of French thought; to its richness, its firmness, its solidity, above all, the severity of its discipline beneath so smooth a surface." Knowledge and discipline were the French lessons for American

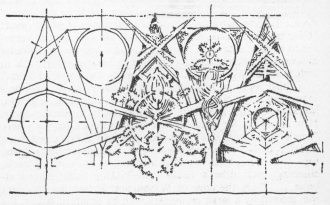

Design for architectural ornament by Louis Sullivan.

artists, especially the architects, and they came back to create a style that, as Fiske Kimball has pointed out, had no equal anywhere at the time, not even in France itself.

At first, it is true, many of the protagonists of the classical returned from France under the archaeological influence of Viollet-le-Duc, an enemy of the Ecole. The two leaders of Picturesque Secessionism, Richardson and Sullivan, were students of the famous school, but many of the men who were accused of being under its influence had never set foot inside the doors. Neither Daniel H. Burnham nor Stanford White attended it. White, after several years in Richardson's office, discovered the classical on a trip through France with Charles Follen McKim and Augustus Saint-Gaudens.

A lesson of the Ecole des Beaux-Arts and, for that matter, of Europe, had been the value of the past. One of the first steps McKim took on leaving the Ecole was to explore our own past by touring New England in 1877 with his future partners, Stanford White and William Rutherford Mead. While Picturesque Secessionism was being acclaimed by fashion after the Centennial Exposition in Philadelphia, they came upon the neglected American Baroque. The revival of the American Baroque (which is still with us in the form of the Colonial Revival Style) stems from that trip. Almost at once Americans began to build in the tradition of their ancestors.

2. *The American Renaissance*

The private palaces, the colossal monuments and the discovery of the American Baroque were milestones along the road to a new taste. Suddenly a vision appeared on the shores of Lake Michigan, springing full-blown like a sudden summer flower. The public rubbed its eyes and came in thousands. Flags waved in the hot midwestern sun, the air was filled with the rush of water from fountains and the murmur of admiring crowds; the vast white buildings were reflected in the giant basin, together with the great statue of the Republic; the monumental peristyle enclosed the Court of Honor and beyond there was a glimpse of the blue Lake Michigan and "the shadow of the dome of pleasure floated midway on the waves . . ." Such was the World's Columbian Exposition of 1893, Chicago's boast to all that, here on the prairie beside the inland sea, had risen an American forum filled with public palaces, rich with ornament and sculpture, to rival even ancient Rome. Some mocked the pretension at the time, and many have mocked it since; yet this temporary world of staff and plaster changed the taste of a nation.

One discerning critic came and left, only to return again, so overwhelmed was he by the spectacle. To Henry Adams "Paris had never approached" such a scene. "Was the American made to seem at home in it? Honestly, he has the air of enjoying it as though it were all his own," runs a passage in *The Education of Henry Adams*. "He felt it was good; he was proud of it; for the most part he acted as though he had passed his life in landscape gardening and architectural decoration," And Adams, recognizing the public taste for this new magnificence, insisted that "Chicago was the first expression of American thought as a unity; one must start there."

The Fair, which was so impressive to Adams and to countless others, has been much condemned, even more than the business age that created it. While the businessmen of the Gilded Age are at present being recognized as the great, if ruthless, organizers of the American Way of Life, their architects, sculptors, painters, landscape architects and city planners are still offered to us as bumbling imitators trained in a French school, who by turning to the tradition of the American Baroque and the American Roman crushed the flower of American art represented by Picturesque Secessionism. If we are now taking a more reasoned view of Rockefeller, Morgan and Harriman, might we not do the same for Burnham, McKim, Saint-Gaudens, Olmsted and the others who participated in designing the Fair and recognize them once and for all as great American artists?

The fascinating story of the Fair has yet to be told in all detail. The initiative of the Chicago businessmen was only the first step. Their master stroke was retaining Frederick Law Olmsted and Daniel H. Burnham among their consultants. To Olmsted belongs the design of the ground plan, to Burnham the unity of the whole and the responsibility for inviting the leading architects, sculptors and painters of the day to join in its creation. Hunt, Saint-Gaudens, McKim and Francis Millet, to name the most prominent, were among them. The co-operating architects unanimously chose the classical tradition for the architecture and decided on a uniform cornice line for the buildings on the Court of Honor. Like Jefferson they turned to the architecture of the ancients, because it had "the approbation of thousands of years . . ." Or as one of them, Henry Van Brunt of Kansas City, put it, they looked to "a uniform and ceremonious style—a style evolved from and expressive of the highest civilization in history" and not "a medieval or any other form of romantic, archeological or picturesque art."

Their triumph stemmed from three conditions: unity of

plan, unity of architecture and magnitude. To these a fourth must be added, collaboration among all the arts. The return to the great classical tradition was well launched. So that when Burnham announced, "There are two sorts of architectural beauty, first, that of an individual building; and second, that of an orderly and fitting arrangement of many buildings; the relationship of all the buildings is more important than anything else," the concept may have been unheard of in American architecture and city planning since the time of Ramée and Jefferson; but the seed fell on cultivated ground.

It is true that a thin thread of government patronage had continued even through the Age of Steam and Iron. While the Picturesque was very much in vogue, the federal government itself had maintained the standards of the American Roman or Federal Style. In 1855 Constantino Brumidi began his herculean work of decorating the Capitol with frescoes. This humble Italian artist, who was driven from his homeland because of his republican principles, completed in 1865 the great "Apotheosis of Washington" which fills the dome. He was then sixty years old. He died fourteen years later, still at work on the frieze; only recently has he received just recognition for his handiwork, thanks to his biographer, Mrs. John R. Murdock. At the mid-century, too, Ammi Burnham Young, now a forgotten architect, succeeded Robert Mills as architect to the Treasury Department (it was in 1852) and from his drawing board came a number of post offices and custom houses, many of them to be found still throughout the country. Best remembered for his designs of the Vermont capitol at Montpelier and the Boston Custom House, Young's government buildings in Portland, Maine, Providence, Rhode Island, Galveston, Texas, and Galena, Illinois, command attention by their beautiful proportions and the classical restraint exercised by this most Roman of American architects.

With the passage of the Tarsney Act in 1893 Congress renewed the tradition of patronage by authorizing the Secretary of the Treasury to obtain designs for public buildings by competition among the leaders of the architectural profession. A fixed fee of 6 per cent of the construction cost was the reward for the winner of the competition. By this law the federal government gave architecture official recognition as an art essential to the community; with the best talent of the country at its disposal government patronage of architecture was soon reflected in the quality of its buildings. (Unfortunately in 1912 a later Congress, under the constant pressure of economy drives, repealed the act, but not before such buildings as the New York Custom House by Cass Gilbert were completed.)

Local governments followed suit with a lively interest in better architecture. One new state capitol arose after the other, especially in the West. Cass Gilbert did the designs for the Minnesota capitol in St. Paul in 1896, and the Arkansas capitol in Little Rock in 1899. The Rhode Island capitol (1895–1901) belongs to McKim, Mead and White; George B. Post and Sons designed Wisconsin's (1906–17) in Madison. One of the more powerful works was the Pennsylvania capitol (1904–6) in Harrisburg by Joseph M. Huston; it is distinguished for its murals by Edwin Austin Abbey and the sculptured groups of George Gray Barnard. In Jefferson City the Missouri capitol completed by Tracy and Swartout in 1917, stands out as perhaps the most Roman of all in scale and character. Despite one or two failures these capitols are magnificent and nowhere more so than in their interiors, where embellishments abound and where all the arts have found a place. In our own time bareness and function have been the chief architectural preoccupations, but these domed capitols invite Americans to the visual splendors of gold and marble not found in the newer state office buildings, or indeed, in any modern government buildings today.

Coinciding with the new interest in monuments and public buildings, the time had come to improve the home of the federal government. L'Enfant's work in Washington, after the initial efforts, had fallen into neglect. The Romantic Revival had invaded the capital city with the Gothic Smithsonian Institution and the Age of Steam and Iron had run a railroad across the Mall. After serving as warehouse and hospital during the Civil War, the federal city was a shambles. The Capitol, "a splendid building, unfolds its repeated colonnades and uplifts its isolated dome at the end of a long vista of saloons and tobacco shops," Henry James noted at the time.

The American people, disregarding Spencerian individualism, were determined that art should bring order to the national capital. The first move was the revival of the L'Enfant plan by the McMillan Commission in 1901. Forty years or so earlier an attempt had been made to create a supervising committee to improve the city on the petition of a group of artists to President Buchanan and Congress, but nothing came of the move. Then in the time of Theodore Roosevelt, Senator James McMillan of Michigan appointed a subcommittee to the senate committee on the District of Columbia, naming as members Burnham, McKim, Saint-Gaudens and

Olmsted. The Washington we see before us today is the result of their work.

They studied the L'Enfant plan, then went abroad to see what the past had to offer and, on their return, incorporated improvements to L'Enfant's work in the plan of 1901. The restoration of the Mall, was first on their list; next came the location of new public buildings, and then memorials, new and old, were related to a general pattern of improvement. Further, the parks were systematized and joined. It was Burnham who persuaded Alexander Cassatt, president of the Pennsylvania Railroad, to remove the station from the Mall. The

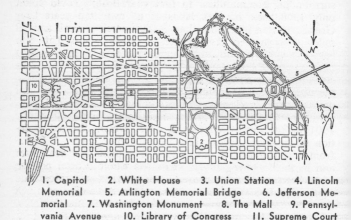

1. Capitol   2. White House   3. Union Station   4. Lincoln Memorial   5. Arlington Memorial Bridge   6. Jefferson Memorial   7. Washington Monument   8. The Mall   9. Pennsylvania Avenue   10. Library of Congress   11. Supreme Court   12. National Gallery of Art

Central portion of present-day Washington, D. C., showing the location of important monuments.

architect suggested a new location south of it, but Cassatt, improving on his idea, and in co-operation with the Baltimore and Ohio Railroad, agreed to build the Union Station where it now stands, well to the north. The heart of Washington was thus restored approximately to the original scheme of the 1790's.

In 1910 on the motion of Senator Elihu Root a National Commission of Fine Arts with seven members was created to advise on and approve future developments in the District of Columbia. President Theodore Roosevelt explained to the American Institute of Architects how it functioned: "Whenever hereafter a public building is provided for, it should be erected in accordance with a carefully thought-out plan adopted long before . . . it should not only be beautiful in itself, but fitting in its relations to the whole scheme of the public buildings, the parks and the drives of the District."

What had begun as part of the training in an atelier of the Ecole des Beaux-Arts in Paris, and then found temporary form in Chicago in 1893, now achieved permanence in the national capital. From Bangor, Maine, to San Diego, California, every city and town attempted self-improvement. Among the first was Greater Boston, which in 1893 created its Metropolitan Park Commission for the central city and its surrounding communities. In that year Boston could count only 1900 acres of park lands as its own; ten years later Greater Boston had more than 13,000 acres of park and 19 miles of ocean shore reserved for the public. Kansas City also began its improvements at the same time by creating a system of parks and boulevards. The improvements in St. Louis stemmed from its 1904 exposition, when the Art Museum, the only permanent building of the fair, was made the focal point for the development of Forest Park. In Cedar Rapids, Iowa, the first suggestions for improvement were offered in 1901 by the city's Commercial Club, which directed attention to the shore development of the Cedar River. A Riverfront Improvement Commission was appointed a year later and in the following fifteen years the whole central portion of the city was changed to an elegant vista of bridges and esplanades. Des Moines, the capital of the state, effected much the same transformation to its waterfront on the initiative of its Civic Improvement and Town Planning Committees. Along with new park systems and waterfronts came the civic centers. The new capitol buildings and town halls would have been ridiculous without civic design. Typical of the changes was the removal of the telephone wires and poles from State Street in Madison, Wisconsin, giving the new domed capitol the approach that was its due. In Harrisburg a similar awakening took place at the turn of the century, and with the completion of the great Pennsylvania capitol other work was pushed. A civic center was planned by the state and the city around the capitol building in 1917 and carried to completion in the twenty years that followed.

Art museums and libraries were built by the score in the City Beautiful period. In 1898 it was decided to consolidate several of New York's privately-endowed public library foundations into one. Among these were the Astor Library, given by John Jacob Astor, and the Tilden Foundation, left by Samuel J. Tilden, Democratic candidate for the presidency

Carrère & Hastings' entrance to the Manhattan Bridge, New York.

in 1876. A competition was held for a new building to bring them together. Carrère and Hastings won, and the great structure, which is one of the city's best-known institutions, was completed in 1911. Hastings was also responsible for the design for the beautiful bronze bases of the two flagpoles that stand before it. They were executed by Raffaele J. Menconi and were cast in the famous Tiffany Studios. Buffalo obtained its handsome Albright Art Gallery, the work of Green and Wicks, in 1905, and many other cities housed their art collections in handsome galleries on the wave of the new interest in the arts.

Church achitecture broke away from the influence of Richardson, and although many new churches were built, relatively few were carried out in the classical tradition. In general the fervent Gothicist Ralph Adams Cram had his way. Preaching Gothic as the only true Christian architecture this latter-day medievalist won many patrons of all sects. To him and his partners Goodhue and Ferguson, we owe the sumptuous St. Thomas's (1908) in New York, the First Baptist (1909) in Pittsburgh and the Fourth Presbyterian (1912) in Chicago. It was the distinction of the church architecture of the period that the evangelical Protestant joined the Episcopal and the Roman Catholic in building decorated houses of worship. (Cram, Goodhue and Ferguson's most outstanding work was the imposing addition, including the chapel, to the United States Military Academy at West Point in 1904.)

The college campus, too, went through a metamorphosis as the Grand Design returned to the "academical village." If we compare Olmsted and Vaux's plan for Berkeley and the University of California (1866) with the former's plan for

Leland Stanford Junior University (1888), the change is astonishing. The first is Downingesque and the second extremely formal. The later plan for the University of California campus (1902) by Emile Bénard and John Galen Howard is in the best classical manner. With the tremendous expansion of American universities many classical campuses were built at this time. The American garden, like the campus, also changed. Largely due to the influence of Charles Adams Platt and Edith Wharton, the Italian garden came to America. One of Platt's best gardens, although neglected, is that of the Harold R. McCormick estate in Lake Forest. The best known example of his influence is Meridian Hill Park in Washington, familiar to music lovers because of its summer concerts. The French formal garden also enjoyed a considerable vogue, and although many of the great ones have gone before the omnivorous subdivider, one or two of those of Jacques Gréber and the younger Olmsted can still be found on the Atlantic seaboard at Newport, on Long Island and in the environs of Philadelphia.

To round out the pageantry of the age came the pyrotechnician. Fireworks abounded on every occasion, public and private. America even had its own celebrated family of pyrotechnical artists, the Pains. Among the many who attended their displays was Theodore Roosevelt, who, it is reported, "couldn't keep his hands off the stuff."

Even the staid railroad corporations were infected by the rage for display. Instead of the smoky depots of the Age of Steam and Iron beautiful stations sheltered the waiting passengers, and the city, which until now had been knocked about by the railroad, had a new embellishment. Burnham

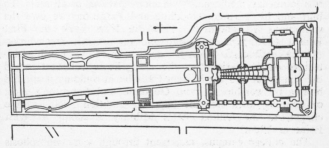

Plan of Meridian Hill Park, Washington, in the Franco-Italian formal manner, cascade on the right. Designed by George Burnap and Horace W. Peaslee with planting by Vitale, Brinckerhoff & Geiffert.

built more than one great station; his Pennsylvania Railroad Terminal in Pittsburgh has a waiting room where gold, a form of ornament too rarely used in the United States, forms part of the decoration. Alexander Cassatt, on a visit to his famous sister, the painter Mary Cassett living outside Paris, had seen how the Paris-Orléans Railroad had electrified its tracks into the French capital, and he was determined that the Pennsylvania Railroad should have its own station in New York. Electrification proved the solution, and in 1906 he commissioned McKim, Mead and White to build the monumental Pennsylvania Station. The New York Central followed suit after electrifying its lines. It retained the architects Reed and Stem and Warren and Wetmore to do the Grand Central. In no small part due to the skillful engineering of Colonel William Wilgus, who devised the method of routing the trains underground, the station is one of the handsomest and most convenient in the world.

In spite of the inevitable unevenness of execution, all of these buildings, even the modest libraries made possible by the philanthropy of Andrew Carnegie, have a character that reveals the stylistic aspirations of the age. This style was in a recognizable classical tradition, essentially a public style, to be embellished by all the arts and to be judged by all the people. "When you get through with your work on the other side and come home to build," wrote McKim in 1909 to Lawrence Grant White, the son of his deceased partner, "you will find opportunities awaiting that no other country has offered in modern times. The scale is Roman and it will have to be sustained."

The age of the City Beautiful was one in which architect-planners dominated. The reward of the architects for first visualizing the City Beautiful in America was the commission to build it. The initiative for improvement came from business and professional groups, and among their fellows the architects and the landscape architects assumed the lead. In every city where there was a chapter of the American Institute of Architects, designs, pamphlets and detailed reports poured forth.

The greatest rewards were reserved for the most prominent of all architect-planners, Daniel H. Burnham. In addition to work at the Chicago World's Fair and in Washington, he did plans for Cleveland, San Francisco (in association with Edward H. Bennett) and Manila in the Philippine Islands. Although his important practice carried him to all parts of the country, the improvement of Chicago was always the great aim of his life. In 1897 he had told the Merchants' Club "that the time has come for Chicago to make herself attractive" and he outlined a number of suggestions. Nothing came of them. Undiscouraged he kept advancing ideas for improvement, for he always believed that the city should be a place "for men and women to live and for children to grow up in; his chief idea was to make conditions for working healthy and agreeable, and facilities for recreation both abundant and available." Then in 1906 the Commercial Club of Chicago in-

A pavilion of Roman scale by Bernard R. Maybeck in the Panama-Pacific Exposition held in San Francisco in 1915. A late example of the influence of the Chicago Columbian Exposition, still standing but neglected.

vited him to prepare a comprehensive plan of the city. In the next three years he devoted himself with the assistance of a large staff to the preparation of the plan, a labor of love on his part for he accepted no remuneration for any of his city plans. The unusual aspect of Burnham's plan was its extent. For one thing, he did not confine planning to the city but carried it to the region beyond. Secondly, he took into consideration railroads, highways, parks, playgrounds, forests and bathing beaches. And a third distinction was the dramatization of the architectural effect possible in skillful planning. At the center he wanted low buildings dominated by the high dome of the city hall; tall buildings would form the outer rim. The plan was magnificently presented to the public by the Commercial Club in the form of a handsome book, the first comprehensive plan for an American city of regional scope and authority. The Wacker Manual, a simplified account of the plan, was later printed in the thousands and used as a textbook in Chicago's schools.

No plan has ever influenced an American city in quite the same way that Burnham's dream captured the imagination of Chicago. Even in the corrupt regime of Mayor "Big Bill" Thompson, its suggested improvements were pushed ahead. The new lakefront, the widening of Michigan Avenue, the creation of the Cook County Forest Reserve and the Wacker Drive are the better known improvements that eventually resulted. Very unfortunately, Burnham's plan for a civic center was not realized and the city is still without one. For all the spread of city planning since, it is a compliment to Burnham's genius that the plan has not yet found its equal, even in the well-known Regional Plan of 1929 for New York City, which dwelt inevitably on administration, engineering and legal problems. The times were changing and there were signs that other matters would occupy the American people. The automobile, until then a sign of wealth, was about to become available to all; Henry Ford made his first Model T in the year that Burnham's plan was published. The well-to-do who were deserting the city for their suburban arcadias were soon to forget the other nine tenths who remained in the center, where the City Efficient was to obscure the importance of the City Beautiful.

Before we leave the American Renaissance, which wrought

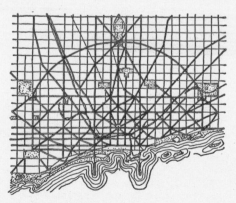

The Chicago Plan of 1909. This abstract of
its Traffic Plan shows the regional character of
the work of Burnham and Bennett.

such a profound change in American architecture as in all the arts, we would do well to recall the famous words of Burnham to city planners, written shortly before his death in 1912. "Make no little plans; they have no magic to stir men's blood and probably themselves will not be realized. Make big plans; aim high in hope and work, remembering that a noble, logical diagram once recorded will never die, but long after we are gone will be a living thing, asserting itself with ever-growing insistency. Remember that our sons and our grandsons are going to do things that would stagger us. Let your watchword be order and your beacon beauty."

Valete, ac plaudite—those words will forever be remembered in the city to which a man of vision brought the blessings of civic design and by generations of American city dwellers yet to come.

130 The City as a Way of Life: The Expanding City I .

PART VII

The City of Towers

1910-1933

THE BRIEF but important period from 1910 to 1933 marks the third stage of finance capitalism, which had begun with the rise of the individual financier, then developed into the giant corporation and now was to take a fresh hold with the rise of mass production. This new stage is best symbolized by the initiative of Henry Ford in 1909, when in the quiet little community of Highland Park, Michigan, he set up the first mass-production plant for automobiles, later to be copied by the great nations of the world. With the new chemical industry, the increasing manufacture of light metals and alloys and the later introduction of the high-speed rolling mill, the age that saw the embryo automobiles and airplanes transformed into daily conveniences was able to couple mass production with its necessary adjunct, mass distribution.

From 1916 the nation's total railroad mileage began to decline, and, although the great age of the automobile was still to come, there were those who saw in the first cross-country highway in 1927 a symbol of the enormous changes the internal combustion engine was already bringing to the nation, and especially to the city. This was the age of the movie palace and the neighborhood theatre, the now spreading chain store, the cafeteria (the first Automat was opened in Philadelphia in 1902), the American drugstore (part pharmacy, part soda fountain and part emporium) and the consolidated high school.

There was a war to end all wars, and America found itself among the world powers. An American statesman, President Woodrow Wilson, was largely responsible for creating the League of Nations, the first concrete attempt at world government. As if to express appreciation of our new role, we raised our skyscrapers still higher. No more interesting or exciting change has ever taken place in the city than the new skyline, created by the whim of American businessmen to reach the clouds. The first really spectacular example was the Woolworth Building, completed in 1913, New York's rival to Paris's Eiffel Tower. The last of the era was the Empire State, 102 stories high and still the tallest man-made structure in the world.

1. *The Skyscraper*

New York Harbor is loveliest at night perhaps [the poet Rupert Brooke wrote home to England in 1913]. On the Staten Island ferryboat you slip out from darkness right under the immense skyscrapers. As they recede they form into a mass together, heaping up one behind another, fire-lined and majestic sentinel over the black gold-streaked waters. Their cliff-like boldness is the greater because to either side sweep in the East River and the Hudson River, leaving the piled promontory between. To the right stands the great stretch of the Brooklyn Suspension Bridge, its slight curve very purely outlined with light; over it luminous trams, like shuttles of fire, are thrown across and across, continually weaving the stuff of human existence. From further off all these lights dwindle to a radiant semi-circle that gazes out over the expanse with a quiet, mysterious expectancy. Far away seaward you may see the low golden glare of Coney Island.

Thousands have described the scene and other thousands will go on describing it. There is nothing to match the tip of Manhattan anywhere in the world; only in America itself can there be found imitators, such as Chicago and San Francisco. This is the characteristic form of the American metropolis as we know it today. A single skyscraper or a group of skyscrapers at the center in most of the cities, or in the larger ones, several groups with scattered towers. The skyline is first low and then suddenly rises in peaks of stone and steel, a jagged vision that is peculiarly American.

It took about twenty-five years after William Le Baron Jenney perfected his steel frame construction for architects to discover how best to shape the tall building. There were the early efforts of McKim, Mead and White and Louis Sullivan in the 1890's, later of Burnham (the Flatiron Building in New York in 1901), Ernest Flagg (the Singer Tower in New York in 1907) and others. Finally in 1913, with the completion of the Woolworth Tower in New York, America had its first effective tower-form skyscraper. Cass Gilbert, architect of classical state capitols, turned to a free form of the Gothic for the tower. With Gothic pilaster and molding he accented the soaring height, and with terra-cotta crockets and finials gave the tower its lacelike form. Trowbridge and Livingston, taking advantage of a corner site on Wall Street, created the Bankers Trust Company Building at about the same time and topped their classical structure with a design taken from the tomb of Mausolus at Halicarnassus. Carrère and Hastings in the Standard Oil Building at the foot of Broadway fitted the façade of a palace of papal Rome to the street's curve; the building is capped by a giant incense burner from which, in the cold of winter, wisps of white smoke and steam wave in the wind.

A second age of the tall building dawned. A new Wall Street of true skyscrapers replaced the older lower buildings; each one has a different tower, often decorated with sculpture, like the grand winged golden figure on the American Telephone and Telegraph Company home office in New York. Chicago, not to be outdone, created a fantastic setting of water, boulevards and towers along the Chicago River. Following the directive of the Burnham Plan, a double level highway on both banks separated commercial and pleasure traffic going to the lakefront, while across the river a $3,000,000 bridge was thrown to carry Michigan Boulevard northward. Around the bridge were grouped new skyscrapers, the London Guaranty Building, the Wrigley Building with its white terra-cotta façade, and the Tribune Tower (1924) by Raymond Hood and John M. Howells. In this last (a free interpretation of the Gothic as in the Woolworth Tower), Chicago has its most beautiful building, and a skyscraper that for the architectural "purist," expresses its skeleton steel construction by continuous unbroken piers. A skyscraper of more modern character, original in design and decoration, with rippled exterior walls, is the Irving Trust Company at number 1 Wall Street in New York, designed in 1929 by the firm Voorhees, Gmelin and Walker (today Voorhees, Walker, and Smith).

A taste for brighter luxury found its way through the country as the skyscraper came to every American city. The new giant could be used for hotels as well as office buildings. The Ritz-Carlton, a product of the New York of 1912, was as sedate as the Plaza of a few years earlier, but more exotic was the later tower of the Sherry-Netherland, which looked as if its designers, Schultze and Weaver, had brought to life a Maxfield Parrish castle. With the march of fashion up Michigan Boulevard in the 1920's, the Drake Hotel (1921, by Benjamin H. Marshall) called the visitor to Chicago to pass his time on the North Side, tempting him from the proud Blackstone built in 1910. In San Francisco the Mark Hopkins lifted its tower on top of Nob Hill, adding one more extravagance to nature's own fantasy around the Golden Gate.

A new building type in the urban scene was the movie palace. Now that the TV set holds Americans to the fireside, they may soon forget the delight they once took in the downtown

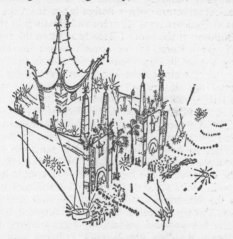

Sid Grauman's Chinese Theater in Hollywood
(1927) by the architects Meyer & Holler, scene
of famous movie premières.

theatres of the decade of Rudolf Valentino. Movie-house operators spared nothing in the embellishing of their palaces. Grauman's Chinese Theater in Hollywood is one of the more unalloyed in its exuberance, but every city had its variant. To go to them is like stepping into a vision of the Bibienas, the imaginative stage designers of the Italian eighteenth century. Even today a visit to the Roxy Theatre (1927) in New York, by the architect Walter W. Ahlschlager, holds one spellbound as the golden columns and decoration carry the eye to the resplendent ceiling.

The splendor unleashed by the American Renaissance died very slowly, as railroad terminals, banks and office buildings continued to be built on a scale unknown outside America. Kansas City had a new Union Terminal by Jarvis Hunt in 1914, Chicago a classic masterpiece in the Union Station

(1924) by Graham, Anderson, Probst and White. The banks responded with special enthusiasm. One of the first signs of the influence of the Chicago World's Fair in the New York area had been Frank Freeman's pedimented Brooklyn Savings Bank, built on Brooklyn Heights in 1894. Twenty years later it was matched across the street by a branch of the Manufacturers Trust, where a columned story is set on a high rusticated base, one of the forgotten triumphs of the architects York and Sawyer. This firm set a new standard of richness in its bank buildings, as any one who has visited the main office of the Guaranty Trust (1912) in New York well knows. The same firm's Bowery Savings Bank (1923) on 42nd Street, has a colossal banking hall that must be unrivaled in the country: the floor is of cosmatesque marble work, there is a high painted and coffered ceiling and columns of rare marble are set against the walls. The American banker, in such buildings, was harking back to a tradition of the Florentine and Venetian merchants of the Italian Renaissance. Pittsburgh, not to be left behind, has the Mellon Bank by Trowbridge and Livingston and also the extraordinary City-County Building, embellished by Hornbostel and Lee with bronze columns. The Soldiers' and Sailors' Memorial Hall by Henry Hornbostel, and the Pittsburgh Athletic Club by Janssen and Cocken (architects of the imposing Mellon Institute done in 1937) are two of the buildings which help make the Steel City a Templed City as well. Even Gopher Prairie in Sinclair Lewis's *Main Street* could boast of a classical bank—the only building in town which gave any pleasure to the heroine's eyes.

Church building, although not quite so extensive as before the war, went on in the 1920's. Some churches, as if in an attempt to rival commercial buildings, went so far as to encase the house of worship in a tall apartment-office building, expecting the income from offices and apartments to meet expenses; these efforts were as undistinguished in their architecture as they were unsuccessful in their finances. An exception is the Chicago Temple Building, with a Gothic spire, built in 1923 by the firm Holabird and Roche, and it proves that the skyscraper church is still worthy of experiment. Cram's message of the "pure" Gothic had by now conquered the American Renaissance, at least in church architecture. He himself continued to design and build, although at a reduced pace. The soaring East Liberty Presbyterian Church in Pittsburgh, where the "social" adjuncts have been skillfully joined to the main structure, is one of his best, although it has a cold quality in its interiors unlike the great medieval prototypes. Together with Ferguson, Cram was responsible for the design of the New York cathedral (Cathedral of St. John the Divine), which replaced the earlier Romanesque project. One of the largest Gothic structures in the world, it stands on Morningside Heights awaiting funds for completion. It is challenged by the nearby Riverside Baptist Church of Allen, Pelton and Collens. This elaborate Gothic pile rises on a magnificent site overlooking the Hudson, enriching the long skyline with its tower and testifying to the piety of John D. Rockefeller. In Brooklyn, Helmle and Corbett, turning from the classical tradition, designed the beautiful St. Gregory's in the manner of an early Christian basilica. Across the country in St. Paul, Minnesota, the New York architect Whitney Warren did not waver in his affection for the classical; in the high altar of the Cathedral of St. Paul with its baldacchino of black and gold marble, he is responsible for one of the most successful decorations in American church architecture. In small churches American Baroque and Greek Revival were favored. Unfortunately their designers were usually afraid to give them the spark of color and ornament that Jeremy Taylor demanded.

The wave of civic design and city planning that stemmed from Chicago's Columbian Exposition was by no means spent. Portions of plans drawn up in Burnham's time were still being carried out, and new plans were being projected under his influence. Among the better known were the plans for Oakland and Berkeley, California, by Werner Hegemann, the plan for New Haven by Cass Gilbert and Frederick Law Olmsted, Jr., those for Norwood and other Massachusetts communities by Arthur A. Shurcliff, the plan for Binghamton, New York, by Charles Mulford Robinson and the ones for Portland, Oregon, and Minneapolis by Edward H. Bennett. Outstanding among these planners was Bennett, who had been a close collaborator with Burnham from 1903 to the latter's death in 1912.

In fact, it was largely due to the initiative of Burnham and Bennett that San Francisco obtained the grandest civic center in the country. After the fire of 1906 the city determined to do something to erase the memory of the disaster. In 1912 John Galen Howard, Frederick H. Meyer and John Reid, Jr., following the precepts of Burnham and Bennett in the Chicago Plan, designed the center very much as we know it today, although the individual buildings were the work of other architects over a long period of time. The high dome of the city hall dominates the low classical forms of the public library, the opera house, the American Legion Building and the others. In the same decade the smaller civic center of

Benjamin Franklin Parkway, Philadelphia, designed by
the French architect-city planner Jacques Gréber in 1918.
The Philadelphia Museum of Art terminates the axis.

Springfield, Massachusetts, was given two classical buildings
and a tall bell tower by the architects Pell and Corbett.

In Philadelphia one of the great avenues of America was
completed in the 1920's, the Benjamin Franklin Parkway. For
some time it had been suggested that the city center be
joined to Fairmount Park stretching to the northwest. Work
was begun in 1910, but the final design was not accepted until
1918, when Jacques Gréber outlined his monumental tree-
lined boulevard. To cap the project Horace Trumbauer, together with Zantzinger and Borie, began the temple-like
Philadelphia Museum of Art in 1918, creating an ensemble
that is only to be matched in Washington.

More typical of the developments of the 1920's was Park
Avenue in New York. After the New York Central Railroad
had electrified its line into New York and built the great
terminal, Park Avenue suddenly became fashionable. Tired
of living in large houses, wealthy New Yorkers sought apartment houses for the days when they had to be in town. From
46th Street to 96th Street, two and a half miles of magnif-

cent monotony of brick and limestone were built. To make
the transition easier for the former homeowners, the duplex,
or double-floor apartment, was invented to provide ample
space and a private stairway, much as in a house. At the foot
of the avenue the architects Warren and Wetmore placed their
New York Central Building tower in 1925 to close the vista.
They sealed off the end with wings in which they placed high-
arched tunnels for automobile traffic; in the middle came the
tall narrow lobby, with its decoration of pink Oriental Jaspe
marble and black-and-gold wrought iron and its red-and-gold

Park Avenue with the tower of the New York
Central Building by Warren & Wetmore
in the distance.

elevators. Chicago joined the parade and created a fashionable apartment house district north of the Tribune Tower on
Lake Shore Drive. Luxurious buildings of limestone stand
along the lake's edge, adding new monoliths to the skyline.

To help the well-to-do arrange their apartments in these
towers came the interior decorator, a professional new in
America. The architects, for some reason, had surrendered
this lucrative side of their art around the turn of the century, when a former actress, Elsie de Wolfe, showed the rich
how to decorate their homes. The profession expanded with
the years and came to be largely dominated by women, a
curious aspect of American culture. The decorators gave apartment house living the elegance that reached its apogee in New
York and Chicago at this time. As Miss de Wolfe, who later
became the famous hostess Lady Mendl, observed of the postwar decade, it was a time of "goings out to goings on."

Certainly the American real estate developer has seldom surpassed his creations on Park Avenue and Chicago's North Side, which only today are being destroyed, as plain glass façades replace ornamented brick and stone.

2. *Speculation and the Automobile*

It was the America of the Jazz Age that loomed so large on the international scene in the decade following the First World War. For the first time Americans were called on to assume responsibilities they had never held before, as they became bankers and manufacturers to the world. J. P. Morgan and Company was working closely with the Banks of England and France; Dillon, Read and Company was financing the coal and steel magnates of the Ruhr; and Henry Ford was scattering subsidiaries like seeds over the face of the earth. New York stood next to London in banking and Paris in fashion. Visitors to America in earlier generations had discovered our capacity to build. Now all could see, as Rupert Brooke maintained, that the art of architecture had become American.

This age, so short and so innocent, although it believed itself so daring, was to transform old cities and create new ones. Los Angeles and Detroit, substantial centers before the First World War, doubled their population in the decade after 1914. In 1911 a moving picture was cranked out in the temperance colony that later became Hollywood, and within the next few years the infant industry had migrated from New York to the sunny West Coast. One more strange setting had been added to the urban scene in America. Less colorful but no less startling was the coming of the automobile industry to Detroit. Hamtramck, once a farming community on the edge of the city and today a city within the city of Detroit, had a population of 3589 in 1910 which jumped to 45,615 a decade later, thanks to the coming of the Dodge Motor plants and to Henry Ford's large factory in nearby Highland Park.

This period has been called the "Age of Frenzied Innocence." How else can one explain the Florida boom that created so many new cities? Modern Florida dates from the 1880's, when railroads began crossing the state for the first time, at the initiative of Henry B. Plant, Atlanta railroad man, and Henry M. Flagler, onetime associate of John D. Rockefeller. The former chose to develop the west coast of the peninsula and the latter the east coast, which proved the more fantastic. Flagler had discovered the state in the course of a pleasure trip and had fallen in love with the possibility of

Ford factory at Highland Park, designed by the
industrial architect Albert Kahn in 1908.

developing a new Eldorado. Backed by Standard Oil millions,
he easily bought railroads and extended them, beginning in
1888 at Jacksonville. Gradually he brought together what
came to be the Florida East Coast Railway and pushed it
south. Whenever it touched an existing town he built a hotel,
and if no town existed he developed one. His first hotel was
the Ponce de Leon in St. Augustine, by the architects Carrère and Hastings; others followed in Palm Beach and Miami,
both towns owing their existence to his railroad. By 1912, the
year in which he died, the tracks had reached Key West.

In 1912 the first real estate company was formed in Miami
Beach, and ten years later one of America's most notorious
publicists, Steve Hannigan, was making the press of the world
accept the man-made islands off Miami as the source of all
bathing beauties. After Flagler's groundwork was finished the
development of Florida continued slowly, confined largely to
the building of hotels. Interest in the state as a winter resort
was growing, and by 1924 real estate was booming everywhere,
particularly in and about Miami. The election of Calvin Coolidge as President that November seemed to announce the
coming of another millenium, and speculation began in full
force. People flocked into the state as they never had before.
All the tricks of previous booms were tried again. Buying and
selling of land and actual construction went on at such a pace
that rail transportation, overburdened with building materials,

broke down. In August, 1925, the Florida East Coast Railway refused to ship anything to Miami but fuel, livestock and food, and the breakdown grew worse as thousands of freight cars collected at Jacksonville that winter. People turned to shipping, but even that ancient method failed when, in January, 1926, a boat rolled over and blocked the channel leading to Miami harbor.

The boom did not stop immediately. Poor people from the Georgia hills, contemptuously called "Crackers," together with the wealthiest families in the country, joined in the hysteria. All either engaged in speculation or in promoting it. Everything was done on the basis of a down payment of 10 per cent, as in Chicago ninety years before. The properties changed hands so fast that the business of recording the sales broke down, and most of the transactions were settled long after the boom had collapsed, when all but the original owner of the property had disappeared. By the middle of 1926 the market was falling fast, and on September 15 the east coast was hit by one of the worst hurricanes in American history. This disaster ended the rout; Florida was not to begin its slow comeback until the mid-thirties.

The real estate boom which overtook the country was to be found, as in previous generations, on the city's outskirts. With improved commuting service and availability of the handy automobile, the migration of the wealthy from the center to the fringes went on at an increasing rate. The building of town houses had stopped, except in rare instances, and those being constructed never deserved the name of private palaces. If the rich built new houses they were suburban houses, country villas and pleasure pavilions. F. Burrall Hoffman and Paul Chalfin designed "Vizcaya" for the farm equipment millionaire James Deering on the outskirts of Miami in 1917. Whole rooms brought from Europe furnished this fabulous villa, which has a large Italian garden with fountains and statues looking out on Biscayne Bay. William Randolph Hearst, extensive buyer of antiques as well as newspaper tycoon, built himself "La Cuesta Encantada," more familiarly known as "The Ranch," the twin-towered palace on the hills of San Simeon above the blue Pacific. Both examples were outstanding in an age of accent on comforts rather than on extravagance. Palm Beach, although in Florida, stood somewhat apart from the boom. It owed its reputation as a fashionable winter playground to the whim of millionaires. Here one sumptuous villa after another in the Hispano-Moresque Style arose on the sandy shores at the inspiration of Addison Mizner. This extraordinary architect, originally from San Francisco, was able to persuade his clients to pour their millions into the resort, and although Palm Beach was eventually touched by the speculative debacle, he left a monument to extravagance which is unrivaled in our time.

It was not so much the coming of the income tax that brought about the change, but the arrival of a new generation, bored and rebellious, which rejected the ritual and the palaces of its parents. The town house was abandoned in the 1920's for the apartment, but even more for the suburban arcadia like Old Westbury and Oyster Bay near New York, and new money swelled the existing suburbs such as Lake Forest near

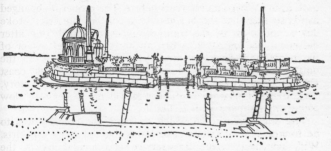

Artificial island off the gardens of the Villa Vizcaya, Miami,
Florida, now the Dade County Museum.
The sculpture is by Alexander S. Calder.

Chicago, or plush Burlingame near San Francisco. In the winter Palm Beach or Santa Barbara proved the safest havens. The Fifth Avenue of the 1900's began to disappear, as Henry James had prophesied it would, in the country that considered change synonymous with progress.

The large suburban houses in the East and the Middle West were mostly in the Modern Colonial of Delano and Aldrich and Charles A. Platt. Grosse Pointe and Grosse Pointe Farms, outside Detroit, have many samples of the latter's best work. On the outskirts of New York and Philadelphia some turned to the Norman Farm House Style as done by Mellor, Meigs and Howe. In New Orleans Richard Koch built delightful homes in the local Greek Revival manner, while in Pasadena and in Southern California generally the Missions furnished inspiration for suburban dwellings. Although not as grand as the earlier town houses, those built in this period gave a distinction to suburban life which is absent in our own time.

3. *Planned Communities*

The automobile appeared in increasing numbers in the twenties and soon a huge second-hand car market gave warning to Henry Ford and other manufacturers of cheap cars that they were facing increased competition. But in spite of the number of automobiles the mass-dormitory suburb was still the exception rather than the rule. Construction continued within the cities. Rows and rows of houses were built on the vacant land of larger cities where tax exemption or municipally furnished public utilities encouraged development, especially in Brooklyn, Philadelphia, Baltimore, Chicago and Los Angeles. These were without benefit of planning, but the age was notable for employing the planner elsewhere. Forest Hills Gardens in Queens, New York, was designed by Grosvenor Atterbury and the Olmsted brothers in 1910, as a demonstration project financed by the Russell Sage Foundation. Using the commuters' railroad station they laid out an orderly village of brick, with an interesting square as a focal point and with tree-lined streets. During World War I the federal government had to provide homes for workers in defense industries and some notable planned towns sprang up, such as Yorkship Village near Camden, New Jersey, by Electus D. Litchfield and Atlantic Heights above Portsmouth, New Hampshire, by Kilham and Hopkins.

The inspiration for much of this planned work came from the Garden City movement of England, which saw a solution of the problems of modern living by combining the best best features of country and town. In America the Garden City influence was felt strongly after 1905. For the first time residential towns were designed by trained planners and architects, and the gridiron plan was discarded in favor of the Romantic curvilinear street pattern.

In addition to the new communities in the suburban belt, planning spread to the industrial towns in the South and West, where corporations were forced to provide homes for their employees, despite the earlier reaction to the Pullman strike. Kingsport, Tennessee, planned by John Nolen as early as 1910, got its start when in 1920 the Tennessee Eastman Corporation built its plant there. The town's development was guided by an improvement company. Kohler, Wisconsin, the home of bathroom fixtures, was another carefully planned town. One such community, Tyrone, New Mexico, had unusual architectural distinction. In 1917 Bertram Goodhue was called in by the Phelps Dodge Corporation to build a town for copper miners. The architect was at the height of his powers, having just completed the design for the San Diego Exposition of 1915; as he had done in the exposition, he accepted the Spanish Baroque of the Southwest as his style and laid out a plaza with a railroad station, office building, stores, movie theatre, church and hotel. Arcades joined the principal buildings, giving unity to the design and shade to the citizens. Tyrone was never finished; mining operations slackened with the end of World War I, but it remans one of the most successful industrial towns in America in its design. In the neighboring state of Arizona, at Ajo, today owned by the same corporation, another town was built by the architects Kenyon and Maine; although well designed, it is not the equal of Goodhue's.

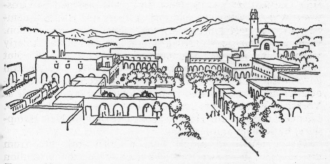

Tyrone, New Mexico. Center of the planned mining town, designed for the Phelps Dodge Corporation by the architect Bertram G. Goodhue in 1917.

In the spreading suburban scene the emphasis was on neo-Romantic planning and on greenery and too rarely on architecture. Only in the well-known suburb of Lake Forest did Howard van Doren Shaw in his arcaded market square (1913) attempt to give the suburb a solid architectural core. Much of the planning, when it broke away from the gridiron, confined itself to laying out streets and only occasionally a town center. The actual building was left to small developers or to future homeowners. "To the north of Zenith, among wooded hills above the Chaloosa River, there was being laid out one of the astonishing suburbs which have appeared in America since 1910," Sinclair Lewis relates in his novel *Dodsworth*. "So far as possible, the builders kept the beauties of forest and hills and river; the roads were not to be broad straight gashes but-

ting their way through hills, but winding byways, very inviting
. . . if one could only kill off the motorists. Here, masked
among trees and gardens, were springing up astonishing
houses . . ." Sam Dodsworth, the novel's hero, thought "that
there was something slightly ridiculous about mixing up Spain
and Devon and Norway and Algiers and transplanting them
to the sandy hills of a Midwestern town, where of late the
Yankees had trapped the Indians . . . but it was all a fantastic
play to him, very gay and bright after the solemn respectabilities and the disapproving mansard roofs of the older residential avenues of Zenith.

"Here, at least, he reflected, was all the color and irregularity
he had gone abroad to seek . . ."

New architectural groupings came to the suburb with the
migration of the apartment house from the central city.
Around 1910 Andrew J. Thomas, a New York architect, had
devised what he called "the garden apartment." Instead of
placing the front of his building flush to the street, he set it
back from the property line, having a spot of green in the form
of grass and shrubs about it. For the Queensboro Corporation at Jackson Heights, Long Island, he designed a large number of garden apartments facing on interior gardens. Thomas,
who also is credited with inventing the kitchenette, was able
to offer his clients a variety of economies by rearrangement of
the traditional apartment house plan, but in the process he
sacrificed architectural distinction. Unfortunately his imitators have not proved as conscientious in their work or as generous in the amount of space allotted to the apartments; the
result is that American suburbs are often burdened with extremely ugly multiple dwellings.

The most spectacular of the developments of this period,
dependent as they all were on good commuting service, was
Shaker Heights outside Cleveland. In 1916 Oris Paxton and
Mantis James Van Sweringen, two brothers who rocked the
financial world of the 1920's with their railroad operations,
bought 256 acres of farmland (later to be greatly expanded)
and built a rapid transit line to the heart of the city. Instead
of breaking up their land into lots of the same size and price,
they skillfully divided it with winding roads and preserved
the trees. They were thus able to dispose of lots of different
sizes to meet the needs of a wide income group. The future
citizens of Shaker Heights could then build their own houses,
fitting their needs and their incomes. Although they permitted freedom of style in the houses built, the Van Sweringens
took precautions to see that the designs were of a high standard and even had a board of architects pass on them before

they could be built. Colonial, English and French styles, reflecting suburban taste of the era, were favorites. Apartment houses were built near the station for those who wanted country living but did not want to own houses. Like so many American suburbs, Shaker Heights emphasizes greenery and nature rather than architecture and continues the tradition of the open lot which is so characteristic of the suburban scene. In many places in the East and all over the Middle West it is still considered unfriendly to build a fence or plant a hedge between one's neighbor and oneself.

Unlike the more spectacular Shaker Heights, the modest experiment of Radburn, New Jersey, closely echoed the cosy English Garden Cities of Letchworth and Welwyn. Many architects and planners contributed to the design, among them the architects Andrew J. Thomas, Henry Wright, Robert D. Kohn, Clarence S. Stein, Frederick L. Ackerman, and Thomas Adams. As at Forest Hills, a railroad station was nearby, but with the addition of two highways the community announced itself to the world as "The Town of the Motor Age." One of the main objects was to keep traffic at a minimum in the community, separating the pedestrian and the automobile, and to reserve as much space as possible for playgrounds and parks. This the designers accomplished by using dead-end streets with green walk-ways behind the houses. In contrast to Shaker Heights, Radburn has single-family dwellings of uniform Colonial design, some garden apartments, a small shopping center and schools. Despite the lack of financial success and the fact that it is swallowed today in the expanding suburbia of northern New Jersey, it remains a conspicuous offspring of the English Garden City in America.

By the time Radburn had been completed, the postwar building boom had ended, foreshadowing the depression of the 1930's. But the suburb had come to rival the city as a way of life. Magazines, newspapers, department stores, radio and salesmen began to give their undivided attention to this rich new market that was growing up outside the older centers. Interior decorators here found some of their best customers, and a new school of landscape gardeners, represented by Umberto Innocenti, Marian Cruger Coffin, Beatrix Farrand and Robert Ludlow Fowler, offered variations on the formal of the previous era for the large informal homes of the age. This world had its novelist in F. Scott Fitzgerald; he gives us pictures in *The Great Gatsby* of the Prohibition decade on Long Island's North Shore. The groundwork was being laid for the mass suburbs that were to come with the highways, with greater dependence on the automobile and truck, and with the easier home financing of the Federal Housing Administration.

4. The City Efficient

While the American city continued to rise at its center and to spread at its edges, an important change was taking place in its administration. An inherent part of the coming of age of the American city in the previous generation had been the call for good urban government. Gradually the movement gathered momentum as more and more people came to believe that mere political reform was not enough and that only scientific administration would meet the complex problems of the modern city. Great impetus was given the movement by the spectacle of Galveston ruined by a tidal wave in 1900 and helplessly disorganized after the disaster. One result was the creation of the so-called "commission" form of city government in which the municipality was governed by a small group of all-powerful elected commissioners without a mayor. The science of city government is as subject to fashion as anything else; a decade later the political scientists were extolling the council-manager form over all others. First instituted in Dayton in 1914, this system provides for an elected council and mayor who choose an expert, preferably a specially trained outsider, to govern the city much as the board of directors employs a president to administer the affairs of a corporation. America was harking back to a city official once popular in Italian municipalities of the Middle Ages, the famous podesta. The National Municipal League, under the leadership of Richard S. Childs and others, took up the new system, and except in the very largest cities it is today widely used throughout the country.

Paralleling these efforts came the creation of municipal reference libraries, private bureaus of municipal research, planning boards, unified budget systems and all the modern appurtenances of local government. Around 1913 universities began to train men as municipal administrators. In this way city governments followed in the wake of the federal and state governments on the march to efficient administration, until by the 1920's the scientific spirit reigned in the administrative field, and the timid efforts of the turn of the century were a thing of the past. The City Efficient was accepted as normal. Even city governments ruled by political machines saw that the people expected at least a minimum of service and employed engineers and other experts in responsible positions.

In the process the City Beautiful gradually disappeared. The "efficient" administrator had no time for the arts, which as often as not were termed "window dressing." Besides, some of America's better improvements had in the course of their construction been subject to corruption. The magnificent Pennsylvania capitol was touched by a scandal that occupied Harrisburg for a decade, although corruption had been exaggerated, as Governor Pennypacker proved. In carrying out the Chicago Plan the notorious machine of Big Bill Thompson profited by the large expenditures; the great work of Burnham was, in the end, brushed by scandal. The result was that the new efficiency refused to marry with the arts or forgot that they were a necessary part of the urban scene.

Typical of the changed attitude was the transition from civic design to zoning after 1916. The American Renaissance at its height had always seen city planning in visual terms, along with giving people more light, more air and better living conditions. The City Efficient saw city planning in terms of legal controls of the height and use of buildings, otherwise known as zoning. Zoning, like the organization of better municipal adminstration, has been a most valuable step forward, but it is only one of many instruments for building better cities.

A product of the City Efficient was the well-known Port of New York Authority, created by the states of New York and New Jersey in 1921. Despite its great harbor New York's port facilities had developed in a most haphazard fashion, as had the rail network supplying it. In 1917 100,000 freight cars backed up in the Jersey yards because of a near-breakdown at the port. In an effort to overcome the local municipal particularism and the railroad competition, the two states decided to create an administrative body to deal with special problems in and about the harbor. The first work of the Authority was an attempt to unify the railroad and the port facilities with belt lines, including freight tunnels under Manhattan, but its efforts came to nothing because of the opposition of the railroad corporations. The Authority, which is so powerful today, then turned to building facilities for automobile traffic. In 1929 it took over the Holland Tunnel built two years before; thanks to the revenue from the fifty-cent toll tax, it was able to build other tunnels, new bridges and connecting highways. The rise of the Authority began in that year, and today it is almost a government unto itself in the New York area. Enjoying quasi-independence and having its own tax system in the form of tolls, it continues its plans for redevelopment, leaving the railroads to fend for themselves.

Public works, chiefly highway building and street widening, held the attention of the City Efficient. Modern scientific road building began around 1912; four years later the Federal Aid Road Act was passed, foreshadowing generous government allocations for improved roads. Total revenue spent on highways went from over a billion dollars in 1921 to two billion by 1928. In the latter year the first cloverleaf intersection was built in New Jersey and two years later saw the construction of the Pulaski Skyway across the Jersey flats. At the turn of the century France had the best highway system in the world; thirty years later America was far in the lead. Efficiency and highway building went hand in hand. "The problem of housing, clothing and feeding the destitute loomed large neither in the public consciousness nor in local government," Robert Averill Walker has written of the 1920's. "In other words, the public works department far overshadowed the welfare department, and planning in confining itself to the former was completely in step with the times."

An embodiment of the new scientific spirit of that age is Robert Moses, who has played and continues to play so large a role in the affairs of New York City. A student at Yale, Oxford and Columbia, he worked for many years in private organizations devoted to bringing efficient methods to public administration. When Alfred E. Smith was governor of New York State, Moses entered government service, where he has remained ever since, making his great reputation as administrator of parks and highways. The man who had obtained his doctorate at Columbia University with the thesis, *The Civil Service of Great Britain*, was showing Americans the better European methods of good government. Today, although efficient administrative experts abound, he stands out as the great example of the "expediter" of the 1920's in contrast to the civic designers of the City Beautiful, Frederick Law Olmsted, Charles Follen McKim and Daniel H. Burnham, who were artists.

The shift thus passed to the legal, administrative and sociological side of city planning. Despite the insistence of Herbert Hoover that "enormous losses in human happiness and in money . . . have resulted from lack of city plans," and that "our cities do not produce their full contribution to the sinews of American life and national character," businessmen had lost interest in planning except in its utilitarian aspects that affected their own business. Zoning as a universal panacea actually proved a hindrance to planning, since it tended to fix the pattern of cities, just as it takes the emphasis off stricter regulation of housing conditions. Besides, there came the cry, ever more insistent on the part of the business community, that planning was a form of government interference with private enterprise. Escaping to the suburb at night, the businessman did not have to sleep in the city he had created. This attitude was reflected in the courts, where even zoning was not fully accepted until the early thirties. Private covenants, with their racial restrictions, were upheld as late as the 1940's, blocking any effective city planning in many places.

The most important contribution of the City Efficient at this time was the monumental *Regional Plan of New York and Its Environs*. Begun in 1922 and finished in 1929 under Charles D. Norton, Frederick A. Delano and Thomas Adams, a survey was made of 5528 sq. mi. with a resident population of 9,900,000, comprising northern New Jersey, southern New York State and southern Connecticut, and counting 500 municipalities. Thanks to the generous support of the Russell Sage Foundation, it was exceptional in its thoroughness and detail. In eight well-documented and illustrated volumes it dealt with the following subjects: Major Economic Factors in Metropolitan Growth and Arrangement; Population, Land Values and Government; Highway Traffic; Transit and Transportation; Public Recreation; Buildings—Their Uses and the Spaces about Them; Neighborhood and Community Planning; Physical Conditions for Public Services. Here, as in Burnham's plan for Chicago, the region was proposed as the base for the master plan, and although it was a private venture, it has had some influence in the later work carried on in and about the city. For example, it laid out the pattern of parkways and regional parks now almost completed around New York City.

5. *The New City Pattern*

The spread of efficiency in the 1920's was by no means universal. The largest cities wallowed under regimes of hopeless corruption, but no one seemed to mind any more than they objected to the bootleggers defying Prohibition. Few were aware of what was going on in the urban pattern, although sociologists were noticing alarming changes. For one thing, there was the migration from the city center. The wealthy had been the first to move, but the less affluent followed, to a new part of the city and not to a suburb. The teeming pre-1914 slums were emptying as the recent immigrants began to improve their position, and their children, dissatisfied with the old urban "side-glooms," found new homes elsewhere.

Further, the slums were not filling up as they had before the war, because immigration from Europe had been effectively cut off by the Immigration Act of 1924. It is true that Negro slums continued to increase in number and population and, in many places, rivaled the earlier holes. In Chicago gangsters committed murder in open daylight; people of position were horrified but went home to their suburbs with a sense of security. Beneath the prosperity which filled the air, a close examination showed that the problems were serious.

The late Professor Eduard C. Lindeman and Nels Anderson observed at the time that American cities appeared to be taking on a function-pattern which had the shape of concentric rings about a central core. The downtown central area served for offices, department stores, hotels and large theatres, marked by one skyscraper or a cluster of them. Then came a ring of slum dwellings, often once substantial houses and buildings that had been abandoned by the well-to-do, and in some instances being abandoned by the working people; here lived poor transients and here were marginal industries, cheaper stores and markets. The next ring consisted of the lower-income groups who lived near their work. Apartment houses and modest homes, and some industries, were to be found in the third. The fourth ring was made up of single residences, while the fifth and last zone consisted of residential suburbs, industrial towns and real estate developments. The pattern varied from city to city but was common to all of them in this period. Only with the crisis of 1929 did the rosy light disappear along with prosperity, and Americans discovered that their cities were riddled with blight and misery.

Despite the falling off of construction after 1925 and the warnings sounded by an agricultural slump, business was good and buildings continued to rise within the city. Many of the nation's tallest skyscrapers were begun in 1928 or 1929, to be finished after the collapse of the country's economy. The Cities Service Tower, the Bank of Manhattan Trust Company, the Irving Trust Tower, and the Chrysler Building were among the many in New York. In Pittsburgh the architect Charles Z. Klauder was supervising the construction of the "Cathedral of Learning." This forty-story tower, which was eventually to lodge the University of Pittsburgh, is said to have been inspired by John Ruskin; the architect rather seems to have looked to William Beckford, author of *Vathek,* for have we not here a Fonthill Abbey made permanent in steel and stone? (It contains wrought iron work by Samuel Yellin, the greatest American name in the art.) Chicago continued to build apartment houses on the near North Side, and the great statue of Ceres was not raised to the top of the imposing Board of Trade Building until 1930. This skyscraper is the focal point of Chicago's greatest canyon, putting a finishing touch to the monumental La Salle Street. New York led inevitably in the competition for the title of having the "Tallest Building in the World." The noise of pneumatic hammers filled the air with a confident note even in 1930. It is not difficult to imagine the enthusiasm of the architects Shreve, Lamb, and Harmon, watching the Empire State Building brought to reality. The project was so efficiently organized by the construction firm of Starrett Brothers and Eken that the steel was trucked to the site from the New Jersey railroad yards and hoisted directly into place without stopping traffic. The steel frame rose at the rate of a story a day for the whole 102 stories. In order not to lose time in letting the work gang of 3500 lunch away from the building, a temporary restaurant was established as the building progressed upward, much as Brunelleschi had arranged for the convenience of his artisans while raising the dome of Santa Maria del Fiore in fifteenth-century Florence. In 1930 the building was completed, to be for long a white elephant in a city that already had more than enough office space. But it was and remains the tallest building in the world and a monument to the age of the City of Towers.

The emphasis on construction, the bareness of the latter-day skyscraper, the low ceilings, and the poverty of decoration in the lobbies warned of a new trend. The classical was still there, but it was being stripped of all attraction, as painting and sculpture were being stripped of content. The American Renaissance had come to an end, even though one last private palace was to come to New York in 1932 in the home of William Goadby Loew on 93rd Street off Park Avenue, designed by the architects Walker and Gillette. The days of the great skyscraper were numbered. When they came to be built again, they would be shorn of their rich towers and left to stand uncrowned in the city. Forty years after Rupert Brooke's encomium, another famous English writer, Sacheverell Sitwell, was forced to remark that all of New York's new buildings seemed to be unfinished at the top, a trend which was confirmed by the example of Rockefeller Center.

Business came to a standstill in the spring of 1933; the old dreams had vanished and with them all traces of the City Beautiful. A new world was to confront the American people after 1933, and to the City Efficient would now fall the task of trying to solve a multitude of urban problems and of stemming the growing disorder in the urban scene.

PART VIII

The Regional City

1933-

1. *The New Deal and World War II*

With the collapse of the stock market in October, 1929, the American economy underwent a radical transformation. The system of finance capitalism which had prevailed for seventy-five years was gradually changed into a system of co-operative capitalism in which government, agriculture and even labor joined with business in guiding our economy. As more and more demands were made upon it, the American government, which up to then had largely been a regulatory instrument, began to take on responsibilities of welfare and service. Fiscal policy was geared to joint business and government enterprise as never before.

The first impact of the depression had disastrous results on our cities. Always precarious because of limited sources of city revenue, municipal finances were now burdened with the welfare problem as unemployment mounted to the alarming figure of 13,000,000 in 1933. Welfare, a service that had been the stepchild of the municipalities, now for a time took precedence over public works, as the unemployed continued to crowd into the cities.

At the same time a belated revolution occurred in American transportation. Despite the construction of extensive highways in the 1920's, the automobile, bus and truck had so far only begun to challenge the power of the railroad. Now the locomotive was deserted wholesale for the internal combustion engine, which was proving to be cheaper for haulage of people and goods. In 1926, for example, bus income was less than one fifth the passenger income of the railroads; by 1931 it was twice that of the steam giant. The shift to trucking was more significant because freight, after all, is the main source of railroad revenue. In the 1920's trucks confined

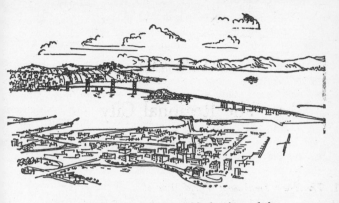

View of San Francisco Bay with the city and the
San Francisco-Oakland and Golden Gate Bridges.

themselves to transporting high-cost items within a fifty-mile
area; after 1929 they accepted cheaper goods for longer distances. In 1928 only 1.9 per cent of the cotton going to Houston, Galveston and Texas City was carried by truck; four
years later close to half the cotton moving to Houston alone
was hauled by highway. The automobile, the bus and the
truck now became necessities in the American economy.

When Franklin D. Roosevelt began the vast New Deal
program to relieve unemployment, highway construction was
among the first items on the list—especially the highways
going in and out of our great cities. Federal expenditure was
matched by state and city, and new authorities were created
in imitation of the pioneering Port of New York Authority.
New limited-access highways were built in and around New
York, making it easy to get in and out of the city from the
suburbs. The program gained momentum, and shortly before
America entered World War II the first modern long-distance
highway had been completed, the first link of the Pennsylvania Turnpike, which now runs from Philadelphia to Pittsburgh and beyond to the Ohio State line. A measure of the
growing size of all these improvements is the San Francisco-
Oakland bay bridge, eight and one-quarter miles long, completed in 1937. It was only under the New Deal that the
superhighway took an undisputed place in American life.
Until the early 1930's suburbs and real estate developments
generally stuck close to streetcar lines and railroads, as in the

instance of Shaker Heights. With the upswing of business after 1935 people discovered that the new highways had made the automobile handier for commuting, and real estate men began to build home developments away from transit and railroad lines.

For all the virtues of the automobile, the new expansion on the urban fringe would not have been possible had not home-financing been made easier and cheaper. High interest rates, second mortgages, short-term financing and other restrictions had made houses costly to buy for many Americans before 1933. With the creation of the government-guaranteed mortgage the whole financial picture changed. The innovation had no precedent here or abroad; the Roosevelt administration introduced the device as a means of reviving the construction industry in its fight on unemployment. In return for a small annual fee from the home-owner, the Federal Housing Administration (FHA) guaranteed the mortgage; with this backing, the mortgagee—a savings bank, life insurance company or other financial institution—asked only 4 per cent interest and fixed the repayment of the loan over a period of twenty-five years. This was in sharp contrast to 6 or 7 per cent interest, five-year terms, and second mortgages of the previous decade. By 1939 this New Deal instrument was creating the popular suburb on a scale never seen in America before.

Trying desperately to combat unemployment, the New Dealers with their legislation indirectly transformed the American physical scene. A case in point was Roosevelt's introduction of the forty-hour week legislation in 1933. The laborer may have joined the merchant on the Brooklyn ferry in the 1820's, but he was rarely to be found in any great numbers on the railroad, the horsecar or trolley going to the suburbs. Despite Harriet Beecher Stowe's expository on the virtues of the suburban cottage in the 1870's, the suburb remained the rich man's paradise until after 1933. What good were the railroad and the early highway if the American employee had to put in an average of sixty hours a week in 1910? Not until the 1930's did the forty-hour week become standard. Now the average American could commute daily like his wealthier neighbor and he had the weekend free to devote to his family and to home improvements. New shopping facilities followed the city migrant to the suburb; in the late thirties branches of downtown department stores were to be found in White Plains and Greenwich outside New York and in Evanston outside Chicago. Factories joined the migration as plant owners discovered that their workers could arrive by car. This last migration was especially noticeable in Southern California, which came to depend entirely on the automobile.

The physical planning of the New Deal brought important advances beyond the limited range of highways and public works. "It is time to extend planning to a wider field," announced President Roosevelt in 1933, and in this case he meant "a corporation clothed with the power of government, but possessed of the flexibility and initiative of a private enterprise." This was the Tennessee Valley Authority—a dream of Senator Norris's since 1922—which brought regional planning to the Tennessee River drainage basin. With thorough planning and carefully supervised projects, ranging from soil erosion and malaria control to the production of cheap electric power and improved navigation, a whole river valley has been transformed. The TVA proved its worth in World War II and today, despite some opposition and whittling down, its electrified farms and atomic cities stand before the world as outstanding examples of American ingenuity.

Among the men around Franklin Delano Roosevelt was the late Harold L. Ickes, former Republican and Bull Mooser, who carried on the tradition of an earlier Roosevelt in his work for preserving national parks and reservations. Shortly after the introduction of the TVA in 1933 Ickes, as Secretary of the Interior, appointed a National Planning Board (which eventually came to be known as the National Resources Planning Board), with instructions to outline suggestions for the development of the nation. Important studies were made of the American economy in all its facets, and for the first time the federal government recognized our cities as a key factor in the national economic life. It was a signal for the re-emergence of city planning from the doldrums into which it had fallen in the 1920's. In the first wave of the City Efficient, cities had turned to private consultants, who proved the chief figures in city planning in the 1920's. In the thirties, with the new interest in planning coming from the federal government, municipal commissions were revived and multiplied. Thanks to the unemployment relief funds at their disposal, cities were able to make thoroughgoing studies of local problems and, whenever possible, to direct their spending properly to answer the unemployment need and to improve conditions. The American people had become aware of the social and economic problems in their cities and they were determined to find out the exact nature of these problems and then proceed to solve them. The result was that planning became accepted by most municipal governments as an essential part of the administrative process, and although the results were often indirect, the city planning commissions, then as now, cannot be underestimated in their usefulness to city officials and city government.

One of the revelations of the new research was the extent of urban blight. Concomitant with the revival of city planning came the renewed interest in slum clearance and better housing. A start had been made by the President's Conference on Home Building and Home Owning created by Herbert Hoover. It had now become obvious to all that regulatory legislation was insufficient because private enterprise was not able to meet the needs of low-income housing. Only the government could provide adequate shelter for those unable to pay for homes and apartments, an extension of government authority now accepted as beneficial by leading real estate men. Publicly financed, publicly owned but built by private construction firms, a series of housing developments was begun by the federal government as part of the general works program in 1934. At the same time state and local governments set up special housing authorities. In 1937 the United States Housing Authority, since absorbed by the Housing and Home Finance Agency, was created by the federal government to subsidize local housing efforts. It was put under the direction of the able New York businessman, Nathan Straus. Whole sections of the worst slum lands in American cities were cleared and rebuilt, offering many Americans the minimum amenities at modest rent. With the coming of World War II the public housing program was co-ordinated with that sponsored by the Federal Housing Administration, "to see that the Army and Navy get what they need, when they need it, with no if's or but's." Despite the injunction for speed, design was not necessarily sacrificed in the process. As the administrator pointed out, "the defense housing program can create neighborhoods which contribute to decent living." All told, approximately 1,200,000 family units were built under the program, and despite the pressure of war, quality was maintained. By the end of the war, in addition to the numerous Federal Housing Administration agencies, there were 448 local public housing authorities in the cities and 368 in the counties.

In reviewing the projects built since the mid-thirties it is clear that the government went beyond the duty of supplying shelter and attempted to create a decent living environment for tenants and homeowners. Outstanding were the attempts of the Resettlement Administration in building "garden suburbs"—Greenbelt near Washington, Greendale near Milwaukee and Greenhills near Cincinnati. In the urban housing projects the South supplied the most interesting designs, notably in Jacksonville, Florida, by M. C. Greeley and Associates, and Robert Mills Manor in Charleston, South Carolina, by a group of seven local architects of whom Samuel Lapham was designated Chief Architect. In the redevelopment of the blighted area, a number of fine old buildings in the neighborhood, including the Marine Hospital and Jail by Mills, were successfully incorporated into a unified project. Of the war housing, the most discussed and approved example was Baldwin Hills Village in Los Angeles, by Reginald Johnson, Lewis Wilson, Edwin E. Merrill and Robert Alexander. This attractive "village" has the unusual feature of a strictly formal plan, a Jeffersonian concept rare in our time.

The public-housing projects differ radically from those built with the help of FHA mortgages on the question of segregation. The first important breakdown of racial segregation took place in certain public-housing projects in the late 1930's—a giant step forward—and although progress has been slow, the policy has spread to some private developments aided by the government.

The life insurance company housing that followed in the wake of government initiative has also produced changes in some cities. Beginning in New York in 1939 the Metropolitan Life Insurance Company built Parkchester with a population of 75,000 at a cost of $30,000,000. This was followed by the more famous Stuyvesant Town on the lower East Side, which tripled the density of the area it was built on. Chicago, Los Angeles, San Francisco and other cities can also point to life insurance company housing which is meeting the needs of middle-income families, although their overpowering masses of brick and steel may not point the way to better city planning.

Under the New Deal far more was done to improve cities and towns in America than at any period since the heyday of the City Beautiful movement. Parks, playgrounds, public swimming pools, paved sidewalks, new schools, better street lighting, art galleries and other necessities of a modern community were built all over the country. It is a fact that the American city took on new life during the administrations of the two Roosevelts, whose paramount interest was the conservation of our great forests and other natural resources.

Part and parcel of government relief for the unemployed, which was the key to the whole Roosevelt program, was the government support of the arts. Thanks to the initiative of the artist George Biddle and the enlightened administration of Edward Bruce, Forbes Watson and Holger Cahill, who

instituted broad new artistic policies, work relief was extended
to architects, painters, sculptors, writers, actors and musicians.
Many important projects were carried out, among which are
such landmarks in American culture as the American Theatre
projects, the Index of American Design, the Historic American Buildings Survey, and the federal guidebooks to our cities
and states. The decoration of public buildings, which had been
neglected in the 1920's, was carried out in hundreds of communities whose citizens had scarcely heard of the word "artist." There have been objections to much of the work done,
but it must be remembered that most of the artists were easel
painters, unaccustomed to mural work, and that experimentation was forced upon them. Over 3000 artists were employed,
and others were put to work on the recovery of our national
heritage. Numerous ancient buildings were restored and re-
paired, thus preserving them for future generations, and historic parks were brought back to life. The tragedy of the
art program lay in the fact that it was not made permanent;
its short life ended in 1943. Our tradition of government
patronage is sporadic; America is rare among nations in having no continuing public support of the arts.

2. *Victory and After*

Even for Americans World War II was an astonishing revelation of the nation's industrial power. Production reached
new heights, old industries developed new methods, and new
industries were created. The discovery and production of
atomic energy was the most spectacular development of all.
Many parts of the country, hitherto neglected, came to life
under the impetus of war production, the most conspicuous
being those in which the atomic energy towns were located.
Huge plants were built with the entire process of production
carried on under one roof, and whole cities rose to house the
large working force. In Oak Ridge, Tennessee, and Hanford,
Washington, the government built communities that made
the towns of World War I appear to be villages in comparison.

Equally astonishing was the increase of production after
the war. With employment at a high level, a million and
more homes a year became the rule, new highways joined
cities together, and new factories appeared on what had been
farmland only a few years before.

As a result the city has been touched by an explosion outward of wider scope than ever before. People are migrating
from the city center by hundreds of thousands. While the
population of the central cities rose 13 per cent between 1940

and 1950, their suburban population increased 35 per cent. Home ownership today is commonplace. For the first time in this century more than half the families of America live in their own homes, and the rate is climbing yearly. This would not be possible without the assistance to private industry and homeowners offered by the government-guaranteed mortgage, notably in the case of veterans' housing. The actual houses remain basically of balloon-frame construction with the addi-

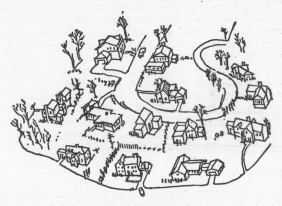

A high-income subdivision at
Great Neck, Long Island.

tion of some new materials. The suburban community is today built as a unit by one or two developers, whereas formerly individuals bought lots from the developer and built their own houses. Standardization and factory-made parts have brought unusual economies, particularly in kitchen and bathroom equipment, but have made for a certain sameness in the final product. Swirling ribbons of houses and lots are strung over the landscape, too often without the protection and softening of trees. The open lot remains standard, although today the garage or carport and its driveway have joined the house on the site. Shrubs and an occasional small garden enhance the setting, giving it a degree of individuality. The unexpected fertility of the new suburban families has made many of them "children's villages"; youth and youth's activities match the newness. School construction has quickly followed home building; education costs have been one of the unforeseen items of the homeowner's budget. To meet the shopping needs of the mass suburb, huge new shopping centers have been built;

most downtown department stores now have suburban branches and the ever present chain stores are well established in the growing suburb. Church building has undergone a rebirth, although the structures seem humble when compared with the earlier church buildings of America; important as religion is in these communities, their inhabitants do not demand elaborate houses of worship.

Today almost every family who can afford the change is moving to a suburb. The present extensive building of superhighways will open up even greater stretches of countryside to the developer, and the homeowner will follow. Working about the home has come to be the occupation of the American in his new-found leisure time. Prior to World War II the amateur house painter counted for little in the paint market; today it is estimated that 65 per cent of the house-paint sales go to the amateur. In the instance of wallpaper, he now buys 60 per cent as against 25 per cent in 1940. New tools have been designed to meet the market. When the paint roller replaced the brush, the amateur could do his own painting with ease. Other recent inventions are quick-drying odorless paints, new wallpapers, new tiles, new small automatic carpentry tools; they all help to make home ownership in the suburbs more attractive. Even post-hole machines pass from homeowner to homeowner in community fence-building programs, much as the lawnmower passed from hand to hand in its earlier days. In the foreseeable future—if the present trend continues and unless construction costs and land speculation price houses out of the market—the American will be found living only in the suburb. America today is not so much an urbanized as a suburbanized society.

Too often we forget that the suburb has been built at a terrifying cost. This lies not primarily in the *loss of the countryside* before the lengthening superhighway and spreading development; that is perhaps inevitable in the face of a growing population and the very natural desire of the American to own his own home. Rather, it lies in *the abandonment of the city,* the center of our civilization. Like the Mad Hatter at the tea party, who moved around the table using only the clean teacups and leaving the dirty ones behind him, we Americans move on to new land once we have exploited the old. The central city has seemingly been worked for all that it is worth and then abandoned for the suburban fringe. What is perhaps more frightening is that the suburban fringe of twenty-five or fifteen years ago is in its turn being worn out.

Urban blight, as we have seen, had long been pointed out by architects, sociologists, city planners, interested businessmen and others concerned with the city. As a whole the business community saw no solution, and it stood aside while the Roosevelt administration attacked the problem. Obviously little could be done unless business co-operated with government in meeting the problem, but there seemed no way to bring them together. Finally, around 1940, leading real estate men came forward with the suggestion that the government subsidize the real estate business in the city in the form of urban redevelopment and so meet the problem of blight. It came to work in this fashion: the municipality, through a special authority that has federal and state government assistance, purchases rundown sections of the city, clears them and then sells or leases them to developers for improvement. The state of Pennsylvania passed the first urban redevelopment act in 1945, and Pittsburgh businessmen were among the first to take advantage of it in rebuilding the "Golden Triangle." The great incentive to the new movement came with the passage of federal urban redevelopment legislation with a $500,-000,000 subsidy. Every city and town in the country has now another reason to examine itself to see how it can prevent further blight and, if possible, save the central districts.

The fact that business is once again taking an active interest in large-scale urban improvements is extremely important. Equally important is the provision in the federal and state laws that no community will receive a subsidy for urban redevelopment unless it is carried out according to a comprehensive city plan. In Philadelphia a comprehensive plan, including improvements to the Independence Hall area, has already been worked out for the whole city, and the urban redevelopment projects, already under way or in the planning stage, are the result of a collaboration among city planners, housers, architects, government departments and business groups.

If modern urban redevelopment, housing and even commercial structures (in some of which could once be found a tradition of art patronage) seem lacking in character and design by comparison with earlier American architecture and planning, the reason is not far too seek. The bare blocks and slabs that today pass for architecture are the result not of economy but of taste. A convenient artistic philosophy fell on starving soil during the Depression, when Thorstein Veblen's harsh condemnation of ornament and all objects dedicated to pleasure found a new vogue; at the same time "functional" architecture arrived from Europe and Frank Lloyd Wright's variations on the theme of Picturesque Secessionism were rediscovered. The new architecture and planning were called vari-

ously the "International Style," "Modern," "Functional,"
"Abstract," and "Organic," but perhaps a term applied to a
companion school of painting suits it best, Non-Objective. In
any case the movements stemmed from one root—the "form
follows function" theory and the emphasis on structure of
the nineteenth-century restorer, Viollet-le-Duc. The new taste
fitted perfectly the vogue for informality and casualness of the
artistic rich, who were the first to build in the Non-Objective
manner. Classicism has been stripped bare, construction has
been exposed, and a "casualness" of layout that is more dis-
orderly than any planning of the Age of Steam and Iron is
everywhere around us. The movement today shows signs of
exhaustion and is being subjected to criticism from many of
its earlier exponents, as well as from the public. The poverty
of a style that allows only "organic" nature as decoration—
a simple piece of driftwood in the lobby or a spindly tree
against a plain glass wall—appears poorer still when viewed
in the light of the variety and richness in which Americans
have built and will continue to build when they have rediscovered their past and their versatility.

3. *Traffic, Parking and City Planning*

Apart from the taste of the times, it is quite obvious to any-
one who has eyes, ears, feet, a home or a pocketbook that
today's city leaves much to be desired. Let us take the most
publicized problem and the one incurring the heaviest expenditures of public funds: *traffic*. In the next few years Detroit plans to spend $195,000,000 on expressways, or enough
to build a dozen large housing projects. Other cities have
highway programs of comparable size. If railroads were the
most spectacular contribution of the Picturesque Era to our
cities, then the new highways may be considered the major
contribution of our time. But they should not be welcomed
unquestioningly. The great highways have often created as
many new problems as those they were built to solve. Granted
that the new suburbs must have access to the central city,
we must be careful to see that we are not creating pythons
to strangle the suburbs as they are already strangling the city.
The conveniences of the highway—freeway, superhighway,
limited-access highway, parkway, turnpike, throughway—are
familiar to everyone; in fact, the modern city could not exist
without them. The task is to see that highway planning is
allied with city planning, a marriage of joint interests which
does not always take place today.

A commercial parking lot and a traffic jam.

In addition to the highway there is another unresolved dilemma facing the community. In an effort to get the automobile off the streets, city governments and private interests have created what is probably the worst blot on the American scene since the coming of the railroad yards—the open-air parking lot. The city can no longer smile, because so many of its teeth are missing. If Athena, the protectress of cities, should suddenly transform all these parking lots into beautiful public gardens, the resulting enchantment would still be mitigated by the fact that the holes in the urban fabric have prevented an orderly architectural grouping. Destructive of architectural effect and ugly to contemplate, these gaping holes of black-top or cinders, often with an attendant gas station, occur everywhere except in the most densely profitable shopping or financial districts. There, parking garages with cars in tiers or in underground excavations reveal the profit to be derived from high hourly charges to businessmen and shoppers.

Looking down from a skyscraper outside the golden center of a certain Midwestern city, it is possible to see that almost 50 per cent of the land, excluding streets, is today given over to parking lots. This is not where the drivers want to be—they have business nearer the central office blocks or in the department stores—but they have no choice. Few people realize that the lots given over to parking are often more profitable than building, and what was once the best residential area of the city is now a no man's land of shiny steel auto tops, broken occasionally by a mansard roof, a short brick row, or an ugly "diner." The place is empty at night, ghostly and silent like a painting by Edward Hopper, when the cars have all gone home to the suburbs and the only activity that gives it any life is absent.

Since the automobile will be with us for a very long time to come, and since our cities are becoming larger and more dependent than ever on the internal combustion engine, it behooves Americans to consider traffic routes in relation to the city as a whole. Instead of letting the useful machine take charge, we should relegate it to a position where it cannot imperil our nerves and our bodies or destroy the American city and suburb. If our cities were properly planned, we could ensure that traffic ran in its proper groove, separated from pedes-

Entrance to underground parking garage, Union Square, San Francisco.

trian movement and child play. We should ensure that fast-moving and slow-moving traffic be kept separate, so that high-speed routes did not run through residential neighborhoods. We could build more underground garages for cars, right beneath the buildings where the owners wanted to go, as San Francisco has done under Union Square or Buenos Aires below its opera house. Costly as they may be, we should build sunken and tunneled highways, like those crossing Central Park, instead of surrendering valuable park land to the cement ribbon and then calling it a parkway. We could attack the problem of overcongestion of downtown streets in a way that would render the automobile a slower and less efficient method of transportation—by reviving the idea of rapid transit, a public service that began in the hands of a "traction ring" and has fallen like a broken toy into the laps of local transit authorities.

It is ridiculous that urban transportation in New York City,

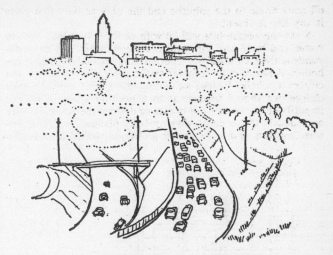

Cars disappearing into Los Angeles smog.

by fiat of the state legislature, is divided between a subway authority on the one hand and authorities for highways, bridges and tunnels on the other. The New York City Transit Authority and the Triborough Bridge and Tunnel Authority, for instance, should be combined and the tax collected on automobile drivers used to improve the city's rapid transit system, and both should be made responsible to the mayor and the Board of Estimate rather than to the state. The Port of New York Authority should pay a subsidy from its rich toll-tax revenue to the dilapidated Hudson Tube system, which provides rapid transit between New York and New Jersey. The neglect of rapid transit in favor of the "bossy" highway, as Henry James would have called it, is one of the follies of our time, especially in view of the tremendous improvement that has taken place in America's great railroad system, now almost wholly dieselized or electrified. It is the height of inefficiency, too often condoned by "efficiency experts," to accept the departmentalizing of urban transport which appears to be part of the mania for "independent authorities." Certainly the new Oxy-Muffler, a catalytic device invented by Eugene Houdry to destroy leaded gasoline fumes, should be made mandatory for all automobiles, buses and trucks operating within city limits. There are many ways to make the American city and the automobile more compatible, ranging from super-blocks, in which the car impinges only on the edges, to eliminating noxious gasoline fumes, and they all involve an acceptance of the principle of city planning which, with civic design, has proved to be the only way of making any community safe, beautiful and attractive to live in.

Looking down on the scenes of present-day disorder, the American may shake his head and wonder how chaos can ever be replaced by planned amenity. In the bustling, the moving about, the tearing down and the building up, the occasional reward seems to be overwhelmed by discouraging cost. But there is reason to be hopeful; our history shows that we have been equal to extraordinary emergencies, *once we have realized their nature and problems.* If this book has emphasized the more interesting aspects of man-made America, it is to give us some notion of our rich tradition in town and city building, forgotten or denied. It is true that today our city has few champions among us and our town is sacrificed to the booming highway. *But this is because we have been looking in another direction.* "Even the small town is too large," warns Frank Lloyd Wright, who paradoxically enough is building a Non-Objective museum in the heart of New York City. "It will gradually merge into the general non-urban development. Ruralism as distinguished from urbanism is American and truly democratic." This illusion of rural America lingers on among architects, critics, novelists, soap-opera fans, editorial writers and movie-makers. "Soapland," the country of the "soap opera," as James Thurber reminds us, is largely "the perpetuation of the ancient American myth of the small town" of rural America, although it comes to us over the airwaves from the big city radio and television station. Those who find rural life more desirable must today bring the city with them. It is part of our bag and baggage, and there is no escaping from it. Wright may find refuge in the Wisconsin hills or the Arizona desert, but the American housewife, in her kitchen, must confine her dream of the good life to the soap opera. The anodyne has obscured the reality that is all around.

We have seen that the two major forces of technology which have created the new landscape are the railroad and the automobile, with their accompanying inventions of steel construction, electric power and electronics in the form of telephone, radio, television and the airplane. They made new cities inevitable and exploded old cities outward from their centers. A new and most certainly more important development in technology, atomic power, by the inevitable variety of its uses brings only the realization that the city can now be expanded still further. Decentralization, as the city planners call it, is a force no longer to be resisted. If it is true, as the advocates of smallness insist, that these new technological forces can be directed toward the abolition of the city and the creation of smaller living and working units scattered over the face of the country, it is equally true that "recentralization" can accompany "decentralization" to create a more palatable and realistic answer to the problem, a solution involving a proper relationship between city, town and country, with less dislocation and loss of cultural momentum. "Smallness" is no answer to our problem today; it was a necessity that the city in our time should break up the small community in which "the range and diversity of interests are kept within the bounds and forms of a narrow context." The pattern today is an expanding one that, with creative transformation, will grow in range, complexity and richness. There is no need to be afraid of "bigness"; it is a challenge and contains rewards if we are willing to master its problems.

Americans have been hesitant to accept the contribution of the urban community, just as in the 1900's they could not grasp the meaning and value of the giant business corporation. The giant corporation, which enabled us to raise our standard of living by producing great quantities of goods more cheaply, made inevitable the rise of the labor union, an instrument for human rights in the face of advancing technology. The mass production of automobiles, among other results, has brought forward the engineer and his techniques to provide in the superhighway, the cloverleaf and the great tunnels and bridges a suitable form for rapid vehicular transport. The conservationist has helped us preserve whole sections of the American countryside for our pleasure and for the preservation of our natural riches. Contractors build the tallest buildings in the world, part boast, part enterprise, part necessity, to show that building can use technology to human ends. Man has conquered space and time, making the world one. But in the city the expansion to twentieth-century measurements has not yet occurred, except in a crude and timid form. The instruments are there, with some adaptations to be made and a few new ones to be created.

Everyone knows by now that New York is not just Manhattan Island but that, since 1898, it has been officially and politically five great boroughs extending into Long Island and including the whole of Staten Island. Other cities,—Boston, with its Metropolitan District Commission, and Los Angeles with its county planning commission—have attempted to recognize and deal with "bigness" in various ways, such as annexation, state and federal assistance, the creation of autonomous authorities and other devices. However, it is not generally recognized, except by experts, that *all over the country* wherever a city of any size exists there is a magnet and a concentration which is the heart of possible regional expansion, much of which has already occurred without preconceived planning or attention. There are at least 178 of these concentrations, and probably many others whose influence is much greater than their mere size would indicate. Furthermore, many of these are coterminous or so closely spaced that they effectively combine into a unit larger than themselves. As Professor Victor Jones of Wesleyan has pointed out, an urban core runs from Bridgeport, Connecticut, to Springfield, Massachusetts, which contains 1,500,000 people in an area actually smaller than many single large cities. People travel back and forth in this urban area to work and play; they live on its edges in what are still considered country towns and, to all intents and purposes, are part of what we shall call a *Regional City*. In the future, the city will have the geographical aspect of a region, an area, let us say, within a fifty-mile radius of the main center of the metropolis. It is the area whose boundary is set by the local radio and TV station, by the commuting distance, and by the circulation of the metropolitan newspaper. Although the Regional City will assume the name of the metropolis, every community within the region will retain its importance, and new communities will be created, even within the metropolis, to meet the local needs of the people.

To take full advantage of the assets of this Regional City, much has to be done to remove inequalities, ignorance and prejudice—the "small-town" thinking that exists instead of twentieth-century urban thinking. Industries in the area pay taxes to the local community in which they settle, while other communities having no industries must house workers of those same factories and find the wherewithal to provide schools for the children. Other communities, beginning as exclusive residential areas, have zoned themselves to keep out not only industry but low-income families. In creating exclusively residential suburbs they have discovered that their revenue is too small to pay for the facilities demanded by irate families, who in the city had at least a few cultural facilities to which they could turn and now find themselves paying heavily for schools, roads and a new library. The desire to keep out industry—to make a never-never land of classless American homeowners on standard plots—has had its inevitable result. A small house that yields perhaps $50 for

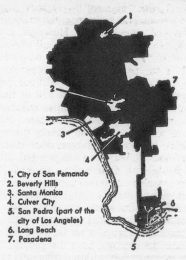

1. City of San Fernando
2. Beverly Hills
3. Santa Monica
4. Culver City
5. San Pedro (part of the city of Los Angeles)
6. Long Beach
7. Pasadena

Map of the city of Los Angeles, including its port of San Pedro and the communities engulfed by the municipality.

school purposes in taxes annually may contain two children who cost $200 each to maintain in the public schools for a year. Apart from recognizing the necessity of a revision of the taxing system, authorities and the public must be convinced of the desirability of having noiseless, smokeless, industrial plants strategically located in suburban communities, to contribute to the tax roll and school costs, provide welcome employment and reduce commuting distances. Warehousing, research laboratories and printing firms have already been accepted in some communities, but the list must be expanded.

The exclusively residential community also creates problems it does not have to solve, and a chain reaction sets in. Beside every Scarsdale there is a Tuckahoe, where people who work for the well-to-do live. How different this is from our earlier American tradition, which allowed people of all classes to mingle together, as they still do in communities where people live as well as work! Something of this mixture should be retained in new communities; it is healthier for democracy, which will surely suffer if residential suburbs continue to refuse public housing projects, business firms, industry and rest camps. Without these they will remain smug, lackluster backwaters, and the city will suffer along with them.

The Regional City will mean co-operative effort for certain services, taxes and administration, and local autonomy for others. It need not mean "bigness" in little affairs that are best handled locally; in fact the voice of the people may be heard louder and more effectively when incompatibilities between town and city or town and town are ironed out. Certainly, in all the history of urban life, co-operation has been most noticeable when an aim is clearly stated and understood. But the idea that in order to have a better life the unit, now existing, must be expanded into a larger whole is not yet grasped by many people, including those in high places who are unable or unwilling to recognize change when they see it taking place before their eyes. We are stumbling in the throes of another expansion, and there is not yet the vision to control it as there was in the time of Andrew Haswell Green, who fitted the instrument of government to the situation of an expanding city at the turn of the century.

The "Higher Provincialism" of the American philosopher Josiah Royce, which today would be called "Regionalism," could find its instrument in the Regional City. "The present state of civilization, both in the world at large, and with us, in America, is such as to define a new social mission which the province alone, but not the nation, is able to fulfill." The vigorous development of a highly organized provincial life today can only take place in the Regional City, containing as it does all the elements—industry, homes, farming, services, higher educational and cultural institutions—that are necessary for twentieth-century life. "As our country grows in social organization, there will be, in absolute measure, more and not less provincialism among our people." Just as Royce thought the province could save the individual in the early 1900's, so today the Regional City can encourage individual development and social co-operation—if it is once recognized as the new unit of society and national life.

How will the Regional City be different enough from the city as it exists to capture the imagination, stir the pride and give the pleasure that is necessary but lacking in the city we know? First, it will have a wide geographical area to include all the territory within the range of influence of the urban centers. Second, it will have a considerably diversified economic base, including heavy and light industry, large and small business, agriculture and services (administrative, medical, educational and cultural). Third, it will be large enough to include the essential facilities for all types of human activity, from the processing of raw materials to the enjoyment of wild nature, as well as opera, ballet, symphony, art museums, scientific museums, art schools, and institutions of higher learning. Fourth, the present cities and towns within the Regional City will have their own governments, over which will be an instrument similar in form to a metropolitan council to govern the whole. The towns might come to have the status of boroughs, and the central city be broken up to form similar boroughs, each with their elected officials. The new Metropolitan Corporation of Toronto in Canada points the way. In any event, the state governments must give the municipalities greater home rule and a greater share of the tax revenue. For example, the gasoline tax, which in many states is reserved for highway construction, should be also allocated for urban redevelopment and improved rapid transit. Fifth, the Regional City will have the benefit of planning, so that the smaller units will be properly related to larger ones, so that expansion can be controlled, so that a form can be achieved employing all resources, and so that the local communities will preserve their individual qualities within the great metropolitan whole. Sixth, the arts will have a decisive role in reviving the American tradition and making our communities more beautiful in every way.

4. The American Tradition

The role of the arts is the most neglected of all the instruments needed for the creation of the new city. While school-building programs and highway plans receive their fair share of attention today, the fine arts are not yet given their due in the United States. This is partly because art is linked with tradition, and the American tradition in the arts is not yet widely known. "By studying the works of the old masters," the painter Washington Allston advised a student, "you will imbibe their spirit insensibly, otherwise you will as insensibly fall into the manner of your contemporaries."

Many Americans today are unaware how useful a knowledge of tradition can be—to fuse the Future into the Past, as Emerson advised, and to save that which seems worth saving, not only in the form of physical salvage, but in the realm of ideas. If methods of colonial town planning can guide us in the building of new industrial towns, or vanished American residential squares can serve as a model for building in the Atomic Age, then we would be foolish to ignore the lesson. Constant reminders of better things are visible everywhere in the United States; a Boston house plan, proportions of a room

in Westover, a street in Santa Fe, even the sorriest collection
of frame buildings calling itself a town in Minnesota may be
the theatre of some festival or custom, adding color to the
drab surroundings. We should be loath to lose all this, and
yet we do not know or cherish the smallest part of what we
can now call with certainty a great cultural heritage, a heritage
covering the entire country and reaching out into other lands
and periods. This heritage is being destroyed all around us.

Arrows show proposed rerouting of traffic around old
Colonial town center, Ridgefield, Connecticut, in a
study sponsored by the local League of Women Voters
and undertaken by planning students at Yale University.

Fortunately a beginning has been made in this country to re-
discover the architectural and decorative art traditions: in
the pages of the *Architectural Record* from 1891 to 1920, in
the Index of American Design, in the Historic American Buildings Survey, by the historians of the National Park Service
and in the work by individual art and architectural historians
who, since World War II, have turned to their own country's
past as well as to Europe's. Fortunately, also, at Newcastle,
Delaware, at Winston-Salem, North Carolina, at Economy,
Pennsylvania, at Williamsburg, Virginia, at Deerfield Village,
Massachusetts, at New Salem, Illinois, and elsewhere, the
restorer and preserver has been put to work to save a few
examples of town building for future eyes to enjoy. Of how

much more remains to be explored and evaluated, this book has given some indication. With the reservoir of the past to draw upon, the future can be given some direction.

It is not generally known that in most areas of the country a community not only has power to control the land uses within its boundaries but also, and this is entirely constitutional, to control esthetic appearance. While it is arguable that much harm can be done in the name of esthetic control, such considerations based on a firm knowledge of the arts and tradition have great validity. A community might start by making a checklist of dangers, losses and needs, a balance sheet of its resources in civic art, from the humblest park bench to broad-scale esthetic problems, fitting the scale of action—be it federal, state, municipal, institutional or private enterprise—to the discoveries made. A short checklist follows:

Are the town approaches cluttered with objectionable signs, shoddy roadside stands and automobile graveyards? Have unsightly poles and utility wires been replaced by underground cables?

Is there a well-planned and beautiful civic center that reflects the spirit of the community? Does it contain adequate cultural facilities? Have mural decorations and historical paintings been considered for public buildings? Are these fountains, gateways, arches or other evidences of civic art placed where people can enjoy them as part of the city plan?

Has sculpture been made part of the town's architecture and public squares? Has the community honored local and national figures and events by statues and other memorials? (The sculptor Bartholdi intended to gild the Statue of Liberty in the manner of the ancients. Should not his intention be honored in our own time?)

Are there facilities and settings in the community for pageantry, displays, celebrations and demonstrations? New Orleans has a city decorator for its Mardi Gras pageant—is the city in question decorated for important local festivals? Are the Fourth of July and other national occasions being celebrated in the great American tradition?

Does the community have a cast and model museum, like the one in the Carnegie Institute in Pittsburgh, where all can see copies of great sculpture and whole façades, as well as models, of famous buildings? Paris and Rome have their cast museums, why not a museum for Ameri-

can and foreign monuments in every city in the country?
Copies of the great works (pictures included) will serve
to inspire civic design.

Is there a civic art commission, as well as a city planning commission?

Are the parks sufficient in size and distribution for the
population? Are the existing ones run down? Do they
contain enough public diversions? Have recreation areas
outside the city been acquired? Is the park system being
invaded by new highways?

Are slum areas being cleared and replaced by well-
planned housing? Are those responsible working in the
best traditions of American design or are they building
soulless blocks in monotonous rows? Has any attempt been
made to renew and rehabilitate blighted areas worth saving? If so, are the restorations being done with imagination?

Has factory design and location been considered by
the community?

Do the suburbs have proper central squares identified
by a beautiful civic building? Has consideration been
given to building suburban houses around courts and
squares instead of in endless ribbons? Have all the possibilities of different buildings types and arrangements
been studied? Has subdivision control been properly exercised?

Is there a well-organized restoration program, either
private or municipal, for preserving buildings and parts
of the community of historic or architectural interest?
(For information on how to go about saving important
historic or architectural structures, the reader is advised
to write to the National Trust for Historic Preservation,
712 Jackson Place, N. W., Washington, D. C.) Is there
a state or local ordinance preventing demolition or change
in areas which the community cherishes, as in the historic district of Charleston or the Vieux Carré in New
Orleans?

And all Americans might ask themselves the following questions concerning the federal city:

Has the embellishment of our national capital been made
a continuing effort? Does Washington have an opera house
with a permanent opera company, a ballet theatre, several
repertory theatres, an adequate concert hall, and all the other
appurtenances of a great capital city? Is Washington being
beautified in the spirit of Jefferson, Brumidi and Burnham?

Have the elements of grandeur, magnificence and glory, as well as beauty, been accepted here as American?

And how can the blessings of art be brought to the American city? The United States is becoming too big and important to hope that our cities will be improved by private help alone. Everything should be done to encourage joint business and government enterprise, with one proviso: government must do more than it is doing today.

The late urban sociologist Louis Wirth gives the reason: "Coupled with the archaic basis of urban revenue, the flight from the older areas has brought many of our cities to the verge of bankruptcy. The municipalities, having inherited the liabilities of those who have fled from the city and being unable to tap the assets that are piling up in the suburbs, are unable, without the aid of the states and the federal government, to maintain the minimum services for their people."

This is the key to the situation: the federal government aids in housing, urban redevelopment and other civic enterprises; so do the state governments. The cities cannot undertake these responsibilities alone, and it is not likely that they can or will develop civic art programs on the scale that is needed by themselves. The whole question of civic art should be tackled on the national and state levels, as well as on the municipal level, if the cities are to be saved from blocks of barrack-like housing and unimaginative urban redevelopment projects.

As Max Wehrly of the Urban Land Institute reminded Americans recently, "We are *just beginning* the mammoth job of revamping our older areas to bring them into line with our current demands for urban use." There are going to be tremendous changes in the cities in the next twenty years, and it would be a tragic mistake to rebuild them, forgetting the concept that cities are, or can be, man's supreme creation. The cities can and should pay a conscious tribute to our civilization instead of being an unconscious revelation of it. Artists should be employed in all urban redevelopment projects, not only to embellish the buildings but to collaborate on their form and design, as Michelangelo collaborated on the Campidoglio in Rome and Augustus Saint-Gaudens on the plan of the Mall in Washington.

To this end it will be necessary to set up federal and state aid programs for civic art, and one of the first steps should be the creation of a Department of Fine Arts in Washington. The Congress is not unaware of this necessity, several bills with this aim having been introduced in recent years, among them a bill by the Honorable Charles R. Howell, which in addition would ensure that artists be employed on public buildings in order "to encourage and assist in surrounding our houses, grounds and towns with a maximum of beauty." These are Jefferson's words—a reminder, where the arts are concerned, that there is still much to be done on all levels of government.

Encouragement from the national level would require local participation to make it real. In a democracy the well-springs of popular taste should above all else be considered. Public buildings, streets and parks all need the inspired hand of the artist, and there is good reason to hope that, as in seventeenth-century France and in the period of the young Republic in America, the creation of public works of art would encourage the initiative of businessmen and private patrons along these lines. On the state and local level we need a revival of civic art commissions. We now have over 2000 local planning commissions in the United States, but they have not taken on the functions of the municipal art commissions. The municipal art commissions in San Francisco, Baltimore, Philadelphia and New York are among the very few left. We need the muralist in our cities, the mosaicist and the sculptor, the artist in metal, wood, cloth, glass and ceramics, and the other decorative arts; we need a re-emphasis of symbolism and allegory to touch the springs of national and local pride; we need these things on the street corner, the housing project, on the very pavement of the city itself. We will not get much public support for improving our cities unless we include in our aim the positive attempt to make them more beautiful. People will not be persuaded to return to the central city—they will not even take an interest in the city—unless in future programs of redevelopment there is a renaissance of civic art and a collaboration of artists to embellish it. That is why it is necessary to revive the idea of the City Beautiful, broadening it to include the concept of art for everybody, and subsidizing the artist along with housing, urban redevelopment and public works, which we have been subsidizing since the end of the war and which today indeed cannot be carried out in any other way.

More than mere planning for economic and social necessities is needed to meet our expanded ideals of today. It is not enough to examine the economic conditions of Americans and to improve their material well-being; only the embellishment of the community and the presence of the arts will feed its pleasures, its spiritual hunger and its local patriotism. "Finally, let the province more and more seek its own adornment," continues the appeal of Josiah Royce.

Here I speak of a matter that in all our American communities has been until recently far too much neglected. Local pride ought above all to center, so far as the material objects are concerned, about the determination to give the surroundings of the community nobility, dignity, beauty . . . We Americans spend far too much of our early strength and time in our newer communities upon injuring our landscapes, and far too little upon endeavoring to beautify our towns and cities. . . [He had here his native San Francisco in mind.] I can strongly insist that no community can think any creation of genuine beauty and dignity in its public buildings or in its surroundings of its towns and cities too good a thing for its own deserts. For we deserve that in such realms we can learn how to create or enjoy, or to make sacrifices for. And no provincialism will become dangerously narrow so long as it is constantly accompanied by a willingness to sacrifice much in order to put in the form of great institutions, of noble architecture, and of beautiful surroundings an expression of the worth that the community attaches to its own ideals.

Memorial column on Beacon Hill in Boston, designed by Charles Bulfinch in 1789.

An early proponent of world government, the philosopher well knew that the universal community depends for its strength on the happiness and well-being of its smallest units.

We Americans have dangerously neglected the visual reflection of the love we hold for our country. Whereas in the time of Washington and Jefferson the planning and embellishing of the community often went hand in hand with that love, we have forgotten that our aims and aspirations must have symbols, made permanent by the genius of the artist, in the form of great squares, great avenues, carefully tended forests, monumental buildings, great historical murals, allegorical paintings, noble settings, beautiful fountains, triumphal arches and columns.

Columns? On Beacon Hill in Boston, behind the Massachusetts State House, there is a Doric column bearing an American eagle. Designed by Charles Bulfinch, the monument was raised in 1790 on what was then a bare hilltop to commemorate the heroes of the Revolution. Today, in the shadow of the State House, it stands in the middle of a parking lot. Let the curious pick their way through the parked cars to examine it close at hand. Here is the message at its base, reserved for the silent automobiles:

AMERICANS

WHEN FROM THIS EMINENCE

SCENES OF LUXURIANT FERTILITY

OF FLOURISHING COMMERCE

AND THE ABODES OF SOCIAL HAPPINESS

MEET YOUR VIEW

FORGET NOT THOSE

WHO BY THEIR EXERTIONS

HAVE SECURED TO YOU

THESE BLESSINGS

Our columns are in parking lots, our city plans and civic designs are scattered before the onrush of the highway and our art is confined to museums. Bulfinch's column is symbolic of our neglect. Let us explore America again, for if we are to know where to aim, we must see what has gone before us. We must discover the origins of American communities, see the forces that have shaped them, learn to respect the countryside about them and study the arts that have given them beauty. With the economic opportunity at hand, we will create new communities, new towns and new cities that can be at once the pride of the region, the pride of the nation and the glory of the America we offer to the world.

PART IX

The Seven Eras of the American City

A key to significant related factors in the growth, structure and planning of the American community.

Developments are noted in their period of greatest importance and not necessarily at the time of their inception.

The obverse of the Seal of the United States. Benjamin Franklin, among others, was responsible for its design. It is most commonly seen on the one-dollar bill.

FIRST ERA OF CITIES   1607–1776

The Colonial Pattern

NATIONAL
ECONOMY:

Colonial Mercantile Capitalism

POLITICAL AND
SOCIAL FACTORS:

Calvinism
Anglican Protestantism
Slavery
Indentured Servants
Proprietors' Land Holdings
Squatters
Long-lot System of Farming
Immigration: English
      Negro
      Scotch-Irish
      Germans

TRANSPORTATION:

Ocean and River
Stagecoach and Wagon

TECHNOLOGY:

Handicrafts
Small Water Mills
Forges

BUILDING TYPES:
(Structural and
Functional)

Mortised and Tenoned Frame Construction
Log Cabin
Three-Story Brick House
Plantation House

ARCHITECTURAL
STYLE:

Echo of the Medieval
American Baroque (Colonial)
The Formal Garden

PLANNING AND
CIVIC DESIGN:

Orthogonal, or Gridiron, Plan
Baroque Planning (traces of radial planning)
Pennsylvania "Dutch" Linear Towns
Fortification Plans
Public Greens and Squares

URBAN FORMS AND
EXAMPLES:

Agricultural Market Town (New England "Village," Southern Town)
Religious Communities (Bethlehem, Pa.)
Seaports and Mercantile Cities (Boston, Newport, New York, Philadelphia, Charleston)
Southern Courthouse Towns (Gloucester and Yorktown, Va.)
Colonial Capitals (Annapolis, Md., Williamsburg, Va.)
Stagecoach Towns (Morristown, N. J.)
Head-of-Navigation Towns (Hartford, Conn., Richmond, Va.)
Fortified Towns (Albany, N. Y., Fredericka, Ga., St. Augustine, Fla.)

SECOND ERA OF CITIES   1776–1825

The Young Republic

NATIONAL ECONOMY:	National Mercantile Capitalism
POLITICAL AND SOCIAL FACTORS:	American Revolution (1776–1781) First Westward Movements beyond Alleghenies Freehold System of Land Ownership Louisiana Purchase (1803) War of 1812 Immigration: English French
TRANSPORTATION:	Ocean and River Turnpikes
TECHNOLOGY:	Small Industrial Plants Textile Mills
BUILDING TYPES: (Structural and Functional)	Urban Row House Wooden Factory Buildings Merchants' Exchange Government Building Colleges Athenaeums Theatres
ARCHITECTURAL STYLE:	Continuation of American Baroque American Roman English Landscape Garden Urban Pleasure Gardens
PLANNING AND CIVIC DESIGN:	Monumental Radial Plan (Washington, Buffalo, Detroit, Indianapolis) Residential Squares
URBAN FORMS AND EXAMPLES:	Market Town (Rome, N. Y., Lexington, Ky.) Small Industrial Town (Pawtucket, R. I.) Mercantile City (Baltimore, Md.) State Capitals (Montpelier, Vt., Columbia, S. C.) The National Capital (Washington, D. C.) Spas (Ballston, N. Y., Saratoga, N. Y., Virginia Springs, Va.)

THIRD ERA OF CITIES 1825–1850

The Romantic Era

NATIONAL
ECONOMY:
   Industrial Capitalism

POLITICAL AND
SOCIAL FACTORS:
   Rise of Roman Catholicism
Mormonism
American Industrial Revolution
Opening of Erie Canal (1825)
Mexican War (acquisition of Texas and California)
California Gold Rush
Immigration: Irish
            German
            Continued English

TRANSPORTATION:
   Steamboat Transportation
River and Canal
Horse-drawn Omnibus
Short-distance Railroad Lines

TECHNOLOGY:
   Large Water-power Mills
Gas Light
Coal Mining (anthracite)

BUILDING TYPES:
(Structural and
Functional)
   Balloon-frame Construction   Banks
Southern Mansion House   Hotels
Customs Houses   Villas
Warehouses

ARCHITECTURAL
STYLE:
   Romantic Revivals: Greek Revival
                Gothic Revival
                Tuscan Revival
The Romantic Garden (Andrew Jackson Downing)
The "Rural Cemetery" (Mt. Auburn Cemetery, Cambridge, Mass.)

PLANNING AND
CIVIC DESIGN:
   Courthouse Square of the Midwest and Deep South (Peoria, Ill., Oxford, Miss.)
Riverside Promenade (New Richmond, Ohio)

URBAN FORMS AND
EXAMPLES:
   Industrial Town (Lowell, Lawrence, Mass.)
Mercantile and Industrial City (New York, Philadelphia)
River and Canal Cities (Cincinnati, O., St. Louis, Mo., Rochester, N. Y.)
Early Mining Towns (Pottsville, Carbondale, Pa.)
Lumber Towns (Bangor, Me.)
Utopian and Sectarian Communities (New Harmony, Ind., Oneida, N. Y.)
Metal Industry Towns (Housatonic Valley Towns, Conn.)
Linear Road Towns (New Concord, O., Centerville, Ind.)

FOURTH ERA OF CITIES   1850–1880

The Age of Steam and Iron

NATIONAL
ECONOMY:
Finance Capitalism, First Period: Rise of the Financier

POLITICAL AND
SOCIAL FACTORS:
Civil War (1861–1865)
Emancipation of Slaves
Homestead Act (1862)
Three Railroad Lines Cross Alleghenies (1852)
Transcontinental Railroad (1869)
First Great Strikes
Immigration: German   Swedish
           Irish   Jewish
           English   Canadian

TRANSPORTATION:
First Railroad Age (beginning of the railroad network)
Horsecar
Steel Bridges
Trunk Railroad Lines

TECHNOLOGY:
Steam-powered Mills   Telegraph
Coal Mining (bituminous)   Oil Drilling
Non-ferrous Metal Mining   Pressed Brick
Cast-iron Construction

BUILDING TYPES:
(Structural and
Functional)
Wood and Brick Tenements
Cast-iron Front
Brownstone Houses (eastern)
Commercial "Blocks"
Department Stores
Gasometer
Primary Public Schools

ARCHITECTURAL
STYLE:
Picturesque Revivals:
       Ecclesiastical Gothic
       Ruskinian Gothic
       Second Empire (mansard roof)
       Viollet-le-Duc   ⎫
       Eastlake   ⎬ Gothic
       R. Norman Shaw ⎭
       Queen Anne
       Richardsonian Romanesque
The Picturesque Park (Frederick Law Olmsted)

PLANNING AND
CIVIC DESIGN:
Curvilinear Suburban Plan (Llewellyn Park, N. J., Riverside, Ill.)
The Residential Avenue
Picturesque Landscaping

URBAN FORMS AND
EXAMPLES:
The Railroad City (Philadelphia, Chicago)
Bituminous Coal Towns (Connellsville, Pa.)
Western Mining Towns (Virginia City, Nev.— silver; Placerville, Cal.—gold; Butte, Mont.— gold, silver, copper)
Oil Boom Towns (Titusville, Pa.)
Resort Towns (Newport, R. I., Atlantic City, N. J.)

FIFTH ERA OF CITIES 1880–1910
The Expanding City

NATIONAL
ECONOMY:

Finance Capitalism, Second Period: Rise of The
Corporation

POLITICAL AND
SOCIAL FACTORS:

Consolidation of Standard Oil Empire (1879)
J. P. Morgan's Leadership of New York Money
Market (1879–1910)
Rise of Mass Distribution (first Woolworth store,
1879)
The Salvation Army
Henry George's Single-tax Theory (1879)

The Social Church	Factory Legislation
YMCA and YWCA	Rise of Trade Unions
Vocational Education	The Country Club
The Settlement House	Amusement Parks

Tenement Law

Immigration:	Italian	Swedish
	Czechoslovakian	Norwegian
	Hungarian	Greek
	German	Japanese
	Jewish	Polish
	Irish	Canadian

TRANSPORTATION:

Second Railroad Age (the completed rail network)

Elevated Railroad	Cable Car
Electric Trolley	Subway

TECHNOLOGY:

Skeleton Steel Construction	Telephone
Electric-powered Mills	Terra-cotta Tile
Electric Light	Business Machines
Elevator	

BUILDING TYPES:
(Structural and
Functional)

"Tall Buildings" (early skyscrapers)
Apartment Houses ("French flats")
Public Libraries
Art and Science Museums
Large Town Houses
Steel-frame Office Buildings
Steel-sash Factories
Consolidated Railroad Terminals
General Hospitals

ARCHITECTURAL
STYLE:

American Renaissance, First Phase: Hunt, Mc-
Kim, White, Burnham, Gilbert
Picturesque Secessionism (Sullivan, Wright, Pur-
cell and Elmslie, Greene and Greene)
Formal Garden Revival (Platt, Gréber)

PLANNING AND
CIVIC DESIGN:

Monumental Planning	
(the City Beautiful)	Railroad Plazas
Civic Centers	University Campuses

URBAN FORMS AND
EXAMPLES:

The Metropolitan City (New York)
Railroad Industrial Cities ("Cities of the Calu-
met," Ind.)
Railroad Residential Suburbs (Greenwich, Conn.,
Chestnut Hill, Pa.)
Railroad Market Towns (Crete, Dorchester,
Neb.)
Steel Towns (Gary, Ind., Aliquippa, Pa.)
Southern Textile Towns (Kannopolis, N. C.)

SIXTH ERA OF CITIES   1910–1933
The City of Towers

NATIONAL ECONOMY:	Finance Capitalism, Third Period: Rise of Mass Production

POLITICAL AND SOCIAL FACTORS:	Henry Ford Introduces Mass Production of Automobiles (1913)
	Rockefeller Foundation (1913)
	World War 1 (1914–1918)
	The Holding Company
	Rise of Public Relations and Advertising
	Progressive Education
	Federal Income Tax (1916)
	Prohibition
	Cross-country Highway (1927)
	Negro Migration from the South to Northern Cities
	Falling off of Immigration:
	    Italian Polish
	    German Canadian
	    Irish Mexican
	    English

TRANSPORTATION:	Rail and Automobile Age Highways Automobile, Truck and Bus
TECHNOLOGY:	Motion Picture Radio Chemical Industry Light Metals and Alloys High-speed Strip-steel Mills
BUILDING TYPES: (Structural and Functional)	Tower-form Skyscrapers Electric Power Station Movie Palaces Cafeteria Drugstore Consolidated High School Medical Centers Gas Station, Garage Garden Apartments
ARCHITECTURAL STYLE:	American Renaissance, Second Phase: Collegiate and Skyscraper Gothic Colonial and Classic Revivals Hispano-American Revival Arts Décoratifs "Modern" Interior Decoration as a Profession Variations on the Formal Garden
PLANNING AND CIVIC DESIGN:	Land-use Master Plans The Garden City and Suburb Zoning
URBAN FORMS AND EXAMPLES:	The Automobile City (Detroit, Mich., Los Angeles, Calif.) Oil-refining Towns (Bayonne, N. J., Texas City, Texas) Speculative Residential Communities (Coral Gables, Fla., Long Beach, N. Y.) War Housing Communities (The Fairview section of Camden, N. J.) Metal-processing Towns (Middletown, O.) Garden Suburbs (Forest Hills Gardens, N. Y., Radburn, N. J.)

The Regional City

NATIONAL ECONOMY:	Co-operative Capitalism: Joint Business and Government Enterprise in Banking, Farming, Home Financing and Scientific Research
POLITICAL AND SOCIAL FACTORS:	The Great Depression (1929–1936) Reconstruction Finance Corporation (1932) The New Deal Tennessee Valley Authority (1933) Federal Housing Administration (1934) United States Housing Authority (1937) Government Aid to the Arts (1933–1941) Social Security Public Health Services Industrial Unionism World War II (1939–1945) United Nations Federal Aid in Urban Redevelopment (1949) Urban Renewal (1954)
TRANSPORTATION:	The Automobile Age Expressways Truck and Bus Pipelines Long-span Bridges Aviation Vehicular Tunnels
TECHNOLOGY:	Construction Machinery Mass-produced Consumer Durables Perfection of Mass Distribution Television Atomic Energy Electronics
BUILDING TYPES: (Structural and Functional)	Low-cost Housing Factory-produced Houses Motels Trailer Homes Regional Shopping Centers One-story Industrial Plants Serviced by Interior Truck
ARCHITECTURAL STYLE:	Astylar Functionalism Functional Era Industrial Design Trends Stripped Classic
PLANNING AND CIVIC DESIGN:	Regional Planning Metropolitan Area Planning Subdivision Control Highway Planning Urban Redevelopment
URBAN FORMS AND EXAMPLES:	The Regional City Mass-dormitory Suburbs (Levittown, N. Y.) Private and Public Housing Projects (Stuyvesant Town, New York, Jane Addams houses, Chicago) Urban Redevelopment (Golden Triangle, Pittsburgh, Temple Street Area, Philadelphia, Pa.) Greenbelt Towns (Greendale, Wisc.) Atomic Energy Towns (Oak Ridge, Tenn., Hanford, Wash.) New Industrial Towns (Morrisville, Pa.)

FURTHER READING

For information on civic art, architecture, planning and history of his local community, the reader should consult his public library, historical society or museum library. The non-syndicated Sunday supplements of the daily newspaper often contain valuable information about the community. Particularly useful for pictures and views are the *National Geographic Magazine* and *Holiday Magazine*, which frequently devote a whole article to a city or town. More specialized material can be found in the *Journal of the Society of Architectural Historians*, the *American City Magazine*, *Business Week, Engineering News-Record, Journal of the American Institute of Planners*, the annual volumes of the American Society of Planning Officials, *Landscape Architecture* and *Landscape*. The American Guide Series, prepared originally by the Federal Writers' Projects of the Works Progress Administration and kept up to date by the several publishers, remain the best single source on the American community. The *Dictionary of American Biography* is an invaluable reference work on American civic designers, artists, architects and engineers.

The following list is a guide to some of the more useful works on the history and art of the townscape in America:

AMERICAN TRADITION OF CITY PLANNING AND CIVIC DESIGN

Thomas Adams, *Outline of Town and City Planning*. New York: Russell Sage Foundation, 1935

American Institute of Architects, Committee on Town Planning *City Planning Progress in the United States, 1917*. Washington, D.C. *Journal of the American Institute of Architects, 1917*

Daniel H. Burnham and Edward H. Bennett, *Plan of Chicago Prepared Under the Direction of the Commercial Club*. Chicago: Commercial Club, 1909

Werner Hegemann and Elbert Peets, *The American Vitruvius: An Architect's Handbook of Civic Art*. New York: Architectural Book, 1922

Walter Dwight Moody, *Wacker's Manual of the Plan of Chicago . . . Especially Prepared for Study in the Public Schools of Chicago*. Chicago: Printed by Sherman, 1911

Christopher Tunnard, *The City of Man*. New York: Scribner, 1953

ARCHITECTURE, LANDSCAPE ARCHITECTURE
AND THE ALLIED ARTS

Edward Bruce and Forbes Watson, *Art in Federal Buildings: An Illustrated Record of the Treasury Department's New Program in Painting and Sculpture.* Washington, D.C.: Govt. Printing Office, 1936

George Harold Edgell, *The American Architecture of To-day.* New York and London: Scribner, 1928

Talbot Faulkner Hamlin, *The American Spirit in Architecture.* New York: Yale, 1926

——, *Greek Revival Architecture in America.* New York: Oxford, 1944

Samuel Isham, *The History of American Painting . . . New Edition with Supplemental Chapters by Royal Cortissoz.* New York: Macmillan, 1942

Sidney Fiske Kimball, *American Architecture.* Indianapolis and New York: Bobbs-Merrill, 1928

Alice B. B. Lockwood, ed., *Gardens of Colony and State: Gardens and Gardeners of the American Colonies and of the Republic before 1840.* New York: Scribner, 1931. 2 vols.

Hugh Morrison, *Early American Architecture, from the First Colonial Settlements to the National Period.* New York: Oxford, 1952

Montgomery Schuyler, *A Critique of the Works of Adler & Sullivan, D. H. Burnham & Co., Henry Ives Cobb.* New York: Architectural Record Co., 1896

——, *Works of the Late Richard Morris Hunt, The Architectural Record,* vol. 5, 1895, pp. 97–180

Lorado Taft, *The History of American Sculpture . . . New Edition with a Supplementary Chapter by Adeline Adams.* New York: Macmillan, 1930. 2 vols.

BIOGRAPHIES OF CIVIC DESIGNERS AND ARTISTS

Carl Bridenbaugh, *Peter Harrison, First American Architect.* Chapel Hill: University of North Carolina, 1949

Ralph Adams Cram, *My Life in Architecture.* Boston: Little, Brown, 1936

Agnes Addison Gilchrist, *William Strickland, Architect and Engineer, 1788–1854.* Philadelphia: University of Pennsylvania, 1950

Henry-Russell Hitchcock, *The Architecture of H. H. Richardson and His Times.* New York: Museum of Modern Art, 1936

Sidney Fiske Kimball, *Thomas Jefferson, Architect.* Boston: Privately Printed, 1916

Charles Moore, *Daniel H. Burnham, Architect, Planner of Cities.* Boston and New York: Houghton Mifflin, 1921. 2 vols.

——, *The Life and Times of Charles Follen McKim.* Boston and New York: Houghton Mifflin, 1929

Frederick Law Olmsted, Jr., and Theodora Kimball, eds., *Frederick Law Olmsted: Landscape Architect, 1822–1903.* New York and London: Putnam, 1922–28. 2 vols.

Charles A. Place, *Charles Bulfinch, Architect and Citizen*. Boston and New York: Houghton Mifflin, 1925

Charles Herbert Reilly, *McKim, Mead & White*. New York: Scribner, 1924

Augustus Saint-Gaudens, *The Reminiscences of Augustus Saint-Gaudens. Edited and Amplified by Homer Saint-Gaudens*. New York: Century, 1913

D. B. Steinman, *The Builders of the Bridge: The Story of John Roebling and His Son*. New York: Harcourt, Brace, 1945

Everard M. Upjohn, *Richard Upjohn, Architect and Churchman*. New York: Columbia University, 1939

Marianna G. Van Rensselaer, *Henry Hobson Richardson*. Boston and New York: Houghton Mifflin, 1888

John Lloyd Wright, *My Father Who Is on Earth*. New York: Putnam, 1946

AMERICAN SCENE AND BACKGROUND

Wayne Andrews, *The Vanderbilt Legend: The Story of the Vanderbilt Family, 1794–1940*. New York: Harcourt, Brace, 1941

Donald Joseph Bogue, *The Structure of the Metropolitan Community*. Ann Harbor: University of Michigan, 1949

Carl Bridenbaugh, *Cities in the Wilderness; The First Century of Urban Life in America, 1625–1742*. 2nd edition. New York: Knopf, 1955

——, *Cities in Revolt; Urban Life in America, 1743–1776*. New York: Knopf, 1955

—— and Jessica Bridenbaugh, *Rebels and Gentlemen: Philadelphia in the Age of Franklin*. New York: Reynal and Hitchcock, 1942

H. Paul Caemmerer, *Historic Washington, Capital of the Nation*. Washington, D.C.: Columbia Historical Soc., 1948

Carl Carmer, *The Hudson*. New York and Toronto: Farrar and Rinehart, 1939

Thomas Childs Cochran and William Miller, *The Age of Enterprise*. New York: Macmillan, 1942

Miles Lanier Colean, *Renewing Our Cities*. New York: Twentieth Century Fund, 1953

James Fenimore Cooper, *Notions of the Americans*. Philadelphia: Carey, Lee & Carey, 1828. 2 vols.

Everett Dick, *The Sod-House Frontier, 1854–1890*. New York and London: Appleton-Century, 1937

James Ford and others, *Slums and Housing, with Special Reference to New York City: History, Conditions, Policy*. Cambridge: Harvard, 1936. 2 vols.

Anthony N. B. Garvan, *Architecture and Town Planning in Colonial Connecticut* New Haven: Yale, 1951

Henry-Russell Hitchcock, *Rhode Island Architecture*. Providence: Rhode Island Museum, 1939

Mark Holloway, *Heavens on Earth: Utopian Communities in America, 1680–1880*. New York: Library Publishers, 1951

Richard Hubbard Howland, *The Architecture of Baltimore: A Pictorial History*. Baltimore: Johns Hopkins, 1953

Homer Hoyt, *One Hundred Years of Land Values in Chicago: The Relationship of the Growth of Chicago to the Rise in its Land Values, 1830–1933*. Chicago: University of Chicago, 1933

Henry James, *The American Scene*. New York and London: Harper, 1907

Victor Jones, *Metropolitan Government*. Chicago: University of Chicago, 1942

Walter H. Kilham, *Boston after Bulfinch: An Account of Its Architecture, 1800–1900*. Cambridge: Harvard, 1946

John Atlee Kouwenhoven, *The Columbia Historical Portrait of New York: An Essay in Graphic History in Honor of the Tricentennial of New York City and the Bicentennial of Columbia University*. Garden City, N.Y.: Doubleday, 1953

Jean Labatut and Wheaton J. Lane, eds., *Highways in our National Life*. Princeton: Princeton, 1950

Lewis Mumford, *Sticks and Stones, a Study of American Architecture and Civilization*. New York: Boni and Liveright, 1924

Stuart Alfred Queen and David Bailey Carpenter, *The American City*. New York: McGraw-Hill, 1953

Beatrice St. Julien Ravenel, *Architects of Charleston*. Charleston, S.C.: Carolina Art Assoc., 1945

Aaron Morton Sakolski, *The Great American Land Bubble*. New York and London: Harper, 1932

Herbert Wallace Schneider, *A History of American Philosophy*. New York: Columbia University, 1946

William Warren Sweet, *The American Churches: An Interpretation*. New York and Nashville: Abingdon-Cokesbury, 1948

Robert Averill Walker, *The Planning Function in Urban Government*. Chicago: University of Chicago, 1941

Dixon Wecter, *The Saga of American Society: A Record of Social Aspiration, 1607–1937*. New York: Scribner, 1937

Thomas Jefferson Wertenbaker, *The Old South: The Founding of American Civilization*. New York: Scribner, 1942

Theo B. White, ed., *Philadelphia Architecture in the Nineteenth Century*. Philadelphia: University of Pennsylvania, 1953

Coleman Woodbury, ed., *The Future of Cities and Urban Redevelopment*. Chicago: University of Chicago, 1953

INDEX

215